Taylor's Guides to Gardening

Barbara W. Ellis

FRANCES TENENBAUM, Series Editor

Taylor's Guide to

Bulbs

HOW TO SELECT AND GROW
480 SPECIES OF SPRING
AND SUMMER BULBS

HOUGHTON MIFFLIN COMPANY

BOSTON   NEW YORK   2001

Taylor's Guide is a registered trademark of Houghton Mifflin Company.

Library of Congress Cataloging-in-Publication Data
Ellis, Barbara W.
Taylor's guide to bulbs : how to select and grow 480 species of spring and summer
bulbs / [Barbara W. Ellis].
    p. cm. — (Taylor's guides to gardening)
  ISBN 0-618-06890-2
   1. Bulbs. I. Title: Bulbs. II. Title. III. Series.
SB425 .E45 2001
635.9'4—dc21   00-053884

Illustration on page 5 from *Taylor's Dictionary for Gardeners,*
illustrations copyright © 2001 by Steve Buchanan

Special thanks to Brent Heath of Brent and Becky's Bulbs
for his help reviewing the bulbs included in this book.

Cover photograph by Derek Fell
Book design by Anne Chalmers
Typefaces: Minion, News Gothic

Printed in Singapore
10 9 8 7 6 5 4 3 2 1

❧ Contents

❧Introduction

Versatile, colorful, easy to plant and even easier to grow, bulbs belong in every garden. There are bulbs for both sun and shade, hot climates and cold, as well as selections perfect for every style of garden, from formal perennial borders to casual woodland or shade plantings. Planted *en masse*—arranged in either blocks or free-form drifts—bulbs make it easy to paint sheets of color over the landscape. Most are simple to tuck in among clumps of perennials, plant between the roots of trees, or naturalize in grass or wild gardens. Many make easy and stunning container plants, too. There are also many bulbs that thrive in difficult sites: in the pages of this book, you'll find plenty of choices for spots that are hot and dry in summer, for example. Fortunately, bulbs also are relatively inexpensive, putting stunning displays within the reach of nearly every gardener's budget. They are inexpensive enough that many are commonly grown as annuals—tulips and gladiolus are two examples. Growing bulbs as annuals makes it easy to change a garden color scheme for a single season, and it also makes experimenting practical: try out species you haven't grown before to find out what performs well in a particular site, for example.

This book contains information on hundreds of bulbs. It is designed to help you sample the amazing variety of these plants and determine which ones to add to your beds, borders, and container gardens. Both the photographs and the individual entries are listed in alphabetical order by botanical name: *Crocus, Curcuma, Cyclamen,* and so forth. See the index if you need to locate a plant by its common name. The photographs are accompanied by captions that summarize essential information about the plants and give page numbers for the encyclopedia entries, where they are covered in more detail. The encyclopedia entries, located in the back of the book, include general information on each genus as well as a How to Grow section and individual accounts of outstanding species and cultivars, with descriptions and page references back to corresponding photographs. The How to Grow information covers essential site and soil requirements as well as other important cultural information, including planting time and depth, overwintering tips, and propagation information. When is the best time to plant the bulbs? How deep should they be planted? How do you overwinter them if they are not hardy in your area? What are the best methods for propagation?

🌿 WHAT IS A BULB?

Gardeners and botanists differ in their use of the word "bulb." For botanists, bulb means a specific botanical structure consisting of a stem surrounded by fleshy, modified leaves. Onions, daffodils, tulips, and lilies all grow from true bulbs. Botanists further divide true bulbs into two general types: tunicate and fleshy. See Bulb Terms for definitions of various bulb structures as well as other terms relating to bulbs. Knowing the specific type of structure that a bulbous plant grows from is a valuable piece of information to have if you want to propagate it. See "Propagating Bulbs" for specifics on techniques that work with different types of structures.

When gardeners use the word "bulb," they commonly are referring to plants that grow from a variety of underground structures, including true bulbs, corms, tubers, tuberous roots, and rhizomes. For simplicity's sake, in this introduction, the word "bulb" is used in this general sense. In the encyclopedia entries, however, the various structures are referred to by their correct botanical names: a bulb is a true bulb and a tuber is a true tuber, for example. In the nursery trade, the term "bulb" is commonly used to refer to bulbs, corms, tubers, and other structures that can remain alive for two months out of the soil. Nursery owners use this definition because it means bulbs (and other structures) can be stored, packaged, and sold in a similar way and are typically offered in general bulb displays.

Bulbs also are often grouped according to when they bloom—a characteristic that is often more important to gardeners than the specific structure they grow from. See "Deciding What to Grow" on page 6 for more information on spring, summer, and fall bulbs.

(text continues on page 6)

BULB TERMS

BULB. A true bulb is a storage organ, usually underground, that is made up of fleshy scales, which are actually modified leaves, attached to a basal plate that gives rise to the roots. At the center of the bulb is a compressed stem containing an embryonic shoot or flower. The fleshy scales store food for the plant. Bulbs made up of a solid mass of tightly packed scales covered by a papery tunic are called tunicate bulbs. The tunic protects the bulb from being damaged or drying out. *Narcissus* spp., *Tulipa* spp., *Allium* spp., and *Hippeastrum* spp. all have tunicate bulbs. (In some cases, these bulbs are very poorly developed: many *Allium* spp. have bulbs that simply look like fleshy stems.) *Lilium* spp. and some *Fritillaria* spp. grow from bulbs that are not covered by a tunic and have loose scales. These are called scaly or nontunicate bulbs. Not only do they dry out more quickly, they also are damaged more easily than tunicate bulbs.

BULBIL. A small bulb that forms above ground, such as in the leaf axil of a plant.

BULBLET. A small bulb that forms below ground, such as along a plant's stem or around the base of a larger bulb.

BULBOUS. In gardening, this term is used to refer to any plant that bears swollen or rounded roots that resemble bulbs, whether the actual structures are true bulbs, corms, or tubers.

CORM. A bulblike organ for storing food that actually is a swollen, solid, underground stem. Unlike bulbs, corms are not constructed of layers of scales. They are usually covered with a papery tunic. The best-known plants that grow from corms are glads (*Gladiolus* spp.) and crocuses (*Crocus* spp.). Most corms live only one year: once the parent corm has bloomed, it withers and dies, and a new corm forms on top of the old corm.

CORMEL. A small corm that forms underground near the base of a parent corm.

OFFSET. A small bulb, shoot, or plant that is produced near the base of a parent plant.

PERIANTH SEGMENTS. Perianth is a collective term for both the calyx (sepals) and the corolla (petals) of a flower and is most commonly used when these two parts of a flower are similar in appearance. The "petals" of a flower with similar-looking sepals and true petals are correctly called perianth segments.

RACEME. A single-stemmed inflorescence (flower cluster) made up of flowers carried on individual stalks, called pedicels.

RHIZOME. A specialized, horizontal stem that runs underground or on the soil surface. Rhizomes contain nodes and internodes and also produce roots at the nodes. Plants that grow from fleshy rhizomes often are included in the general category of bulbs, including bearded irises (*Iris* bearded hybrids). Lily-of-the-valley *(Convallaria majalis)* also spreads by rhizomes, in this case thin ones called pips. Since the rhizomes can be stored and sold while they are dormant, these plants are often included in bulb catalogs and displays.

SCALY BULB. *See* Bulb.

SPIKE. A single-stemmed inflorescence (flower cluster) made up of flowers that are either attached directly to the main stem without a stalk or are nearly stalkless.

STEM TUBER. These structures are formed from swollen stem tissue, and, unlike conventional tubers such as potatoes, they have an upright orientation in the soil, with leaf and flower buds arising from the top and roots from the sides or bottom. Stem tubers are perennial and increase in size each year, but they do not produce offsets. Tuberous begonias *(Begonia × tuberhybrida)* and cyclamen *(Cyclamen* spp.) both grow from stem tubers.

TEPAL. A tepal is a petal-like perianth segment (collectively, the calyx, sepals, and corolla, or petals, of a flower). In a flower with tepals, the true sepals and petals are indistinguishable. Lillies *(Lilium* spp.), tulips *(Tulipa* spp.), and crocuses *(Crocus* spp.) all bear flowers with tepals rather than distinct sepals and petals.

TRUE BULB. *See* Bulb.

TUBER. A modified underground stem that is fleshy and swollen, stores food for the plant, and is also a reproductive organ. (Potatoes are the best-known example, but *Caladium* species also grow from tubers.) Tubers are true stems and have all the parts of a typical stem, including buds (called eyes) marking the nodes. They form at the tips of underground stolons or rhizomes.

TUBEROUS ROOTS. Like other bulbous structures, tuberous roots are overwintering and food-storage adaptations. In this case, they are fleshy, swollen sections of roots that have the internal and external structure of a root. They lack nodes and internodes and have buds only on the end near the crown or stem of the plant. Dahlias (*Dahlia* spp.) grow from tuberous roots. That's why it is important to include part of the main stem or crown of the plant when dividing or propagating dahlias: the individual fleshy roots do not have buds and cannot sprout. Tuberous roots usually are biennial—they form and overwinter the first year, sprout the following spring, and then shrivel and are replaced the second year.

TUNICATE BULB. *See* Bulb.

UMBEL. An inflorescence (flower cluster) in which all the individual flowers are borne on stalks that arise from the same point at the tip of the main stem. Umbels are flat or rounded on top. Ornamental onions (*Allium* spp.) bear their flowers in umbels.

❧ DECIDING WHAT TO GROW

Perhaps the best guideline to follow when deciding which bulbs to grow is "the more the better." After all, it's hard to have too many snowdrops or daffodils in spring. And did you ever hear anyone complain about too many lilies in summer or autumn crocuses in fall? The wider the variety of species and cultivars you grow, the longer the bloom season you'll enjoy. Especially large genera—*Allium* (ornamental onions), *Lilium* (lilies), *Narcissus* (daffodils), and *Tulipa* (tulips)—offer a wide range of species and cultivars you can use to plan weeks (and sometimes months) of color in the garden. See the individual entries for suggestions on selecting plants that will lengthen the bloom season.

Another guideline to keep in mind when planting bulbs is the tried-and-true rule "match the plant to the site." In other words, when selecting plants to grow, use your garden's sun, soil, and weather conditions to guide your choices. (With bulbs that are overwintered indoors—either dry or in containers—available space in winter may play a deciding role in what you grow!) Bulbs selected because they thrive in the conditions available in your yard inevitably perform better than ones that have to struggle to survive.

If you are not already familiar with the conditions your garden has to offer, take time to study the sun and shade patterns in your yard on a typical day. Bulbs that require full sun need a site that offers at least 8 hours of direct sun per day. Ones that require light or partial shade need either good light all day or full sun for part of the day and shade for the rest of the day. Sites that receive direct sun for a few hours in the morning or afternoon and dappled shade the rest of the day will keep many species happy. Dappled shade cast by deciduous trees is fine for many spring-blooming bulbs, which thrive in the full sun available before the trees leaf out. Most are dormant by the time these sites are fully shaded in early summer. Deep-rooted species such as oaks are best for underplanting with bulbs: few plants can compete with the dense mat of roots produced by maples and other shallow-rooted trees. A site with deep, all-day shade, such as one shaded by evergreens, isn't suitable, and even shade-loving bulbs won't succeed there.

When evaluating sites, also dig a few test holes to find out about the soil. Most bulbs prefer well-drained soil and rot in a spot with damp, heavy clay or one that remains constantly wet. You can improve the drainage of any soil by double digging and adding organic matter such as compost. For sites with very poor soil or chronic drainage problems,

Allium unifolium, which blooms from late spring to early summer, is just one of the many ornamental onions in the genus Allium. *With a little planning, it's possible to fill the garden with species and cultivars of* Allium *that bloom from spring right into fall.*

raised beds may be the answer. Many bulbs also thrive in the perfectly drained conditions of a rock garden.

If you are planning to grow some of your bulbs as annuals, keep in mind that you may need to provide ideal conditions for only part of the year. A spot that is hot and dry during summer dormancy is ideal when growing tulips as perennials, but if you are planning to enjoy them for a single season and then replace them, all you need to worry about is keeping them happy from winter through the following spring. In this case, they won't do well in a bed that is wet all winter, but one that is kept moist all summer is fine because the tulips are going to be replaced anyway.

Bulbs for Season-long Bloom

While nearly everyone is familiar with hardy spring bulbs such as daffodils and tulips, there are also many other spring bulbs to choose from, along with a wide array of summer- and fall-blooming species invaluable for adding extra pizzazz to the garden. With a little planning, it's possible to have bulbs in bloom from late winter right through fall. Use the following three groups to help guide your choices:

SPRING BULBS. It's hard to imagine a spring garden without the bright colors of spring bulbs. Of these, the best known are hardy species such as daffodils (*Narcissus* spp.), tulips (*Tulipa* spp.), crocuses (*Crocus*

(text continues on page 10)

SCHEDULING SPRING BULBS

The list below divides some of the most common species of spring-blooming bulbs by bloom season. Use it to select a wide range of bulbs — both different species and various cultivars within a particular genus to extend the spring blooming season from late winter right into summer. Bear in mind it's hard to generalize about bloom seasons, especially for spring-blooming bulbs. Not only does the exact time of bloom vary depending on where you live, but planting location also affects bloom time. In general, bulbs planted in a south-facing site next to a wall or fence (look for the sites where snow melts first) will bloom first. The same species, planted in a protected, north-facing site may be delayed by several weeks. There is lots of overlap among the various cultivars within the highly hybridized genera — most notably *Narcissus* (daffodils) and *Tulipa* (tulips). The list below includes specific types of daffodils and tulips, but also look for specific cultivars in bulb catalogs and displays that are rated "early," "midseason," and "late," then plant some of each.

LATE WINTER TO VERY EARLY SPRING
Chionodoxa. Glory-of-the-snow.
Crocus. C. chrysanthus (snow crocus), *C. angustifolius* (cloth-of-gold crocus) and *C. tommasinianus,* followed by *C. biflorus* (Scotch crocus) and *C. vernus* (Dutch crocuses).
Cyclamen coum. Hardy cyclamen.
Eranthis. Winter aconite.
Galanthus. Snowdrops.
Iris reticulata. Reticulated iris.

EARLY SPRING
Anemone. A. blanda (Grecian windflower).
Puschkinia scilloides. Striped squill.
Narcissus. Cyclamineus, Triandrus, and Trumpet daffodils.
Scilla. Squill.
Tulipa. T. kaufmanniana, T. fosteriana, T. greigii, and their cultivars.

EARLY TO MIDSPRING
Hyacinthus. Hyacinth.
Muscari. Grape hyacinths.
Narcissus. Small- and Large-cupped daffodils, Tazetta daffodils.
Tulipa. Single Early, Triumph, Darwin Hybrid, and Double Early
tulips. Also *T. clusiana, T. humilis, T. tarda,* and *T. turkestanica.*

MIDSPRING
Anemone. A. nemorosa (wood anemone) and *A. sylvestris* (snow-
drop anemone).
Fritillaria. Fritillary.
Hyacinthoides. Bluebell.
Narcissus. Double, Poeticus, and Jonquilla daffodils.
Tulipa. Lily-flowering tulips. Also *T. bakeri, T. batalinii, T. saxatilis.*

LATE SPRING TO EARLY SUMMER
Allium. Ornamental onions, *A. aflatunense* (Persian onion), *A.
caeruleum* (blue globe onion), *A. christophii* (star of Persia), *A.
giganteum* (giant onion), *A. moly* (lily leek), and *A. schoenopra-
sum* (chives).
Anemone canadensis. Meadow anemone.
Camassia. Camassia.
Erythronium. Dogtooth violet.
Leucojum. Snowflake.
Lilium candidum. Madonna lily.
Ornithogalum. Star-of-Bethlehem.
Tulipa. Darwin, Fringed, Bouquet or Multiflowering, Parrot, and
Peony tulips.

spp.), and hyacinths (*Hyacinthus* spp.), but there are many more. See "Scheduling Spring Bulbs" on pages 8–9 for a list of many spring-blooming species and when they bloom. There are also tender bulbs that bloom in spring where they are hardy and can be grown outdoors year-round — *Babiana* spp., *Chasmanthe* spp., and *Ixia* spp. are examples. When grown in areas where they are not hardy, these usually fall into the category of summer bulbs because they are planted outdoors after the last spring frost and generally bloom in early to midsummer.

The so-called little bulbs are a subset of hardy spring bulbs. This term refers to a range of small species including snowdrops (*Galanthus* spp.), winter aconites (*Eranthis* spp.), squills (both *Scilla* spp. and *Puschkinia* spp.), grape hyacinths (*Muscari* spp.), glory-of-the-snow (*Chionodoxa* spp.), and snowflakes (*Leucojum* spp.). Dwarf and species forms of daffodils (*Narcissus* spp.), tulips (*Tulipa* spp.), and crocuses also are sometimes included in discussions of "little bulbs."

In general, hardy spring bulbs require similar conditions to grow well and are carefree plants well worth the little bit of effort it takes to plant them. See "Growing Bulbs" on page 16 for general culture and refer to the individual entries for specific requirements.

SUMMER BULBS. This group includes many hardy species as well as a wide range of tender ones. Hardy summer-blooming bulbs include many ornamental onions (*Allium* spp.), lilies (*Lilium* spp.), crocosmias (*Crocosmia* spp.), summer hyacinths (*Galtonia* spp.), gayfeathers (*Liatris*

Despite the common name summer snowflake, Leucojum aestivum *bears its dainty clusters of bell-shaped flowers in spring. Closely related* L. autumnale *flowers from late summer into fall.*

Little bulbs, such as glory-of-the-snow (Chiono-doxa forbesii), *are most effective when planted in large drifts. Fortunately, their bulbs are quite inexpensive, and nearly anyone can afford adding a hundred or two to the garden.*

spp.), hardy gloxinia *(Incarvillea delavayi)*, and alstroemerias (*Alstroemeria* spp.). A wide array of tender bulbs (that may be hardy, depending on where you live) also fall here. These include belladonna lily *(Amaryllis belladonna)*, tuberous begonias *(Begonia × tuberhybrida)*, caladiums (*Caladium* spp.), cannas (*Canna* spp.), crinum lilies (*Crinum* spp.), dahlias (*Dahlia* spp.), glads (*Gladiolus* spp.), pineapple lilies (*Eucomis* spp.), gloriosa lilies *(Gloriosa superba)*, Peruvian daffodils (*Hymenocallis* spp.), and naked ladies (*Lycoris* spp.). Heat-loving tropical plants also are considered summer bulbs. These include *Alocasia* spp., *Amorphophallus* spp., *Colocasia esculenta,* and gingers such as *Curcuma* spp., *Globba winitii,* and *Hedychium* spp.

There are summer bulbs for all sorts of growing conditions, including species for sun and shade as well as dry soil and wet soil. See "Overwintering Tender Bulbs" on page 21 for information on keeping these plants from year to year. Refer to the individual encyclopedia entries for specific cultural information and suggestions for handling them season by season.

FALL BULBS. All too often overlooked, fall bulbs are a great way to add color to the garden at the end of the season and are well worth the effort it takes to search them out. Many genera that include well-known spring-blooming species include fall-blooming ones as well. There are fall-blooming ornamental onions (*Allium* spp.), crocuses (*Crocus* spp.), cyclamen (*Cyclamen* spp.), lilies (*Lilium* spp.), snowflakes (*Leucojum* spp.), and squills (*Scilla* spp.). Autumn daffodils *(Sternbergia lutea)* and

Although commonly known as autumn or winter daffodils, Sternbergia lutea *bears crocuslike flowers. The golden yellow blooms grace the garden in fall, and leaves last through the winter.*

colchicums (*Colchicum* spp.) are other indispensable fall-bloomers. See "Growing Bulbs" for general information on the cultural requirements of these species, and refer to the individual encyclopedia entries for specifics on planting times, site and soil, and other requirements.

❦BUYING BULBS

Always inspect bulbs before you buy, or examine mail-order shipments carefully as you unpack them. Reject any that show signs of rot, fungus, or mildew. They should be firm to the touch, never slimy, and of uniform weight (unusually light bulbs are often afflicted with dry rot). They also should never smell moldy. The papery tunic on tunicate bulbs should be intact or nearly so.

While cheap, undersized bulbs are never a good buy, there are ways to stretch your bulb budget and buy top-quality bulbs at the same time. Take advantage of volume discounts offered by suppliers. While 50 or 100 of any one cultivar may seem like a lot, most spring bulbs are best planted *en masse*, and you can always join forces with fellow gardeners to make bulk orders.

Collections offer another great buying opportunity. You'll find all manner of them in catalogs, and they are ideal for adding a wide range of bulbs to your garden. Color is a popular theme — you'll find all-pink collections featuring daffodils, tulips, hyacinths, and glory-of-the-snow (*Chionodoxa* spp.) for example, along with collections of bulbs selected especially for length of bloom or for growing in a lawn, the rock garden, or woodland garden. Naturalizing mixtures of unnamed bulbs offer lots of color for the money, but if you like to know your bulbs by name and want to plant them in drifts of a single cultivar, look for collections made up of 5 or 10 bulbs each of a set number of cultivars. In general, the bigger the collection, the better the deal per bulb.

Buying Bulbs of Native Plants

A number of the bulbs listed in this book are native species. Do not add any of these plants to your garden by digging them from the wild yourself, and buy them only from a reputable nursery that sells nursery-propagated, not wild-collected, plants. Also avoid plants described as nursery grown, because these may have been wild collected and then grown at the nursery for a year or two. The end result is the same: individuals who collect wild plants decimate natural areas, and buying collected plants puts money in their pockets. Many of these species are sold in pots in displays of perennials. Nursery-propagated plants look uniform and healthy, while wild-collected ones often have a just-potted-up look, with an off-center crown and broken or wilted leaves or stems. Other signs of wild-collected plants include weeds in the pots and unusually cheap prices for the size of the plants offered. If in doubt, ask the owners where the plants came from, and shop elsewhere if you receive an unsatisfactory response. Nurseries that propagate their own native plants are proud of the fact and will publicize it — either in their catalogs or in signs in their nursery area. Plant sales of local native plant societies, conservation associations, and botanical gardens are other good sources for native plants. They offer propagated plants or specimens rescued from areas that are about to be developed.

☙ HARDINESS

Throughout this book, you'll find hardiness zones listed for each species, along with the USDA Plant Hardiness Zone Map on page 414. The map lists zones from coldest (Zone 1) to warmest (Zones 10 and 11), and photo captions and individual plant entries in this book list a range for each species. In each range, the first zone listed indicates the northern limit of hardiness, while the second gives a guideline for how far south a plant can be grown. While heat tolerance may be the deciding factor here, for many bulbs it is the number of hours in winter below a certain temperature. In the warmest southern zones, for example, most hardy spring bulbs don't receive enough cold winter temperatures to bloom.

To determine which tender bulbs you can grow in areas where they are not hardy, look at both the hardiness information and the cultural suggestions in the How to Grow section of each entry. Many tender bulbs — gladiolus, for example — are easy to grow even in areas where they are not hardy. Simply plant them in spring, let them bloom in summer, and either dig them in fall for overwintering indoors or replace them annually. (In hot climates, many of these plants bloom naturally in winter — or can be scheduled to do so.) Year-round container growing also is an option for bulbs that are not hardy. In areas with rainy summers and/or winters, container culture is also a good alternative for many bulbs that require dry soil when they are dormant.

Experimenting with Hardiness

Gardeners use hardiness information in various ways. Some stick to plants that fall well within their hardiness zone, an approach that gives good insurance that the majority of bulbs will reappear year after year. Others look at hardiness as a challenge and continually try to test the limits of the plants they grow. Here are some strategies for experimenting with hardiness:

CHOOSE PROTECTED SITES. Plant marginally hardy bulbs in a protected site, such as at the base of a south-facing wall.

MULCH FOR WINTER PROTECTION. Provide winter cover in the form of a protective layer of mulch. In this case, coarse mulch is best. Use materials such as evergreen boughs, salt hay, pine needles, or coarse leaves that won't flatten down too much over winter (oak leaves are ideal). Install mulch in late fall after the soil has frozen. Remove the mulch carefully in spring when temperatures warm and growth resumes.

PLANT DEEPLY. Deep planting sometimes gives plants the protection they need to survive winter lows. This technique works for *Amaryllis,* for example. See the How to Grow sections in the individual encyclopedia entries for suggestions on other plants to try this technique with and suggested depths, then experiment with other species.

CHECK DORMANCY REQUIREMENTS. Many bulbs fail to survive not because of temperature, but because they need dry soil conditions during their dormant season. Species from South Africa and the Mediterranean commonly fall into this category. Species native to western North America also need hot, dry summers. Gardeners in areas where summers and/or winters are rainy have several options for growing these plants: grow them in containers, which makes it easy to simply move plants to a dry spot when they are dormant; dig them after they bloom and their foliage fades, then store them indoors; or grow them as annuals. The How to Grow information in each entry explains the options for each species.

Although Curcuma alismatifolia, *commonly known as Siam tulip, is a tender perennial hardy only to Zone 8, gardeners in the tropics and subtropics aren't the only ones who can grow this exotic-looking plant. In the North, plant the rhizomes out in spring after the soil has warmed up, then dig them in fall to overwinter them indoors.*

ENSURE WELL-DRAINED SITES. Some bulbs that prefer dry soil in winter will do fine in a raised bed or rock garden, both of which offer very well drained conditions. With these species, amending the soil with coarse (builder's) sand or grit at planting time is a good idea. Use granite chips or pea gravel as mulch, both of which protect the soil but do not retain excess water. Another option for bulbs that require dry soil in winter is to mulch them in fall and then cover the site with roofing paper or plastic to ward off excess rain.

LOOK FOR COOL SITES. Other species—especially those native to the Pacific Northwest—fail in warm climates because of summer heat rather than winter cold. To experiment with these species, look for cool sites in your garden. Spots with morning sun and afternoon shade are cooler than those in morning shade and afternoon sun, for example. Sites on the north side of your house, a wall, or a low planting also tend to be cooler. Ensuring that soil remains cool and moist also can make the difference between success and failure with a particular plant. In this case, mulching with compost or chopped leaves is beneficial.

LOOK FOR MOIST SITES. A few species—*Curcuma* and *Hedychium*, for example—survive colder temperatures if they are planted in soil that remains moist all winter. In this case, add a layer of mulch in late fall to give the plants extra protection.

❦ GROWING BULBS

The guidelines below will help you keep most bulbs healthy and thriving. See the individual encyclopedia entries for specific cultural requirements for each species.

SITE AND SOIL. As a general rule, plant hardy spring bulbs in full sun to partial shade. A site shaded by deciduous trees is fine for many of these early-blooming plants. That's because they need full sun in spring, but most will have flowered and died back before the trees leaf out enough to cast substantial shade. Limbing up trees can be a practical solution to a too-dark spot. Soil that is rich in organic matter and well drained but evenly moist is ideal for most species. If the soil has been compacted or isn't loose and free-draining, dig in organic matter to a depth of 1 to 1½ feet. Most hardy spring bulbs will stand drier conditions in summer when they are dormant. They rot in wet soil.

PLANTING. Try to get bulbs in the ground as soon as you buy them or receive them in the mail. September is the best time to plant in Zones

2 to 4; October or November in Zones 5 to 7; and November or December in Zones 8 and 9. While earlier planting gives them time to start growing roots before the onset of winter weather, they can be planted up to the time the ground freezes. If you can't plant immediately, store them in a cool, dry place. If you are planting late, cover the beds with a 1- to 2-inch layer of mulch to delay the onset of frozen soil and give them longer to grow roots. If you are running late on planting, try holding the bulbs in a cool, dry place and plant in spring. Plants given this treatment will bloom late the first year but generally perform normally thereafter.

When planting, keep in mind that the roots of most bulbs come out the bottom, and they will grow most vigorously if they are sitting on top of several inches of good soil. This generally isn't a problem if you are planting in an existing bed with improved soil, but if your soil tends to be shallow, work in compost or other organic matter several inches *below* where the base of the bulbs will sit.

There are three different planting approaches. The first option is to dig a separate hole for each bulb. In this case, a trowel or a trowel-sized bulb planter and a kneeling pad are about all you need to plant the so-called little bulbs. A spade or a long-handled bulb planter is effective for digging the deeper holes required by larger bulbs such as daffodils. If you can requisition a helper, it eliminates excess bending to have one person dig the holes and the other, on hands and knees, plant the bulbs. Have the hole-digger push the spade forward and the planter stick the bulb in behind it and then hold it in the ground while the spade is pulled out. Another option is to dig small holes and plant several bulbs in each hole. Or, excavate an entire bed, prepare the soil at the bottom of the excavation (loosen it and work in organic matter such as compost), then set the bulbs in place and refill. This latter option is used for display beds where the bulbs are meant to bloom all together.

Set true bulbs pointed end up with the bottom of the bulb about three times as deep as its diameter. (Keep the papery tunic around true bulbs when planting, because it helps protect the bulb.) With some structures it can be hard to tell which end is up. If in doubt, plant the bulbs on their sides. Don't add fertilizer to the holes as you plant. Instead, topdress the planting site with a balanced organic fertilizer. If the soil surface has been compacted during planting, loosen it with a fork to eliminate spots of dense soil that might prevent the bulbs from emerging in spring. Chipmunks sometimes dig up new plantings of bulbs to see (and sample) what is there. Covering the site with a piece of hardware cloth for a few days after planting helps discourage their curiosity.

FORCING HARDY SPRING BULBS

Forcing bulbs is an easy way to enjoy a dose of spring color in the winter. Forced pots of bulbs also make ideal, relatively inexpensive gifts.

Start with healthy, top-sized bulbs—plant pots with all one color or type of bulb, mix colors (combine two different Darwin tulips, for example), or experiment with interplanting different species that bloom at the same time. You can dig bulbs right out of the garden, too. Grape hyacinths indicate their location in fall because that's when their foliage appears. Established plantings of snowdrops often push bulbs to the surface, or you can mark the locations of bulbs that need dividing and dig them in fall, replanting the ones you don't want for forcing. You'll also need a selection of clay bulb pans or azalea pots, both of which are shallower than normal pots.

Cover the hole in the bottom of each pot with a piece of broken pot—it should be a curved piece (placed curved side up) so water, but not the planting medium, can get out of the bottom of the pots. Spread a layer of soilless potting medium (ProMix is one brand) on the bottom of the pots and set the bulbs so their tips will be just at or slightly above the surface of the medium. Set the bulbs close together for the best show. You can add a second layer of bulbs by placing them between the bulbs in the first layer, after sifting in additional potting medium. Place tulips with the flat side of the bulb to the outside of the pot, because the first leaf comes on that side of the bulb and this creates a pot with an attractive outer ring of leaves. Fill the pots almost to the rim with medium and water them thoroughly.

The bulbs then require a period of cold but above-freezing temperatures (35° to 40°F) to grow roots. During this period, the medium should remain moist but not wet. Set the pots in a cold frame, an unheated garage, a root cellar, or even a refrigerator for this period. In general they need 3½ to 4 months of cool temperatures to grow roots. After that, they can be brought out for forcing, which takes another 2 to 3 weeks before the plants are in full bloom.

When you bring the pots out of cold storage for forcing, set them for about a week in a dark, cool place (55° to 60°F). Then force them either under lights or on windowsills in a cool place (65°F days; 60°F nights). Stake tall plants, such as daffodils and tulips, to keep them upright. (Ringing the pots with small stakes connected by string works fine.) If you plan on saving the bulbs, fertilize with a liquid fertilizer such as fish emulsion every other time you water. After the pots have bloomed, set them in a sheltered corner outdoors after the last spring frost date. Keep the pots evenly moist until the foliage has turned yellow. The bulbs can be dumped out of the pots and planted in the garden in spring or fall. Forced bulbs may take a season or two to resume blooming.

Care Through the Season

Once planted, hardy bulbs can be pretty much left to their own devices. An annual fall feeding helps keep them vigorous—topdress plantings with a balanced organic fertilizer. In good soil, however, most will perform adequately without supplemental feeding. A summertime mulch of chopped leaves, compost, or shredded bark helps keep down weeds and adds organic matter to the soil.

CARING FOR RIPENING LEAVES. After bulbs flower, their foliage remains green for several weeks, then gradually turns yellow and dies back. It's important to let the leaves ripen naturally, because they need time to manufacture food for next year's flowers. With small bulbs, such as crocuses and snowdrops, the yellowing leaves aren't particularly problematic and will simply disappear under surrounding foliage. While the ripening foliage of larger bulbs such as daffodils can be unattractive, do not cut it back until it yellows completely. (Or, don't cut it back at all, and simply leave it in the garden to rot, where it will add organic matter to the soil.) Resist the temptation to braid or tie up the leaves, because this reduces their ability to manufacture food—and lumps of tied-up foliage aren't all that attractive anyway. If you are growing bulbs as annuals, just pull the plants up after they finish blooming.

DEADHEADING. Remove spent flowers to direct energy into next year's flowers. Many smaller bulbs self-sow, and if you would like seedlings scattered about, leave the flowers in place. While improved cultivars won't come true from seed, this is an easy way to increase plantings of species bulbs.

DIVISION. When clumps of bulbs become too crowded and begin to flower less, they need to be divided. Division also is the easiest way to propagate these plants. Dig clumps of bulbs as the leaves turn yellow and begin to die back for the year but before they disappear completely—in late spring or early summer for spring-blooming species. At any season, if you accidentally dig into a clump of bulbs, replant them immediately and they'll probably flower without missing a beat. To avoid slicing into the bulbs by accident, start digging a few inches outside the clump. You'll find clumps consist of large bulbs and offsets of various sizes. The offsets can be left with the mother bulbs or detached and planted individually. They will take a year or two to bloom. Replant all of them immediately. If you can't replant immediately, store the bulbs in a dark, dry, very well ventilated spot until the proper time for replanting. Spread them out to discourage mold from forming.

POTENTIAL PROBLEMS. Inspect bulbs before buying them to avoid those with the common diseases that rot bulbs. Destroy (or return) diseased bulbs that you find in shipments, before the problem spreads to healthy bulbs. Selecting a site with well-drained soil rich in organic matter is another vital key to keeping bulbs healthy. Wet soil leads to rotted bulbs and roots.

A hard, late freeze can destroy flower buds in spring, but most hardy spring bulbs are quite tough and easily withstand frost, even when in bud or bloom. (The flowering of snowdrops and crocuses isn't hampered by a late snowstorm, but heavy, wet snow will flatten taller bulbs such as daffodils.) For fall-blooming species that may or may not bloom before cold weather arrives, keeping plants in containers and moving them indoors if frost threatens is the best option.

Animal pests are probably the biggest problem when it comes to growing hardy bulbs. Mice, voles, and chipmunks all relish bulbs — especially tulips and crocuses. (Moles often are blamed for destroying bulb plantings, but they are strictly carnivorous. Mice and voles give moles a bad rap, because they use mole tunnels to reach bulbs.) To protect bulbs from voracious rodents, surround the bulbs with sharp, crushed gravel at planting time. Planting bulbs in hardware cloth cages is tedious but effective. Daffodils are poisonous, and rodents leave their bulbs alone. Many bulbs in the amaryllis family (Amaryllidaceae), to which daffodils belong, are rodent resistant because the bulbs are poisonous or at least somewhat so.

Overwintering Tender Bulbs

Of course, just which bulbs are tender and which are hardy largely depends on where you live. For bulbs that are not hardy in a particular area, gardeners usually have several growing options. Many tender bulbs are grown as annuals and simply replaced each season. Experimenting with hardiness by looking for a warm site or mulching heavily over winter is another option. Overwintering these plants indoors is also a fairly simple process that is well worth the effort for many species of bulbs. For one thing, overwintered bulbs often give a better show than newly purchased ones. While this isn't necessarily the case with inexpensive corms or tulip bulbs, clumps of overwintered dahlia roots or canna rhizomes nearly always produce bigger, showier plants than newly purchased ones. And a large tub of bulbs such as belladonna lily *(Amaryllis belladonna)* will be more stunning each year. Many gardeners also simply enjoy the process of overwintering plants. Not only does it mark the progress of the seasons, it also provides an opportunity for experimenting with different plants and techniques to discover what works best.

To overwinter bulbs indoors, dig them in either summer or fall just

Where hardy, Amaryllis belladonna can be grown outdoors year-round. The best option for growing them in the North is to plant the bulbs in large containers or tubs. To overwinter them, gradually dry off the soil at the end of the season and store the containers in a cool dry place until the new season begins.

as the leaves turn yellow and begin to disappear. Label them as you dig: piles of bulbs all look remarkably similar several months after you dig them, no matter how sure you are that you'll remember what is what. Net bags make it easy to label a group of bulbs. You can write names directly on structures such as dahlia roots with a felt-tip pen. Store the bulbs dry, packed in either peat moss or vermiculite or simply placed in paper bags, and keep them in a cool, dry place. Keeping these plants in containers year-round is another option. In this case, gradually reduce watering once the leaves begin to turn yellow in summer or fall and store them right in their pots in a cool, dry place. In both cases the storage specifics differ from species to species: see the How to Grow sections in the individual entries for details on recommended soil moisture (some should be kept barely, but not completely, moist) as well as temperature. In all cases, a dry, well-ventilated spot is best.

Inspect overwintered bulbs several times during the winter months. Cut away rotted sections and dust the cuts with sulfur; separate these bulbs from completely healthy ones. Discard any entirely rotted bulbs.

Pot up or plant out bulbs in spring to start the cycle again. Don't move tender bulbs to the garden until after the last frost date, once the weather has settled and the soil has warmed up. Most resent cold, and especially damp, soil when they are just getting started and will simply rot rather than grow. Always water carefully until you see signs that the bulbs are growing actively. To give a head start to plants that thrive in areas with long hot summers—*Curcuma, Caladium, Canna,* and *Hedychium,* for example—consider sprouting them indoors several weeks before the last spring frost date. Starting plants indoors is especially beneficial in areas with short growing seasons. For heat-loving species, setting the pots on a heat mat (the type used to start seedlings) works wonders and encourages the plants to begin growing much more quickly.

☙ PROPAGATING BULBS

The easiest way to propagate clumps of plants that grow from bulbs or corms is to dig the clumps and break apart and replant the individual bulbs or corms. The same is true for plants that grow from tuberous roots, tubers, and rhizomes. Dig bulbs after the foliage has turned yellow but before it disappears completely. With species overwintered indoors, such as dahlias and cannas, wait until spring to divide the rootstocks because the cut edges are more likely to rot over winter.

BASAL CUTTAGE. This technique is used primarily on hyacinths *(Hyacinthus orientalis)* but also can be used with other species including squills (*Scilla* spp.), snowdrops (*Galanthus* spp.), snowflakes (*Leucojum* spp.), daffodils (*Narcissus* spp.), and amaryllis (*Hippeastrum* spp.). Basal cuttage causes bulbs to form large quantities of bulblets. Collect bulbs for basal cuttage in midsummer, after the leaves have died back and dried, discarding any that look diseased.

There are two different techniques for basal cuttage: scooping and scoring. Either way, you damage the basal plate of the bulb and cause it to form numerous bulblets. For scooping, use a spoon with a sharpened edge, such as a grapefruit spoon, or a small-bladed knife to remove the entire basal plate of the bulb and destroy its central shoot. To score a bulb, use a sharp knife to make three cuts, across the base of the bulb, that extend through the basal plate and into the growing point. Dust scooped or scored bulbs with fungicide, then store them upside down in dry sand or on open trays for a week in a warm (70° to 78°F), dry, well-ventilated spot to encourage callus tissue to form. After that, cover the treated bulbs loosely with plastic to increase the humidity to 90 percent. You should be able to see bulblets at the bases of the scales of scooped or scored bulbs in

Like daffodils and many other spring bulbs, hyacinths produce offsets and are easy to propagate by digging and dividing the clumps in late spring after the foliage has turned yellow. To produce an abundance of bulblets from a single hyacinth bulb, consider propagating by basal cuttage.

3 to 4 months. When this happens, plant the mother bulbs, still upside down, in a cool, protected spot with the bulblets just below the soil surface. Scooped bulbs usually produce more bulblets than scored ones, but they take longer to bloom: bulblets from scooped bloom in 3 to 4 years; from scoring in 2 to 3 years.

BULBILS AND CORMELS. Some plants (lilies, for example) produce small bulbs along their stems. Those above the soil are called bulbils; those below, bulblets. These can be detached and grown on into full-sized plants. Plants that grow from corms, including glads and crocuses, also can be propagated by growing on the small corms, called cormels, that they produce around the mother bulbs. Pot up bulbils, bulblets, and cormels in containers and treat them as you would seeds. Or, plant them in a nursery bed until they are large enough to go into the garden. For the corms of summer bulbs such as glads, hold the corms over winter, then replant individually at the proper time for planting full-sized corms. Set bulbils, bulblets, and corms in the soil at a depth of about twice their height.

CHIPPING. This technique, sometimes referred to as bulb cuttings, is a painstaking but useful way to propagate bulbs that are slow to produce offsets, such as snowdrops (*Galanthus* spp.). Collect and dry bulbs from midsummer to fall, discarding any that look diseased. Cut down from the top of the bulb through the basal plate with a sharp knife or razor blade. Cut each piece in half again. (You can continue until you have 16 chips from each bulb, or stop while the individual pieces are fairly easy to handle.) Each piece must have a section of the basal plant. Briefly soak the chips in a liquid fungicide, then let them dry for about 10 minutes. Place the treated chips in a plastic bag with a small amount of vermiculite or perlite. Loosely close the bag and store it in a dark, warm (68°F) place for 3 months. Regularly check for and discard any chips that have begun to rot. After 3 months bulblets should have formed around the basal plate of each chip. Separate them, harden them off, and pot them up. They will take about 3 or 4 years to reach blooming size.

SCALING. You can propagate bulbs with individual scales—such as lilies—by pulling off the scales and planting them one by one. After pulling off the scales, dust the base with a fungicide such as sulfur, and plant in moist vermiculite or a 50-50 mix of coarse sand and peat moss. Cover the pots with a plastic bag. When the new bulbs are large enough to handle, either pot them up and keep them in a protected spot outdoors, move them to a nursery bed, or plant them out in the garden.

GROWING FROM SEEDS. Without doubt, growing bulbs from seeds takes more patience than dividing the clumps, but it is often the best way to acquire an unusual species or raise large quantities of plants. While late winter to midspring is a fine time to sow many bulbs, midsummer and fall are also suitable times to sow seeds of many bulbs. For one reason, many bulbs are best grown from seeds sown as soon as they are ripe to ensure adequate germination.

The easiest way to grow many hardy bulbs from seeds is to sow them in pots and set them outdoors for germination. In this case, sow them just as you would pots to be germinated indoors, then top off the pots with a ¼- to ½-inch layer of fine, washed gravel; the small pebbles sold for use in aquariums usually work well. This layer keeps the mix from drying out quickly, and it also helps prevent mosses from developing and smothering your seedlings. Also add a plastic label (wooden ones rot quickly) marked with the seed name and sowing date. Set the pots in a cold frame, or sink them to their rims in a nursery bed or a protected spot in the garden. Cover them with a piece of fine-mesh hardware cloth to keep mice and other animals from digging in the pots. Natural rainfall will take care of most of the watering, but you will need to water during dry spells. While some perennials germinate in a few weeks, it may take months for others to appear.

Indoors, sow seeds of bulbs as you would annuals in late winter or early spring. Fill containers with moist seed-starting mix, and press the seeds into the surface or cover them with the amount of mix recommended on the packet. Label each pot with the name of the seed and the sowing date. Cover the containers with sheets of clear plastic suspended on a wire frame or with molded plastic "domes" sold for this purpose. Put covered containers under fluorescent lights. Remove the coverings once the seedlings emerge. The seeds of a few bulbs benefit from a brief chilling period before they're germinated. Sow these in pots, place each pot in a plastic bag, close the bag loosely, and set it in the refrigerator for the recommended amount of time. After that, germinate them at the recommended temperature. Keep the pots evenly moist but not wet until seedlings emerge.

Whether sown indoors or out, once your seedlings emerge, remove any covers to allow good air circulation, and give them plenty of light. When the first pair of true leaves has developed, transplant indoor- or outdoor-grown seedlings into individual 2- to 4-inch pots. Use a growing medium that's somewhat coarser — with more perlite and/or vermiculite — than the seed-starting mix. Moisten the growing mix and the pots of seedlings before transplanting. Use a pencil or a plant label to separate individual plants and to make holes in the center of the new containers. Lower seedlings into the holes so they are growing at the same depth they were in their initial pots—you may or may not be able to see a small bulb forming. Gently push the moist mix around the roots until the mix supports the seedling, then lightly tap the bottom of the pot once or twice on your work surface to settle the mix around the roots. Water as soon as possible after transplanting. Keep the pots evenly moist, and start feeding seedlings once they have begun growing again. Use a liquid houseplant fertilizer, diluted to half its regular strength. Feed once a week for 3 to 4 weeks. After that, use the fertilizer full strength every 10 to 14 days until the seedlings are ready for transplanting into the garden or to a nursery bed to be grown on until they reach full size. Before moving seedlings to the garden, be sure to harden them off to minimize transplanting stress. About a week before you're ready to move seedlings to the garden, set them outdoors for a few hours in a shaded location that is protected from wind. Leave them out for a few more hours each day, and gradually move them into a more exposed location. Keep them well watered during this process. The night before you transplant, leave them out all night.

Galanthus elwesii, *commonly called giant snowdrop, produces an abundance of dainty flowers in spring. Where happy, plants self-sow with abandon. Dig the seedlings in spring to spread around the garden, or leave plants to establish large drifts.*

Gallery
of Plants

▲ *Achimenes* 'Peach Blossom'
(inset *A.* 'Minette')

Achimenes, Monkey-faced Pansy,
Orchid Pansy

SIZE: 6 to 8 inches; spreads 1 to 2 feet

Bright shade with protection from direct sun

Rich, evenly moist soil; usually grown in baskets
or other containers

Bears rosy salmon 1½- to 3-inch-wide flowers
from summer to fall

Zones 10 and 11

P. 214

▼ *Agapanthus africanus*

African Lily

SIZE: 2 to 3 feet

Full sun

Fertile, well-drained, evenly moist soil

Bears rounded 6- to 12-inch-wide umbels of
dark purple-blue flowers in late summer

Zones 9 to 11

P. 215

Agapanthus hybrid 'My Joy'
Hybrid Agapanthus
SIZE: 2 to 3 feet
Full sun
Fertile, well-drained, evenly moist soil
Bears umbels of white flowers in mid- and late summer
Zones 7 or 8 to 10
P. 215

Agapanthus hybrid 'Storm Cloud'
Hybrid Agapanthus
SIZE: 3 to 4 feet
Full sun
Fertile, well-drained, evenly moist soil
Bears umbels of dark purple-blue flowers in mid- and late summer
Zones 7 or 8 to 10
P. 215

Allium aflatunense
Persian Onion
SIZE: 2 to 3 feet

Full sun

Well-drained soil

Round 4½-inch-wide clusters of densely packed red-violet flowers in early summer

Zones 4 to 8

P. 217

Allium caeruleum
Blue Globe Onion, Nodding Onion
SIZE: 1 to 2 feet

Full sun

Very well drained soil

Produces 2-inch-wide umbels of densely packed, starry dark blue flowers in early summer

Zones 3 to 8

P. 217

Allium carinatum ssp. *pulchellum*

Keeled Garlic

SIZE: 1 to 1½ feet

Full sun

Well-drained soil

Bears 2½-inch-wide umbels of reddish violet blooms in midsummer

Zones 5 to 8

P. 217

Allium cernuum

Nodding Onion, Wild Onion

SIZE: 1½ to 2 feet

Full sun or shade

Well-drained soil; tolerates heavy soil or sandy conditions

Native North American with 2½-inch-wide umbels of rose-purple, pink, or white flowers in early summer

Zones 4 to 9

P. 217

Allium cristophii
Star of Persia
SIZE: 1 to 2 feet
Full sun
Well-drained soil
Bears ball-like 8- to 12-inch-wide umbels of starry silvery purple flowers in summer
Zones 4 to 8
P. 218

Allium cyaneum
SIZE: 4 to 10 inches
Full sun
Well-drained soil
Produces ¾-inch-wide umbels of 6 to 18 blue flowers in summer
Zones 5 to 9
P. 218

Allium giganteum
Giant Onion
SIZE: 3 to 5 feet
Full sun
Well-drained soil
Produces dense, round 4- to 5-inch-wide clusters of starry rosy purple flowers in summer
Zones 4 to 8
P. 218

Allium giganteum
'White Giant'
SIZE: 3 to 5 feet
Full sun
Well-drained soil
Produces dense, round 4- to 5-inch-wide clusters of starry white flowers in summer
Zones 4 to 8
P. 218

Allium hybrid 'Globemaster'

SIZE: 2 to 3 feet

Full sun

Well-drained soil

Produces long-lasting 10-inch-wide umbels of rich violet flowers in early summer

Zones 4 or 5 to 8

P. 219

Allium karataviense

Turkistan Onion

SIZE: 6 to 10 inches

Full sun

Well-drained soil

In early summer bears 3- to 5-inch-wide clusters of up to 50 starry pale pink flowers

Zones 5 to 9

P. 219

▲ *Allium moly*
Lily Leek, Golden Garlic
SIZE: ½ to 1 foot
Full sun or partial shade
Very well drained soil
Produces loose, showy 2-inch-wide umbels of
starry-shaped golden yellow flowers in early
summer
Zones 3 to 9
P. 219

▼ *Allium oreophilum*
SIZE: 2 to 8 inches
Full sun
Well-drained soil
Produces loose 1½-inch-wide umbels of 10 to 15
pinkish purple flowers in early summer
Zones 4 to 9
P. 220

Allium schoenoprasum
Chives
SIZE: 1 to 2 feet

Full sun

Well-drained soil

Mounds of edible round leaves topped by 1-
inch-wide cloverlike clusters of rosy pink
flowers in summer

Zones 3 to 9

P. 221

Allium schubertii
SIZE: 1 to 2 feet

Full sun

Well-drained soil

Bears striking, round 9- to 12-inch-wide umbels
of pale purple flowers arranged on stalks of
different lengths

Zones 5 to 10

P. 221

Allium senescens

SIZE: 6 to 12 inches
Full sun
Well-drained soil
Bears 1-inch-wide umbels of 20 to 30 mauve-
pink flowers in mid- to late summer
Zones 5 to 9
P. 221

Allium sphaerocephalon

Drumstick Chives, Drumstick Allium, Round-headed Leek

SIZE: 2 to 3 feet
Full sun
Well-drained soil
Produces nearly solid 1-inch-wide clusters of
green to purple or purplish maroon bell-
shaped flowers in midsummer
Zones 4 to 8
P. 221

Allium tanguticum
Lavender Globe Lily
SIZE: 2 feet
Full sun
Well-drained soil
Bears 2-inch-wide lavender-blue flowers in
midsummer
Zones 4 to 9
P. 222

Allium thunbergii 'Ozawa'
SIZE: 8 inches
Full sun
Well-drained soil
Produces 1- to 1½-inch-wide umbels of rose-
purple flowers in fall
Zones 4 to 8
P. 222

Allium triquetrum
Three-cornered Leek
SIZE: 1 foot

Full sun

Well-drained soil

In late spring or early summer bears nodding 1-
to 3-inch-wide clusters of lightly scented
white flowers

Zones 5 to 9

P. 222

Allium tuberosum
Garlic Chives
SIZE: 2 feet

Full sun

Well-drained soil

Bears rounded 2-inch-wide umbels of fragrant
starry white flowers from late summer to
fall

Zones 4 to 8

P. 222

▲ *Allium unifolium*
(inset, close-up)

SIZE: 1 to 1½ feet

Full sun

Well-drained soil

Pacific Northwest native with rounded 2- to 2½-inch-wide umbels of bell-shaped pink to purplish pink flowers in late spring or early summer

Zones 5 to 9

P. 222

▼ *Allium ursinum*

Ramsons, Bear's Garlic, Wood Garlic

SIZE: 6 to 18 inches

Partial shade

Well-drained soil

Bears flattened 2-inch-wide umbels of white flowers in spring

Zones 5 to 8

P. 223

Alocasia hybrid 'Hilo Beauty'

SIZE: 6 to 8 feet

Partial shade; best in a sheltered spot

Deep, rich, evenly moist, well-drained soil

Foliage plant grown for its handsome green
  leaves mottled with cream or light green

Zones 10 and 11

P. 224

Alocasia macrorrhiza

Giant Taro

SIZE: 15 feet and spreads to 8 feet; smaller in
  the North

Partial shade; best in a sheltered spot

Deep, rich, evenly moist, well-drained soil

Foliage plant grown for its glossy, arrow-shaped
  green leaves with leaf blades ranging from 2
  to 4 feet long

Zones 10 and 11

P. 224

Alstroemeria aurea
Peruvian Lily, Lily-of-the-Incas
SIZE: 2 to 3 feet
Full sun in the North, light shade in the South
Rich, moist, well-drained soil
Bears clusters of orange or yellow flowers with
   red-striped tepals in summer
Zones 7 to 10; to Zone 5 with winter protection
P. 225

Alstroemeria ligtu hybrids
Peruvian Lily, Lily-of-the-Incas
SIZE: 1½ to 2 feet
Full sun in the North, light shade in the South
Rich, moist, well-drained soil
Bears clusters of yellow flowers spotted and
   streaked with shades of yellow, white, red, or
   purple in summer
Zones 7 to 10; to Zone 5 with winter protection
P. 225

× *Amarcrinum memoria-corsii*

SIZE: 2 to 3 feet

Full sun or partial shade

Rich, well-drained soil

Produces clusters of long-lived, fragrant rose-pink trumpets in late summer to early fall

Zones 8 to 10, to Zone 7 with winter protection

P. 226

Amaryllis belladonna

Belladonna Lily, Magic Lily, Naked Ladies, Resurrection Lily

SIZE: 1½ to 2 feet

Full sun or partial shade

Average, deeply prepared, well-drained soil; drought tolerant

Produces showy clusters of fragrant pink funnel-shaped blooms in late summer and fall

Zones 8 to 10; to Zone 7 with winter protection

P. 227

Amorphophallus konjac
Devil's Tongue, Snake Palm, Voodoo Lily, Umbrella Arum

SIZE: 3 to 6 feet

Partial to full shade

Very rich, evenly moist soil

Produces leathery red-purple flowers and handsome, deeply lobed, very large leaves

Zones 7 to 10; to Zone 6 with protection

P. 228

Anemone blanda
'Blue Shades' (inset, *A. blanda* 'White Splendour')

Grecian Windflower

SIZE: 6 to 8 inches

Partial or half-day shade

Light, rich, evenly moist soil

Bears fernlike leaves and white, pink, or blue 2-inch-wide daisylike flowers in spring

Zones 4 to 8

P. 229

Anemone coronaria

Florist's Anemone, Poppy Anemone

SIZE: 1 to 1½ feet

Partial or half-day shade

Light, rich, evenly moist soil

In spring bears single or double blooms with black centers in shades of scarlet, violet-blue, or white

Zones 8 to 10

P. 230

Anemone nemorosa

Wood Anemone

SIZE: 4 to 10 inches

Partial or half-day shade

Light, rich, evenly moist soil

Bears white, pale pink, or lavender-blue ½- to ¾-inch-wide flowers in spring

Zones 4 to 8

P. 230

Anemone ranunculoides
Buttercup Anemone, Yellow Windflower
SIZE: 2 to 4 inches
Partial or half-day shade
Light, rich, evenly moist soil
Fast-spreading species with solitary ¾- to 1¼-
   inch-wide blooms in spring
Zones 4 to 8
P. 230

Anemone sylvestris
Snowdrop Anemone
SIZE: 1 to 1½ feet
Partial or half-day shade
Light, rich, evenly moist soil
Bears single white 2-inch-wide flowers in spring
Zones 3 to 8
P. 231

Anemonella thalictroides 'Oscar Schoaf'

Rue Anemone

SIZE: 4 to 8 inches

Partial shade

Average to rich, evenly moist soil

Double-flowered form of a native North American wildflower bearing white or pale pink flowers from spring to early summer

Zones 4 to 8

P. 231

Anomatheca laxa

SIZE: 6 to 12 inches

Full sun

Average, sandy soil

Bears clusters of trumpet-shaped ¾-inch-long red flowers in early summer

Zones 8 to 10

P. 232

Anthericum liliago
Saint Bernard's Lily
SIZE: 2 to 3 feet

Full sun

Rich, well-drained soil

Produces clumps of gray-green grassy leaves
and racemes of starry white flowers in late
spring or early summer

Zones 4 to 7

P. 233

Arisaema candidissimum
SIZE: 14 to 16 inches

Partial shade

Rich, moist, well-drained soil

In early summer bears hooded 3- to 6-inch-
long greenish flowers (spathes) that are
white with pink stripes at the top

Zones 6 to 9

P. 234

Arisaema ringens

SIZE: 10 to 12 inches

Partial shade

Rich, moist, well-drained soil

An early summer–blooming species with
   hooded 4- to 6-inch-long green flowers
   (spathes) striped and tipped with purple

Zones 6 to 9

P. 234

Arisaema sikokianum

SIZE: 1 to 1½ feet

Partial shade

Rich, moist, well-drained soil

Late spring–blooming species with a hooded
   purple-brown flower (spathe) surrounding
   a white club-shaped Jack (spadix)

Zones 5 to 9

P. 234

Arisaema triphyllum

SIZE: 6 to 12 inches or more

Partial shade

Rich, moist, well-drained soil

Native North American wildflower bearing
hooded green flowers (spathes) in spring
and early summer that are often striped
with dark purple

Zones 4 to 9

P. 234

Arum creticum

SIZE: 1 to 2½ feet

Sun or partial shade

Deeply prepared, rich, moist, well-drained soil

Spring-flowering species with arrow-shaped
dark green leaves and fragrant yellow or
creamy white flowers (spathes)

Zones 8 to 10

P. 235

Arum italicum 'Marmoratum' (inset, fruit)

Italian Arum

SIZE: 1 foot

Sun or partial shade

Deeply prepared, rich, moist, well-drained soil

Handsome, arrow-shaped cream-veined leaves, pale greenish white flowers in early summer, and showy spikes of orange-red berries in fall

Zones 6 to 9; to Zone 5 with protection

P. 236

Arum maculatum

Lords and Ladies, Cuckoo-pint, Adam-and-Eve

SIZE: 12 to 15 inches

Sun or partial shade

Deeply prepared, rich, moist, well-drained soil

Glossy, arrow-shaped leaves usually spotted with black or purple, yellow-green flowers in spring, and bright red berries

Zones 6 to 9

P. 236

Asphodeline lutea
King's Spear, Yellow Asphodel
SIZE: 3 to 5 feet

Full sun

Average, well-drained, deeply prepared soil

Bears dense, erect racemes of fragrant, starry bright yellow flowers in late spring or early summer

Zones 6 to 9

P. 237

Asphodelus albus
SIZE: 2½ to 3 feet

Full sun

Average, well-drained, deeply prepared soil

In early summer bears dense, erect racemes of starry white funnel-shaped flowers

Zones 7 to 10

P. 237

Babiana rubrocyanea

SIZE: 2 to 8 inches

Full sun

Light, rich, well-drained soil

Bears spikes of ¾- to 1½-inch-wide red-and-blue flowers in spring

Zones 8 to 10

P. 238

Babiana stricta

SIZE: 5 to 12 inches

Full sun

Light, rich, well-drained soil

Bears spikes of ¾- to 1½-inch-long flowers in spring in shades of blue, purple, mauve, and yellow

Zones 8 to 10

P. 239

Begonia grandis
Hardy Begonia
SIZE: 2 to 2½ feet

Partial to full shade

Rich, evenly moist, well-drained soil

Produces wing-shaped leaves and arching clusters of pink flowers in late summer and early fall

Zones 6 to 10; to Zone 5 with winter protection

P. 240

Begonia sutherlandii
Sutherland Begonia
SIZE: 1 to 2 feet

Partial shade

Loose, well-drained soil rich in organic matter

Mounding species with green leaves and pendent clusters of orange 1-inch flowers all summer

Zones 8 to 10; to Zone 7 with winter protection

P. 240

Begonia Tuberhybrida hybrids
Tuberous Begonia
SIZE: ½ to 2 feet; spreads to ½ to 2 feet
Partial shade
Loose, well-drained soil rich in organic matter`
Bears bright to dark green leaves and single or
    double flowers in summer in yellows, or-
    anges, pinks, reds, and white
Zones 10 to 11
P. 241

Bellevalia pycnantha
SIZE: 1 foot
Full sun or light shade
Rich, well-drained soil
In spring bears dense clusters of small violet-
    blue flowers edged in yellow
Zones 5 to 8
P. 241

Bessera elegans
Coral Drops
SIZE: 2 feet

Full sun

Average, well-drained soil

Bears few-flowered 1½-inch-wide umbels of
    scarlet flowers in late summer or early fall

Zones 9 to 11; to Zone 8 with winter protection

P. 242

Bletilla striata
Chinese Ground Orchid, Hyacinth Bletilla
SIZE: 1 to 2 feet

Partial shade

Rich, evenly moist, well-drained soil

From spring to early summer produces loose
    clusters of up to 12 1-inch-wide magenta-
    pink flowers

Zones 7 to 9; to Zones 5 or 6 with winter pro-
    tection

P. 243

▲ *Bloomeria crocea*
Golden Stars

SIZE: 6 to 12 inches

Full sun or partial shade

Light, sandy soil rich in organic matter

California native wildflowers with umbels of orangy yellow flowers in late spring or early summer

Zones 9 to 10; to Zone 8 with winter protection

P. 244

▼ *Brimeura amethystina* (inset *B. amethystina* var. *alba*)

SIZE: 8 to 10 inches

Full sun or light shade

Rich, well-drained soil

Spring-blooming bulb with racemes of six tubular to bell-shaped flowers

Zones 5 to 9

P. 245

Bulbine frutescens

SIZE: 1 to 1½ feet
Full sun
Sandy, well-drained soil; tolerates poor, dry soil
Bears succulent, lance-shaped leaves and
    racemes of small starry yellow flowers in
    summer
Zones 10 to 11
P. 245

Bulbinella rossii

SIZE: To 4 feet
Full sun or partial shade
Moist, well-drained soil
Produces clumps of succulent, grasslike leaves
    topped by racemes of yellow flowers in
    spring
Zones 8 to 9.
P. 246

Bulbocodium vernum
Spring Meadow Saffron
SIZE: 1½ to 3 inches

Full sun or very light shade

Rich, well-drained soil

Bears showy, crocuslike, rosy purple blooms in
  spring

Zones 3 to 9

P. 247

Caladium bicolor
Caladium, Angel Wings, Elephant Ears
SIZE: 1½ to 2 feet; spreads to 2 feet

Partial to full shade

Evenly moist, well-drained soil rich in organic
  matter

Grown for its handsome, arrow-shaped leaves
  variously patterned in green, white, pink,
  red, and maroon

Zones 10 to 11

P. 248

Calochortus superbus

SIZE: 1½ to 2 feet

Full sun

Very well drained soil

California native wildflower producing loose clusters of cup-shaped cream, lavender-blue, or yellow flowers in late spring

Zones 5 to 10

P. 250

Calochortus venustus

White Mariposa

SIZE: ½ to 2 feet tall

Full sun

Very well drained soil

Native California wildflower with clusters of cup-shaped white, yellow, red, or purple flowers from late spring to early summer

Zones 6 to 10

P. 250

Camassia cusickii
Camass, Cusick Quamash

SIZE: 2 to 3 feet

Full sun or partial shade

Rich, well-drained soil

West Coast native species with showy, erect
racemes of starry blue 2-inch-wide flowers
in late spring

Zones 3 to 10

P. 251

Camassia leichtlinii 'Semiplena'
Leichtlin Quamash

SIZE: 2½ to 3 feet

Full sun or partial shade

Rich, well-drained soil

Selection of a native Pacific Northwest species
with erect racemes of semidouble creamy
white flowers in late spring

Zones 4 to 10

P. 251

Camassia scilloides
Wild Hyacinth, Western Camassia

SIZE: 1 to 2½ feet

Full sun or partial shade

Rich, well-drained soil

Native species from eastern North America with racemes of blue, violet-blue, or white flowers in early summer

Zones 4 to 9

P. 252

Canna 'Phaison'

SIZE: 5 to 6 feet

Full sun

Well-drained, rich, evenly moist soil

Grown for its showy purple leaves striped with yellow and red, topped by orange flowers in summer

Zones 7 or 8 to 11

P. 254

Canna 'Pretoria'

SIZE: 5 to 6 feet

Full sun

Well-drained, rich, evenly moist soil

Produces showy clumps of yellow-and-green-striped leaves edged in maroon topped by orange-yellow blooms in summer

Zones 7 or 8 to 11

P. 254

Canna 'Wyoming'

SIZE: 5 to 6 feet

Full sun

Well-drained, rich, evenly moist soil

Bears burnt orange flowers and handsome burgundy leaves

Zones 7 or 8 to 11

P. 254

Cardiocrinum giganteum

SIZE: 5 to 12 feet

Partial shade

Rich, deeply prepared, moist, well-drained soil

Bears heart-shaped leaves and, in summer, erect racemes of fragrant, nodding, white trumpets striped maroon inside

Zones 7 to 9

P. 255

Chamaelirium luteum

Devil's Bit, Blazing Star, Fairy Wand

Size: 1 to 3 feet

Partial shade

Rich, moist to boggy soil; acid pH is best

Native North American wildflower that bears cylindrical racemes of creamy white flowers from early- to midsummer

Zones 3 to 8

P. 256

Chasmanthe aethiopica

SIZE: 2 feet

Full sun or partial shade

Rich, moist, well-drained soil

Bears racemes of 3-inch-long red or orange flowers with maroon throats in spring to early summer

Zones 8 to 10

P. 257

Chasmanthe floribunda

SIZE: 2 to 4 feet

Full sun or partial shade

Rich, moist, well-drained soil

Bears branched 1-foot-long racemes of 3-inch-long yellow or orange flowers in summer

Zones 9 to 10

P. 257

Chionodoxa forbesii
'Pink Giant' (inset, species)
Glory-of-the-snow

SIZE: 4 to 8 inches

Full sun or partial shade

Average, well-drained soil

Produces loose racemes of blue ½- to ¾-inch-wide flowers with white eyes in early spring

Zones 3 to 9

P. 258

Chionodoxa luciliae
Glory-of-the-snow

SIZE: 4 to 6 inches tall

Full sun or partial shade

Average, well-drained soil

Bears racemes of ½- to 1-inch-wide blue flowers with white centers in early spring

Zones 3 to 9

P. 258

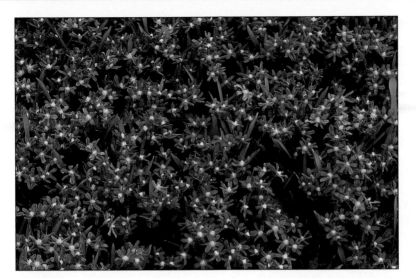

▲ *Chionodoxa sardensis*

Sardenian Glory-of-the-snow

SIZE: 4 to 6 inches

Full sun or partial shade

Average, well-drained soil

Produces racemes of ½-inch-wide bluish purple flowers in early spring that lack white centers

Zones 5 to 9

P. 258

▼ *Chlidanthus fragrans*

Delicate Lily, Fragrant Amaryllis, Peru Chlidanthus

SIZE: 6 to 8 inches

Full sun

Moist, well-drained, somewhat sandy soil

Bears lemon-scented golden yellow flowers in summer that are 3 inches wide and 4 to 5 inches long

Zones 9 to 11

P. 259

Clivia miniata (inset, close-up)
Kaffir Lily

SIZE: 1½ to 2½ feet

Partial shade

Rich, well-drained soil; commonly grown in containers

Evergreen leaves topped by clusters of trumpet-shaped orange, red-orange, or yellow flowers in spring and early summer

Zones 10 to 11

P. 260

Colchicum autumnale (inset 'Alboplenum')
Autumn Crocus, Meadow Saffron

SIZE: 4 to 6 inches

Full sun or light shade

Average, deeply prepared, well-drained soil

In midfall bears from one to six pale lavender-pink 1½- to 2½-inch-long flowers

Zones 4 to 8

P. 261

Colchicum hybrid 'Violet Queen'

Hybrid Autumn Crocus

SIZE: 5 to 6 inches

Full sun or light shade

Average, deeply prepared, well-drained soil

Produces funnel-shaped 2- to 2½-inch-long violet-purple blooms in early fall

Zones 4 to 8

P. 262

Colchicum hybrid 'Waterlily'

Hybrid Autumn Crocus

SIZE: 5 to 6 inches

Full sun or light shade

Average, deeply prepared, well-drained soil

Produces double pinkish lilac blooms with 2- to 3-inch tepals in fall

Zones 4 to 8

P. 262

Colchicum speciosum
Autumn Crocus
SIZE: 5 to 7 inches

Full sun or light shade

Average, deeply prepared, well-drained soil

In fall, bears one to three tuliplike 2- to 3-inch-long reddish violet blooms with yellow anthers

Zones 4 to 8

P. 262

Colocasia esculenta
'Black Magic'
Elephant's Ear, Taro, Dasheen
SIZE: 3 to 7 feet

Partial shade

Deep, rich, wet or constantly moist soil

Foliage plant grown for its heart- or arrow-shaped 2-foot-long purple-black leaves

Zones 10 to 11

P. 263

Colocasia esculenta 'Illustris'
Elephant's Ear, Taro, Dasheen
SIZE: 3 to 7 feet
Partial shade
Deep, rich, wet or constantly moist soil
Foliage plant grown for its heart- or arrow-
  shaped 2-foot-long green leaves with black-
  purple veins and purple leaf stalks
Zones 10 to 11
P. 263

Commelina coelestis
Tuberous Day Flower, Blue Spiderwort
SIZE: 2 to 3 feet; spreads to 1½ feet
Partial shade
Rich, well-drained soil
Bears abundant clusters of small brilliant blue
  flowers from summer to fall
Zones 9 to 11
P. 264

▲ *Convallaria majalis*
Lily-of-the-valley
SIZE: 6 to 9 inches

Partial shade

Evenly moist, rich soil

Bears one-sided racemes of fragrant, waxy white bells in spring followed by round glossy red berries

Zones 2 to 8

P. 265

▼ *Corydalis solida*
(inset 'Beth Evans')
SIZE: 8 to 10 inches

Partial shade

Rich, moist, well-drained soil

Produces mounds of lacy gray-green leaves and clusters of spurred mauve-pink flowers in early spring

Zones 5 to 9

P. 266

Crinum americanum
Southern Swamp Lily, Florida Crinum

SIZE: 1½ to 2 feet

Full sun or partial shade

Very deeply prepared, rich, moist, well-drained
    soil

Southeastern native species bearing umbels of
    large fragrant creamy white flowers from
    late spring to fall

Zones 9 to 11

P. 267

Crinum asiaticum
Poison Bulb, Grand Crinum

SIZE: 2 feet

Full sun or partial shade

Very deeply prepared, rich, moist, well-drained
    soil

Produces large umbels of 20 or more fragrant
    white spidery flowers in summer

Zones 8 to 11

P. 267

Crinum × powellii
Hybrid Crinum
SIZE: 4 to 5 feet
Full sun or partial shade
Very deeply prepared, rich, moist, well-drained soil
Bears showy umbels of fragrant 4-inch-long, pink trumpets in late summer and fall
Zones 7 to 10
P. 268

Crocosmia 'Citronella'
Hybrid Crocosmia, Montbretia
SIZE: 2 to 3 feet
Full sun
Evenly moist soil rich in organic matter
2 to 3 feet
Bears arching spikes of yellow flowers in summer
Zones 6 to 9
P. 269

Crocosmia 'Lucifer'
Hybrid Crocosmia, Montbretia
SIZE: 2 to 3 feet

Full sun

Evenly moist soil rich in organic matter

Bears arching spikes of bright red 1½- to 2-inch-long flowers in summer

Zones 5 to 9

P. 269

Crocosmia 'Venus'
Hybrid Crocosmia, Montbretia
SIZE: 1½ to 2 feet

Full sun

Evenly moist soil rich in organic matter

Bears arching spikes of orange-red and yellow 1½- to 2-inch-long flowers in summer

Zones 6 to 9

P. 269

Crocus ancyrensis
Golden Bunch Crocus
SIZE: 2 inches

Full sun

Poor to average, sandy or gritty, well-drained
   soil

Late winter– to early spring–blooming species
   with bright yellow to orange-yellow flowers

Zones 3 to 8

P. 271

Crocus biflorus 'Miss Vain'
Scotch Crocus
SIZE: 2 to 2½ inches

Full sun

Poor to average, sandy or gritty, well-drained
   soil

Late winter– to early spring–blooming selection
   producing white flowers with pale lilac-blue
   bases and showy orange styles

Zones 3 to 8

P. 271

Crocus biflorus ssp. *weldenii* 'Fairy'

Scotch Crocus

SIZE: 2 to 2½ inches

Full sun

Poor to average, gritty, well-drained soil

Late winter– to early spring–blooming crocus bearing white flowers dusted with violet on the outside

Zones 3 to 8

P. 271

Crocus cartwrightianus f. *albus*

Fall Crocus

SIZE: 2 inches

Full sun

Poor to average, gritty, very well drained soil

Fall- to early winter–blooming species bearing lilac to white flowers with brilliant orange styles

Zones 6 to 8

P. 271

▲ *Crocus chrysanthus* 'Cream Beauty'

Snow Crocus

SIZE: 2 inches

Full sun

Poor to average, sandy or gritty, well-drained soil

Late winter– to early spring–blooming selection bearing creamy yellow blooms that are darker yellow inside

Zones 3 to 8

P. 271

▼ *Crocus chrysanthus* 'Gipsy Girl'

Snow Crocus

SIZE: 2 inches

Full sun

Poor to average, sandy or gritty, well-drained soil

Late winter– to early spring–blooming selection bearing bright yellow flowers striped with bronze-purple

Zones 3 to 8

P. 271

Crocus goulimyi
Fall Crocus
SIZE: 3 to 4 inches

Full sun

Poor to average, sandy or gritty, well-drained
soil

Fall-blooming species with rosy lilac flowers

Zones 3 to 8

P. 272

Crocus imperati 'De Jager'
Italian Crocus
SIZE: 3 to 4 inches

Full sun

Poor to average, sandy or gritty, well-drained
soil

Late winter– to early spring–blooming selection
bearing violet-purple flowers with a yellow
heart and yellow-brown striping

Zones 5 to 8

P. 272

Crocus korolkowii
Celandine Crocus
SIZE: 3 to 4 inches

Full sun

Poor to average, sandy or gritty, well-drained
soil

Late winter– to early spring–blooming species
that bears golden yellow flowers feathered
with brown on the outside

Zones 3 to 8

P. 272

Crocus minimus
SIZE: 3 inches

Full sun

Poor to average, sandy or gritty, well-drained
soil

Late spring–blooming species with rich lilac-
purple flowers and yellow-buff outer petals
marked in dark purple

Zones 3 to 8

P. 273

Crocus sativus
Saffron Crocus, Fall Crocus
SIZE: 2 inches

Full sun

Poor to average, sandy or gritty, well-drained
soil

Fall- to early winter–blooming, bearing lilac-
purple flowers veined in dark purple with
showy red styles

Zones 5 to 8

P. 273

Crocus sieberi
SIZE: 2 to 3 inches

Full sun

Poor to average, sandy or gritty, well-drained
soil

Late winter– to early spring–blooming species
bearing rose-purple flowers with yellow
throats

Zones 5 to 8

P. 274

▲ *Crocus speciosus*
Fall Crocus
SIZE: 4 to 6 inches

Full sun

Poor to average, sandy or gritty, well-drained
  soil

Vigorous fall-blooming species with violet-blue
  flowers veined in darker purple-blue

Zones 3 to 8

P. 274

▼ *Crocus tommasinianus*
SIZE: 3 to 4 inches

Full sun

Poor to average, sandy or gritty, well-drained
  soil

Vigorous late winter– to early spring–blooming
  species bearing pale lilac to red-purple
  blooms

Zones 3 to 8

P. 274

Crocus vernus mix

Dutch Crocus

SIZE: 4 to 5 inches

Full sun

Poor to average, sandy or gritty, well-drained
    soil

Spring-blooming species bearing flowers in a
    range of colors, including white, pale lilac,
    rich purple, violet, and yellow

Zones 3 to 8

P. 274

Crocus vernus 'Mammoth Yellow'

Dutch Crocus

SIZE: 4 to 5 inches

Full sun

Poor to average, sandy or gritty, well-drained
    soil

Selection of a popular spring-blooming species
    that produces rich yellow flowers

Zones 3 to 8

P. 274

Curcuma alismatifolia
Pinecone Ginger, Siam Tulip
SIZE: 1½ to 2 feet
Partial shade
Deeply prepared, moist, rich soil
Bears dark green leaves and small inflorescences
of pink bracts
Zones 8 to 10
P. 275

Curcuma zedoaria
Pinecone Ginger
SIZE: 3 feet
Partial shade
Deeply prepared, moist, rich soil
Bears handsome leaves with a maroon-brown
stripe down the center and bloom spikes
with green bracts tinged maroon-red or
purple
Zones 8 to 10
P. 275

▲ *Cyclamen coum*

Hardy Cyclamen

SIZE: 2 to 3 inches

Partial shade

Loose, rich, well-drained soil

Late winter– to early spring–blooming species with attractive leaves and small white or pink flowers

Zones 5 to 9

P. 277

▼ *Cyclamen hederifolium*

Hardy Cyclamen

SIZE: 4 to 5 inches

Partial shade

Loose, rich, well-drained soil

Fall-blooming species bearing silver-patterned leaves and 1-inch-long pink flowers

Zones 6 or 7 to 9

P. 277

Cyclamen repandum
Hardy Cyclamen
SIZE: 4 to 6 inches
Partial shade
Loose, rich, well-drained soil
Spring-blooming species with attractive leaves and magenta-pink flowers
Zones 7 to 9
P. 278

Cypella herbertii
SIZE: 1 to 3 feet
Full sun
Average to rich, well-drained soil
Bears loose clusters of yellowish orange flowers with inner tepals spotted or lined with purple
Zones 9 to 10
P. 279

Cyrtanthus elatus

SIZE: 1 to 2 feet
Full sun
Average to rich, well-drained soil
Bears umbels of funnel-shaped 3- to 4-inch-
   long scarlet flowers in late summer
Zones 10 to 11
P. 280

Dactylorhiza maculata
(inset, close-up)
Heath Spotted Orchid
SIZE: ½ to 2 feet
Partial shade
Moist, well-drained, deeply prepared soil rich in
   organic matter
Bears green leaves that may be spotted with
   brown or purple and racemes of rose or
   white flowers from spring to late summer
Zones 5 to 8
P. 280

Dahlia hybrid 'Bishop of Llandaff'

SIZE: 3½ to 6 feet

Full sun

Rich, well-drained, evenly moist soil

Bears double orange-red flowers that contrast with handsome maroon foliage

Zones 8 to 11

P. 282

Dahlia Coltness hybrids (dwarf type)

SIZE: 1½ to 2 feet

Full sun

Rich, well-drained, evenly moist soil

Dwarf series that bear single flowers in a wide range of colors and can be grown from seeds

Zones 8 to 11

P. 282

▲ *Dahlia* hybrid 'Figurine'
(waterlily type)

SIZE: 3½ to 6 feet

Full sun

Rich well-drained, evenly moist soil

Pink waterlily-type bloom with fully double,
symmetrical blooms from midsummer to
frost

Zones 8 to 11

P. 282

▼ *Dahlia* hybrid 'Little
Showoff' (collarette type)

SIZE: 3½ to 6 feet

Full sun

Rich, well-drained, evenly moist soil

Cultivar with collarette-type blooms featuring a
ruff of contrasting color in the center

Zones 8 to 11

P. 282

▲ *Dichelostemma congestum*

SIZE: 1½ to 2 feet

Full sun or partial shade

Rich, well-drained soil

Bears dense, rounded 2-inch-wide racemes of
purplish blue flowers in early summer

Zones 6 to 10

P. 283

▼ *Dichelostemma ida-maia*

Firecracker Plant

SIZE: 1 to 2½ feet

Full sun or partial shade

Rich, well-drained soil

In summer, bears exotic-looking umbels of
nodding, tubular flowers that are red with
short rolled-back yellow-green lobes at the
tip

Zones 6 to 10

P. 284

Dierama pendulum
Grassy Bells, Wand Flower
SIZE: 3 to 6 feet

Full sun

Rich, well-drained soil

Produces arching stems of bell-shaped purple-
   pink 1½- to 2-inch-long flowers in summer

Zones 7 to 9

P. 284

Dodecatheon meadia f. *album*
Common Shooting Star
SIZE: 1 foot; to 1½ feet in bloom

Full sun or partial shade

Rich, moist, well-drained soil

A North American native wildflower that bears
   clusters of magenta-pink shuttlecock-
   shaped flowers in mid- and late spring

Zones 4 to 8

P. 286

Dracunculus vulgaris

SIZE: 3 to 5 feet

Full sun or partial shade

Rich, well-drained soil

Bears large lobed leaves marked with white and dark maroon, velvety textured flowers (spathe) in spring or summer

Zones 8 to 10

P. 286

Eranthis hyemalis

Winter Aconite

SIZE: 2 to 3 inches

Full sun to partial shade

Rich, moist — but not wet — soil

A late winter– to early spring–blooming species bearing lobed green leaves and clusters of yellow flowers

Zones 4 to 9

P. 288

Eremurus himalaicus
Himalayan Foxtail Lily
SIZE: 4 to 6 feet

Full sun; a spot protected from wind is best

Rich, well-drained soil

Bears showy, erect 3-foot-long racemes of starry white flowers in late spring and early summer

Zones 5 to 8

P. 289

Eremurus stenophyllus
Foxtail Lily
SIZE: 3 feet

Full sun; a spot protected from wind is best

Rich, well-drained soil

Bears ½- to 1-foot-long racemes of dark yellow flowers from early to midsummer

Zones 5 to 8

P. 289

Erythronium dens-canis
European Dogtooth Violet
SIZE: 4 to 6 inches

Partial or dappled shade

Deeply prepared, evenly moist soil rich in organic matter

Bears green leaves marked with purple-brown
and solitary flowers in spring in shades of
pink, lilac, and white

Zones 3 to 9

P. 290

Erythronium hendersonii
Dogtooth Violet
SIZE: 6 to 14 inches

Partial or dappled shade

Deeply prepared, evenly moist soil rich in organic matter

Pacific Northwest native wildflower bearing
green leaves marked with pale brownish
green bands and racemes of pale lilac flowers in spring

Zones 3 to 9

P. 291

Erythronium revolutum
Western Trout Lily

SIZE: 8 to 12 inches

Partial or dappled shade

Deeply prepared, evenly moist soil rich in organic matter

Pacific Northwest native wildflower with green leaves heavily marked with brown and racemes of lilac-pink flowers in spring

Zones 5 to 9

P. 291

Erythronium tuolumnense

SIZE: 8 to 14 inches

Partial or dappled shade

Deeply prepared, evenly moist soil rich in organic matter

California native wildflower with green leaves and racemes of yellow flowers in spring

Zones 3 to 9

P. 291

▲ *Eucharis × grandiflora*

Amazon Lily, Eucharist Lily, Madonna
Lily, Lily-of-the-Amazon

SIZE: Foliage, 1½ feet; to 2 feet in bloom

Partial, dappled shade; often grown in containers

Bears large glossy dark green leaves and umbels of fragrant white daffodil-like flowers in summer

Zones 9 to 11

P. 293

▼ *Eucomis autumnalis*

Pineapple Flower, Pineapple Lily

SIZE: 8 to 12 inches

Full sun or partial shade

Rich, well-drained soil

Bears erect racemes of greenish white flowers in late summer and early fall

Zones 8 to 10

P. 294

Eucomis comosa
Pineapple Flower, Pineapple Lily
SIZE: 2 to 3 feet

Full sun or partial shade

Rich, well-drained soil

In late summer bears erect racemes of white
flowers edged in purple and with showy
purple ovaries at the center of each bloom

Zones 6 OR 7 to 10

P. 294

Freesia hybrids
SIZE: 1 to 1½ feet

Full sun

Average to rich, moist, well-drained soil

Bears showy racemes of fragrant flowers in a
wide range of colors in late winter and early
spring

Zones 10 to 11

P. 295

Fritillaria affinis

Rice-grain Fritillary

SIZE: 1 to 2 feet

Full sun or light shade

Moist, well-drained soil rich in organic matter

Western U.S. native wildflower with nodding, cup-shaped greenish white flowers marked with red-purple from spring to early summer

Zones 6 to 9

P. 297

Fritillaria davisii

Fritillary

SIZE: 6 inches

Full sun or light shade

Perfectly drained soil and dry conditions when dormant

Bears from one to three 1-inch-long bell-shaped green flowers in spring

Zones 6 to 9

P. 298

Fritillaria imperialis 'Aurora'
Crown Imperial

SIZE: 2 to 4 feet

Full sun or light shade

Moist, well-drained soil rich in organic matter

Vigorous bulb bearing umbels of downward-pointing red, orange-red, or yellow flowers topped by a sheaf of leaflike bracts

Zones 5 to 8

P. 298

Fritillaria meleagris
(inset, 'Alba')
Checkered Lily, Guinea-hen Flower, Snake's Head Fritillary

SIZE: 8 to 12 inches

Full sun or light shade

Moist, well-drained soil rich in organic matter

Bears nodding, broadly bell-shaped pinkish- or red-purple flowers in spring that are checked with dark purple-pink

Zones 4 to 8

P. 299

Fritillaria michailovskyi
Fritillary

SIZE: 4 to 8 inches

Full sun or light shade

Rich but very well drained soil and dry conditions when dormant

Bears pendent, broadly bell-shaped purplebrown flowers edged in yellow in late spring or early summer

Zones 5 to 8

P. 299

Fritillaria pallidiflora
Fritillary

SIZE: ½ to 2 feet

Partial shade

Moist, well-drained soil rich in organic matter

Bears erect clusters of bell-shaped, nodding creamy yellow flowers blushed with green in late spring and early summer

Zones 3 to 8

P. 299

Fritillaria persica
Fritillary

SIZE: 1 to 3 feet

Full sun or light shade; best in a hot, sun-baked site

Moist, well-drained soil rich in organic matter

Produces erect, many-flowered racemes of mauve-purple flowers in spring

Zones 5 to 8

P. 299

Fritillaria pontica
Fritillary

SIZE: 6 to 8 inches

Full sun or light shade

Moist, well-drained soil rich in organic matter

In spring, produces green flowers marked with brown or maroon at the base, either singly or in pairs

Zones 5 or 6 to 8

P. 299

Fritillaria pudica
Yellow Fritillary
SIZE: 3 to 6 inches

Full sun or light shade

Very well drained soil and dry conditions when dormant

Wildflower native to western North America with pendent, bell-shaped golden yellow flowers in spring, either solitary or in pairs

Zones 4 to 9

P. 299

Fritillaria uva-vulpis
Fritillary
SIZE: 6 to 8 inches

Full sun or light shade

Moist, well-drained soil rich in organic matter

Bears solitary, nodding, bell-shaped purple-brown flowers with yellow tips in spring

Zones 5 to 8

P. 300

Galanthus elwesii
Giant Snowdrop
SIZE: 5 to 9 inches

Partial shade

Rich, moist, well-drained soil

Bears fragrant ¾- to 1¼-inch-long white flowers marked with green in spring

Zones 3 to 9

P. 301

Galanthus nivalis
Common Snowdrop
SIZE: 4 inches

Partial shade

Rich, moist, well-drained soil

Bears fragrant ½- to ¾-inch-long white flowers marked with green in late winter to very early spring

Zones 3 to 9

P. 302

Galtonia candicans
Summer Hyacinth
SIZE: 3 to 4 feet

Full sun

Rich, well-drained, deeply prepared soil

Produces erect, showy racemes of fragrant white 2-inch-long flowers in late summer

Zone 6 to 10; to Zone 5 with winter protection

P. 303

Gladiolus callianthus
SIZE: 2 to 3½ feet

Full sun

Light, evenly moist soil rich in organic matter

Produces loose, showy spikes of fragrant, funnel-shaped white flowers with a dark purple-red blotch in late summer and fall

Zones 7 to 10

P. 304

Gladiolus communis ssp. *byzantinus*
Hardy Gladiolus
SIZE: 2 to 3 feet

Full sun

Light, evenly moist soil rich in organic matter

Bears graceful spikes of 2-inch-wide magenta-pink flowers striped with white or pale pink flowers in late spring and early summer

Zones 5 to 10

P. 305

Gladiolus hybrids
Common Gladiolus, Garden Glad
SIZE: 3 to 4 feet

Full sun

Light, evenly moist soil rich in organic matter

Bears dense spikes of showy flowers in summer in a wide range of colors

Zones 8 to 10; Zone 7 with winter protection

P. 305

Gladiolus tristis

SIZE: 1½ to 5 feet

Full sun

Light, evenly moist soil rich in organic matter

In spring, bears spikes of creamy white to pale yellow funnel-shaped, very fragrant flowers often marked pink or another contrasting color

Zones 8 to 10

P. 305

Globba winitii

SIZE: 2 to 3 feet

Partial shade

Deeply prepared, moist soil rich in organic matter

Bears pendent, 6-inch-long racemes of yellow flowers with mauve-pink or purple-pink bracts

Zones 8 to 11; to Zone 7 with winter protection

P. 306

Gloriosa superba 'Rothschildiana'

Climbing Lily, Glory Lily

SIZE: 3 to 6 feet

Full sun

Rich, well-drained soil

Climbing species bearing showy, butterfly-like flowers with reflexed tepals that are red or purple and often margined in yellow

Zones 8 to 10, to Zone 7 with winter protection

P. 307

Habranthus robustus

SIZE: 8 to 12 inches

Full sun; a warm site is best

Deeply prepared, rich, well-drained soil

Bears grassy leaves and solitary pale pink flowers in summer

Zones 7 to 11

P. 308

Haemanthus albiflos
Shaving-brush Plant, White Paintbrush
SIZE: 6 to 12 inches

Partial shade

Evergeen species bearing brushlike umbels of
  many densely packed white flowers surrounded by white bracts with green veins

Zones 10 to 11

P. 310

Haemanthus coccineus
Blood Lily, Cape Tulip
SIZE: 10 to 14 inches

Partial shade

Deciduous species bearing brushlike umbels of
  densely packed red flowers from late summer to fall

Zones 10 to 11

P. 310

Hedychium coccineum
Red Ginger Lily, Scarlet Ginger Lily, Orange Bottlebrush Ginger

SIZE: 4 to 6 feet

Full sun to partial shade

Deeply prepared, moist soil rich in organic matter

Bears fragrant flower clusters from late summer to fall in shades of red, orange-red, orange, pink, and white

Zones 8 to 10

P. 311

Hedychium gardnerianum
Kahili Ginger

SIZE: 4 to 6 feet

Full sun to partial shade

Deeply prepared, moist soil rich in organic matter

From late summer to fall, bears racemes of fragrant yellow flowers that have showy red stamens

Zones 8 to 11

P. 311

Hedychium hybrid 'Elizabeth'
Hybrid Ginger

SIZE: 4 to 6 feet

Full sun to partial shade

Deeply prepared, moist soil rich in organic matter

Bears showy clusters of raspberry pink flowers from late summer to fall

Zones 7 or 8 to 11

P. 312

Hemerocallis hybrid 'Kindly Light'
Daylily

SIZE: 2 to 2½ feet

Full sun or light shade

Average to rich, well-drained, evenly moist soil

Bears yellow 6-inch-wide spider-type blooms with thin tepals in summer

Zones 3 to 10

P. 313

Hemerocallis hybrid 'Living Color'

Daylily

SIZE: 2 to 2½ feet

Full sun or light shade

Average to rich, well-drained, evenly moist soil

Bears 4½-inch-wide rose-pink flowers in summer with a deeper rose-colored eye

Zones 3 to 10

P. 313

Hemerocallis hybrid 'Whooperie'

Daylily

SIZE: 2 to 2½ feet

Full sun or light shade

Average to rich, well-drained, evenly moist soil

Bears showy rose-red flowers in summer with a darker eye zone and green throat

Zones 3 to 10

P. 313

Hermodactylus tuberosus
Snake's Head Iris, Widow Iris

SIZE: 8 to 16 inches

Full sun

Average to rich, very well drained soil; alkaline
  pH is best

In spring, bears solitary, fragrant greenish yellow flowers that have velvety black falls

Zones 6 or 7 to 9

P. 314

Hippeastrum hybrid 'Red Lion'
Hybrid Amaryllis

SIZE: 1 to 2 feet

Full sun to partial shade; commonly grown in
  containers

Deeply prepared, rich, well-drained soil

Bears umbels of up to four very large showy
  bright red flowers in early spring

Zones 8 to 10

P. 315

Hippeastrum papilio
Butterfly Amaryllis

SIZE: 1 to 2 feet

Full sun to partial shade; commonly grown in containers

Deeply prepared, rich, well-drained soil

Bears evergreen leaves and umbels of two or three creamy white flowers heavily striped with maroon in late winter

Zones 10 to 11

P. 316

Homeria collina
Cape Tulip

SIZE: 6 to 16 inches

Full sun

Rich, well-drained soil

From spring to summer bears fragrant, cup-shaped 3-inch-wide flowers that are pink, peach-pink, or yellow

Zones 9 to 11

P. 317

Hyacinthoides hispanica
Spanish Bluebell

SIZE: 10 to 14 inches

Partial or dappled shade

Average to rich, moist, well-drained soil

Vigorous species producing large clumps of leaves and showy clusters of bell-shaped lavender-blue, pink, or white flowers in spring

Zones 4 to 9

P. 317

Hyacinthoides non-scripta
English Bluebell, Harebell

SIZE: 8 to 12 inches

Partial or dappled shade

Average to rich, moist, well-drained soil

Bears dainty, arching, one-sided racemes of bell-shaped lavender-blue flowers in spring

Zones 4 to 9

P. 318

Hyacinthus orientalis (inset 'Amethyst')

Hyacinth

SIZE: 8 to 12 inches

Full sun or partial shade

Average to rich, well-drained soil

Bears showy, dense clusters of extremely fragrant flowers in shades of lavender, violet, white, pink, and yellow

Zones 5 to 9; to Zone 4 with deep planting

P. 319

Hymenocallis harrisiana

Spider Lily

SIZE: 1 foot

Full sun or partial shade

Rich, evenly moist, well-drained soil

Native Mexican species with umbels of starry white green-tinged flowers

Zones 9 to 11

P. 321

Hymenocallis narcissiflora
Peruvian Daffodil, Basket Lily
SIZE: 2 feet
Full sun or partial shade
Rich, evenly moist, well-drained soil
Bears umbels of very fragrant white flowers
sometimes striped with green in summer
Zones 8 to 11
P. 321

Hymenocallis 'Sulfur Queen'
Hybrid Peruvian Daffodil
SIZE: 2 feet
Full sun or partial shade
Rich, evenly moist, well-drained soil
Bears umbels of fragrant yellow flowers with
green-striped throats from late spring to
summer
Zones 9 to 11
P. 321

▲ *Incarvillea delavayi* 'Snowtop' (inset *I. delavayi*)

Hardy Gloxinia

SIZE: 1 to 2 feet

Full sun with shade during the hottest part of the day

Rich, moist, well-drained soil

Bears racemes of white trumpet-shaped flowers from early to midsummer; the species bears pink blooms

Zones 6 to 10

P. 322

▼ *Ipheion uniflorum*

Spring Starflower

SIZE: 6 to 8 inches

Full sun

Average, moist, well-drained soil

Bears starry, fragrant 1½-inch-wide pale blue flowers in spring

Zones 6 to 9

P. 323

Ipheion uniflorum 'Wisley Blue'

Spring Starflower

SIZE: 6 to 8 inches

Full sun

Average, moist, well-drained soil

Bears starry, fragrant 1½-inch-wide dark purplish blue flowers in spring

Zones 6 to 9

P. 323

Ipomoea batatas 'Margarita' (inset, 'Blackie')

Sweet Potato

SIZE: To 10 feet

Full sun

Average, well-drained, evenly moist soil

Vining or spreading plant grown for its heart-shaped chartreuse leaves; 'Blackie' bears purple-black maplelike leaves

Zones 9 to 11

P. 324

▲ *Iris* bearded hybrids (inset, close-up)

SIZE: 8 to 27 inches

Full sun

Average to rich, well-drained soil

In late spring or early summer bears flowers in a rainbow of colors that have fuzzy beards at the top of each fall

Zones 3 through 9

P. 325

▼ *Iris danfordiae*

Danford Iris

SIZE: 3 to 6 inches

Full sun

Average to rich, well-drained soil; warm, dry soil in summer

Bears fragrant yellow 2-inch-wide flowers with brown spots in late winter or early spring

Zones 5 to 8

P. 326

Iris Dutch hybrid 'Oriental Beauty' Dutch Iris

SIZE: 15 to 30 inches

Full sun

Average to rich, well-drained soil

Bears 3- to 3½-inch-wide pale whitish lavender standards and yellow falls from late spring to early summer

Zones 6 to 9

P. 326

Iris Dutch hybrid 'Wedgwood' Dutch Iris

SIZE: 15 to 30 inches

Full sun

Average to rich, well-drained soil

Bears clear blue 3- to 3½-inch-wide flowers in late spring and early summer

Zones 6 to 9

P. 326

Iris histrioides 'George'

SIZE: 4 to 6 inches

Full sun

Rich, well-drained soil

Bears fragrant purple-blue 2½- to 3-inch-wide
  flowers in early spring

Zones 4 to 9

P. 327

Iris reticulata 'Harmony'

SIZE: 4 to 6 inches

Full sun

Average to rich, well-drained soil

Bears fragrant 2-inch-wide deep rich blue flowers with yellow blotches in late winter to
  early spring

Zones 3 to 8

P. 327

▲ *Iris reticulata* 'J.S. Dijt'

SIZE: 4 to 6 inches

Full sun

Average to rich, well-drained soil

Bears fragrant 2-inch-wide purple flowers with red-purple falls; blooms in late winter to early spring, later than other *I. reticulata* selections

Zones 3 to 8

P. 327

▼ *Iris xiphium*

Spanish Iris

SIZE: 15 to 30 inches

Full sun

Average to rich, well-drained soil

Bears white, yellow, or violet flowers from late spring to early summer

Zones 6 to 9

P. 327

Ixia hybrid 'Rose Emperor'
Hybrid Corn Lily, Hybrid Wand Flower

SIZE: 12 to 16 inches

Full sun

Rich, well-drained soil

Bears showy 1½- to 3-inch-wide rose-pink flowers with magenta centers from spring to summer

Zones 9 to 11; to Zone 8 with winter protection

P. 329

Ixia viridiflora
Green-flowered Corn Lily

SIZE: 1 to 2 feet

Full sun

Rich, well-drained soil

Bears spikes of pale green flowers with black centers rimmed in violet-purple from spring to summer

Zones 9 to 11; to Zone 8 with winter protection

P. 329

Kaempferia pulchra
Ginger Lily
SIZE: 6 inches; spreads to 12

Partial shade

Deeply prepared, moist soil rich in organic
matter

Bears handsome dark green leaves marked with
silver and spikes lilac or lilac-pink flowers in
summer

Zones 10 to 11

P. 330

Lachenalia aloides
Cape Cowslip
SIZE: 6 to 12 inches

Full sun

Light, rich, well-drained soil

Bears erect racemes of pendent, tubular yellow
blooms tipped in scarlet in late winter or
spring

Zones 9 to 10

P. 331

Lachenalia bulbifera

Cape Cowslip

SIZE: 1 foot

Full sun

Light, rich, well-drained soil

Bears loose racemes of pendent red or orange
flowers with green and purple tips

Zones 9 to 10

P. 332

Ledebouria socialis

SIZE: 2 to 4 inches

Full sun

Light, rich, well-drained soil

Features evergreen silver-green leaves and
racemes of tiny purple-green flowers in
spring and summer

Zones 9 to 11

P. 333

▲ *Leucojum aestivum* (inset, close-up)

Summer Snowflake

SIZE: 1½ to 2 feet

Full sun or partial shade

Rich, moist, well-drained soil

Bears dainty stems of white bell-shaped ¾-inch-long 1-inch-wide white flowers spotted green in spring

Zones 4 to 9

P. 334

▼ *Leucojum vernum*

Spring Snowflake

SIZE: 8 to 12 inches

Full sun or partial shade

Rich, moist, well-drained soil

Bears white 1-inch-long bell-shaped flowers in early spring either singly or in pairs

Zones 4 to 8

P. 334

▲ *Liatris spicata*
Spike Gayfeather

SIZE: 2 to 5 feet

Full sun

Average to rich, well-drained soil

Native North American wildflowers with erect spikes of densely packed pinkish purple flower heads from mid- to late summer

Zones 3 to 9

P. 336

▼ *Lilium* 'African Queen'
Trumpet and Aurelian Hybrid

SIZE: 4 to 8 feet

Full sun

Rich, evenly moist, well-drained soil

Mid- to late-summer bloomer bearing fragrant trumpets that are brown-purple on the outside and yellow inside

Zones 4 to 8

P. 341

Lilium 'America'
Asiatic Hybrid Lily
SIZE: 3 feet

Full sun

Rich, evenly moist, well-drained soil

Bears clusters of deep burgundy-red flowers
   from early to midsummer

Zones 3 to 8.

P. 339

Lilium auratum
Goldband Lily
SIZE: 2 to 5 feet

Full sun

Requires well-drained, acid soil; dry soil in winter

From mid- to late summer bears fragrant,
   bowl-shaped white flowers with a yellow
   stripe on each recurved tepal

Zones 5 to 8

P. 342

Lilium canadense
Canada Lily, Meadow Lily

SIZE: 3 to 6 feet

Full sun or partial shade

Damp to evenly moist, acid soil

Mid- to late summer–blooming native North American wildflower bearing pendent yellow-orange flowers spotted with maroon

Zones 3 to 7

P. 342

Lilium Candidum Hybrid
Candidum Hybrid Lily, Madonna Hybrid Lily

SIZE: 3 to 6 feet

Full sun

Rich, evenly moist, well-drained soil

Early to midsummer lilies bearing clusters of fragrant, waxy flowers in white or deep red, yellow-orange, and pale yellow

Zones 4 to 9

P. 340

Lilium columbianum
Columbia Tiger Lily, Oregon Lily
SIZE: 5 feet

Full sun

Rich, evenly moist, well-drained soil

Native Pacific Northwest lily with clusters of
    pendent yellow to orange-red flowers spot-
    ted with maroon

Zones 5 to 8

P. 342

Lilium concolor
Star Lily, Morning Star Lily
SIZE: 3 feet

Full sun

Rich, evenly moist, well-drained soil

Midsummer bloomer bearing clusters of erect,
    star-shaped scarlet flowers

Zones 3 to 7

P. 343

▲ *Lilium* 'Corsica'

Asiatic Hybrid Lily

SIZE: 3 feet

Full sun

Rich, evenly moist, well-drained soil

Bears clusters of mauve-pink flowers from early to midsummer

Zones 3 to 8

P. 339

▼ *Lilium* 'Enchantment'

Asiatic Hybrid Lily

SIZE: 2 to 3 feet

Full sun

Rich, evenly moist, well-drained soil

Vigorous cultivar bearing bright orange flowers with brownish speckles in early to midsummer

Zones 3 to 8

P. 339

▲ *Lilium formosanum* var. *pricei*
Dwarf Formosa Lily

SIZE: 1½ to 2 feet

Full sun

Rich, evenly moist, acid, well-drained soil

Late summer– to fall-blooming species bearing white trumpet-shaped flowers

Zones 5 to 9

P. 343

▼ *Lilium* Golden Splendor Group
Trumpet and Aurelian Hybrid Lily

SIZE: 4 to 8 feet

Full sun

Rich, evenly moist, well-drained soil

Bears erect clusters of outward-facing golden yellow trumpets in midsummer marked with burgundy on the outside

Zones 4 to 8

P. 341

Lilium lancifolium
Tiger lily
SIZE: 4 to 5 feet
Full sun
Rich, evenly moist, well-drained soil
Bears orange-red flowers with dark purple-
  black spots from late summer to fall
Zones 3 to 9
P. 343

Lilium Longiflorum Hybrid
Easter Lily
SIZE: 1½ to 3½ feet
Full sun
Rich, evenly moist, well-drained soil
Bears fragrant white trumpet-shaped blooms
  from early to midsummer
Zones 7 to 9; some cultivars hardy to Zone 5
P. 340

Lilium Martagon Hybrid
Martagon Lily, Turk's Cap Hybrid Lilies
SIZE: 3 to 6 feet

Full sun

Rich, evenly moist, well-drained soil

From early to midsummer bears nodding purple-pink 2-inch-wide flowers with recurved
petals and dark spots

Zones 3 to 8

P. 339

Lilium 'Mona Lisa'
Oriental Hybrid Lily
SIZE: 3 to 4 feet

Full sun

Rich, evenly moist, well-drained soil

Bears showy rose-pink blooms with darker rose
at the center and tepals and darker midribs
and freckles in mid- to late summer

Zones 4 to 8

P. 341

Lilium pardalinum
Leopard Lily, Panther Lily
SIZE: 5 to 8 feet

Full sun

Rich, evenly moist, well-drained soil; tolerates alkaline soil

Native lily from the western United States bearing nodding orange-red to red blooms spotted with maroon in midsummer

Zones 5 to 8

P. 344

Lilium pumilium
Coral Lily
SIZE: 1 to 2 feet

Full sun to partial shade

Rich, evenly moist, acid, well-drained soil

Early- to midsummer-blooming species bearing fragrant scarlet flowers with recurved tepals

Zones 3 to 7

P. 344

▲ *Lilium* 'Red Jamboree'
Oriental Hybrid Lily
SIZE: 3 to 4 feet

Full sun

Rich, evenly moist, well-drained soil

In mid- to late summer, bears clusters of bowl-
shaped blooms that are rich rose-red with
white edging on tepals

Zones 4 to 8

P. 341

▼ *Lilium regale*
Regal Lily, Royal Lily
SIZE: 2 to 6 feet

Full sun

Rich, evenly moist, well-drained soil

Mid- to late-summer bloomer with clusters of
fragrant trumpets that are white inside and
purple to wine-colored outside

Zones 3 to 8

P. 344

Lilium 'Tiger Babies'
Asiatic Hybrid Lily
SIZE: 3 to 3½ feet

Full sun

Rich, evenly moist, well-drained soil

Bears loose clusters of salmon-peach flowers
with very recurved, spotted tepals from
early to midsummer

Zones 3 to 8

P. 339

Lycoris radiata
Red Spider Lily
SIZE: 1 to 2 feet

Full sun or partial shade

Deeply prepared, rich, well-drained soil

Bears umbels of deep red or deep pink flowers
in late summer and early fall that have long
spidery, reflexed tepals

Zones 8 to 10

P. 346

Lycoris squamigera
Hardy Amaryllis, Magic Lily, Resurrection Lily

SIZE: 1½ to 2 feet

Full sun or partial shade

Deeply prepared, rich, well-drained soil

Bears umbels of fragrant pale to rich pink trumpets in summer

Zones 6 to 10; to Zone 5 with protection

P. 347

Mertensia pulmonarioides
Virginia Bluebells, Virginia Cowslip

SIZE: 1 to 2 feet

Sun or shade

Rich, evenly moist, well-drained soil

Native North American wildflower; in spring produces nodding clusters of pink buds that open into pale lilac-blue to purple-blue bells

Zones 3 to 9

P. 347

Mirabilis jalapa
Four-o'clock, Marvel of Peru

SIZE: 2 feet

Full sun to partial shade

Average, well-drained soil

Bears fragrant flowers from midsummer to fall
in pink, red, magenta, yellow, or white, each
of which opens in the afternoon and dies by
morning

Zones 10 to 11

P. 348

Muscari armeniacum
'Blue Spike'
Grape Hyacinth

SIZE: 4 to 8 inches

Full sun or light shade

Rich, well-drained soil

Bears dense, cylindrical racemes of fragrant,
double violet-blue flowers in spring

Zones 4 to 8

P. 350

Muscari azureum

SIZE: 3 to 6 inches

Full sun or light shade

Rich, well-drained soil

Bears racemes of bell-shaped flowers in spring
that are sky blue with a darker blue stripe
on each lobe

Zones 4 to 9

P. 350

Muscari botryoides

Grape Hyacinth

SIZE: 6 to 8 inches

Full sun or light shade

Rich, well-drained soil

In spring, bears dense racemes of fragrant flowers that are bright blue with white mouths

Zones 3 to 8

P. 350

Muscari latifolium

SIZE: 8 to 12 inches

Full sun or light shade

Rich, well-drained soil

Produces racemes of urn-shaped dark violet-
blue fertile flowers topped by a cluster of
paler sterile flowers

Zones 4 to 8

P. 351

Narcissus 'Actaea'

Poeticus Daffodil or Narcissus

SIZE: 14 to 18 inches

Full sun to partial shade

Average, well-drained soil

Produces fragrant flowers in mid- to late spring
with broad white petals surrounding a tiny
disc-shaped red-rimmed cup

Zones 3 to 7

P. 356

▲ *Narcissus* 'Avalanche'

Tazetta Daffodil or Narcissus

SIZE: 12 to 16 inches

Full sun to partial shade

Average, well-drained soil

In midspring bears showy clusters of up to 20 small fragrant flowers with white petals surrounding yellow cups

Zones 6 to 9

P. 356

▼ *Narcissus* 'Beryl'

Cyclamineus Daffodil or Narcissus

SIZE: 8 inches

Full sun to partial shade

Average, well-drained soil

In early to midspring bears dainty flowers with reflexed petals that open yellow and fade to white surrounding a yellow cup banded in orange

Zones 4 to 9

P. 355

Narcissus 'Broadway Star'

Split-corona Daffodil or Narcissus

SIZE: 14 to 18 inches

Full sun to partial shade

Average, well-drained soil

From mid- to late spring bears flowers with white petals surrounding a split cup that forms an orange star in the center

Zones 4 to 7

P. 357

Narcissus bulbocodium

Hoop Petticoat Daffodil

SIZE: 4 to 6 inches

Full sun to partial shade

Average, well-drained soil

Produces nearly round, grasslike leaves and in midspring bears yellow flowers with tiny pointed petals surrounding a megaphone-shaped trumpet

Zones 4 to 8

P. 357

Narcissus 'Delnashaugh'

Double Daffodil or Narcissus

SIZE: 14 to 18 inches

Full sun to partial shade

Average, well-drained soil

In midspring, bears very large flowers with white overlapping petals surrounding a cluster of smaller apricot-pink petals

Zones 4 to 8; to Zone 3 with winter protection

P. 354

Narcissus 'Dream Castle'

Small-cupped Daffodil or Narcissus

Full sun to partial shade

Average, well-drained soil

Bears small-cupped all-white blooms

Zones 4 to 8; to Zone 3 with winter protection

P. 354

Narcissus 'Dutch Master'
Trumpet Daffodil, Trumpet Narcissus
SIZE: 12 to 20 inches

Full sun to partial shade

Average, well-drained soil

Bears showy golden yellow blooms in early to midspring

Zones 4 to 8; to Zone 3 with winter protection

P. 353

Narcissus 'Falconet'
Tazetta Daffodil or Narcissus
SIZE: 12 to 14 inches

Full sun to partial shade

Average, well-drained soil

Bears small clusters of fragrant yellow flowers with orange cups in late spring

Zones 5 to 9

P. 356

▲ *Narcissus* 'Fortissimo'
Large-cupped Daffodil or Narcissus
SIZE: 10 to 20 inches
Full sun to partial shade
Average, well-drained soil
In midspring, bears very large blooms that have
  yellow petals surrounding an orange cup
Zones 4 to 8; to Zone 3 with winter protection
P. 354

▼ *Narcissus* 'Foundling'
Cyclamineus Daffodil or Narcissus
SIZE: 10 to 14 inches
Full sun to partial shade
Average, well-drained soil
In early to midspring bears flowers with white
  petals surrounding an apricot-pink cup
Zones 4 to 9
P. 355

▲ *Narcissus* 'Hawera'

Miniature Triandrus Daffodil
or Narcissus

SIZE: 8 inches

Full sun to partial shade

Average, well-drained soil

Bears clusters of three to five yellow flowers
with round cups and slightly reflexed petals
in mid- to late spring

Zones 4 to 9

P. 355

▼ *Narcissus* 'Honeybird'

Trumpet Daffodil, Trumpet Narcissus

SIZE: 12 to 20 inches

Full sun to partial shade

Average, well-drained soil

In early to midspring bears blooms with pastel
yellow petals surrounding a creamy white
yellow-rimmed trumpet

Zones 4 to 8; to Zone 3 with winter protection

P. 353

▲ *Narcissus* 'Ice Follies'
Large-cupped Daffodil or Narcissus
SIZE: 10 to 20 inches

Full sun to partial shade

Average, well-drained soil

Bears delicate-looking blooms with white petals surrounding a yellow cup

Zones 4 to 8; to Zone 3 with winter protection

P. 354

▼ *Narcissus* 'Jack Snipe'
Cyclamineus Daffodil or Narcissus
SIZE: 10 to 14 inches

Full sun to partial shade

Average, well-drained soil

Bears dainty flowers in early to midspring with white reflexed petals surrounding a yellow cup

Zones 4 to 9

P. 355

Narcissus jonquilla
Wild Jonquil
SIZE: 12 inches

Full sun to partial shade

Average, well-drained soil

Bears very fragrant flowers in late spring that are golden yellow with pointed petals and a small flat cup

Zones 5 to 9

P. 357

Narcissus minor
SIZE: 4 to 6 inches

Full sun to partial shade

Average, well-drained soil

Bears 1¼-inch-wide yellow flowers in early spring that point slightly downward

Zones 5 to 8

P. 358

Narcissus × odorus
Campernelle Jonquil
SIZE: 10 to 12 inches
Full sun to partial shade
Average, well-drained soil
Bears one or two very fragrant 1½-inch-wide
    yellow flowers per stem in early spring
Zones 5 to 8
P. 358

Narcissus × odorus 'Plenus'
Double Campernelle Jonquil
SIZE: 10 to 12 inches
Full sun to partial shade
Average, well-drained soil
Bears one or two very fragrant double yellow
    flowers per stem in early spring
Zones 5 to 8
P. 358

Narcissus 'Orangery'

Split-corona Daffodil or Narcissus

SIZE: 14 to 18 inches

Full sun to partial shade

Average, well-drained soil

From mid- to late spring bears flowers with white petals surrounding a pale tangerine orange cup with wavy petal edges

Zones 4 to 7

P. 357

Narcissus 'Petrel'

Triandrus Daffodil or Narcissus

SIZE: 12 to 14 inches

Full sun to partial shade

Average, well-drained soil

Bears clusters of three to five extremely fragrant white flowers that have bell-shaped cups in mid- to late spring

Zones 4 to 9

P. 355

Narcissus 'Pink Charm'
Large-cupped Daffodil or Narcissus
SIZE: 10 to 20 inches

Full sun to partial shade

Average, well-drained soil

In midspring, produces white-petaled flowers with a white cup that sports a dark pink band

Zones 4 to 8; to Zone 3 with winter protection

P. 354

Narcissus 'Quail'
Jonquilla Daffodil or Narcissus
SIZE: 12 to 16 inches

Full sun to partial shade

Average, well-drained soil

Bears clusters of two to four bronzy yellow blooms with small cups in mid- to late spring

Zones 4 to 9

P. 355

Narcissus 'Rip van Winkle'
Miniature Double Daffodil
SIZE: 4 to 6 inches

Full sun to partial shade

Average, well-drained soil

Early-flowering cultivar with yellow dandelion-
like blooms that have many pointed perianth segments and green interspersed with
the yellow

Zones 4 to 8; to Zone 3 with winter protection

P. 354

Narcissus 'Romance'
Large-cupped Daffodil or Narcissus
SIZE: 10 to 20 inches

Full sun to partial shade

Average, well-drained soil

In midspring, bears attractive blooms that have
white petals surrounding a rose-pink cup

Zones 4 to 8; to Zone 3 with winter protection

P. 354

Narcissus 'Sabine Hay'
Small-cupped Daffodil or Narcissus
SIZE: 16 to 18 inches

Full sun to partial shade

Average, well-drained soil

Bears showy flowers with coppery orange petals
surrounding a coral red cup

Zones 4 to 8; to Zone 3 with winter protection

P. 354

Narcissus 'Sir Winston Churchill'
Double Daffodil or Narcissus
SIZE: 14 to 18

Full sun to partial shade

Average, well-drained soil

In midspring, bears fragrant creamy white flowers with petals interspersed with smaller orange petal segments

Zones 4 to 8; to Zone 3 with winter protection

P. 354

Narcissus 'Stratosphere'
Jonquilla Daffodil or Narcissus

SIZE: 18 to 24 inches

Full sun to partial shade

Average, well-drained soil

Bears clusters of two to three fragrant golden yellow flowers in mid- to late spring

Zones 4 to 9

P. 355

Narcissus 'Tête-à-Tête'
Miniature Daffodil or Narcissus

SIZE: 5 to 6 inches

Full sun to partial shade

Average, well-drained soil

Bears yellow flowers, usually in pairs, in early spring

Zones 4 to 9

P. 357

Nectaroscordum siculum
Honey Garlic
SIZE: 3 to 4 feet
Full sun or partial shade
Average to rich, well-drained soil
In summer bears creamy white flowers that are green at the base and flushed with purple
Zones 6 to 10
P. 359

Nerine bowdenii
Nerine
SIZE: 1½ feet
Full sun
Rich, very well drained soil
Bears umbels of musky-scented, funnel-shaped 3-inch-long pink flowers in fall
Zones 8 to 10, to Zone 7 with winter protection
P. 361

Ornithogalum arabicum
Star-of-Bethlehem
SIZE: 1 to 3 feet

Full sun or light shade

Average to rich, well-drained soil

Bears rounded racemes of fragrant, cup-shaped
1½-inch-wide pearly white flowers in early
summer

Zones 8 to 10

P. 363

Ornithogalum dubium
Star-of-Bethlehem
SIZE: 8 to 12 inches

Full sun or light shade

Average to rich, well-drained soil

From late winter to early spring, bears racemes
of cup-shaped flowers in shades of golden
yellow, orange, red, and white

Zones 8 to 10

P. 363

Ornithogalum nutans
Nodding Star-of-Bethlehem
SIZE: 8 to 18 inches

Full sun or light shade

Average to rich, well-drained soil

In spring, bears one-sided racemes of fragrant,
   funnel-shaped white flowers striped with
   green on the outside

Zones 5 to 10

P. 363

Ornithogalum saundersiae
Giant Chincherinchee
SIZE: 2 to 3 feet

Full sun or light shade

Average to rich, well-drained soil

From late winter to early spring bears rounded
   racemes of cup-shaped white flowers

Zones 7 or 8 to 10

P. 363

Ornithogalum umbellatum
Star-of-Bethlehem
SIZE: 6 to 12 inches

Full sun or light shade

Average to rich, well-drained soil

Bears rounded racemes of starry white flowers in early summer that are striped with green on the outside

Zones 4 to 9

P. 364

Oxalis adenophylla
Wood Sorrel, Oxalis
SIZE: 4 inches

Full sun to partial shade

Sandy to gritty, well-drained soil

Bears leaves with up to 20 leaflets and solitary, funnel-shaped purple-pink flowers in late spring

Zones 6 to 8

P. 365

Oxalis bowiei
Wood Sorrel, Oxalis
SIZE: 8 to 10 inches
Full sun to partial shade
Sandy to gritty, well-drained soil
Bears leathery, cloverlike leaves and clusters of funnel-shaped purple-pink to rose-red flowers from summer to fall
Zones 8 to 10
P. 365

Oxalis purpurea 'Garnet'
Wood Sorrel, Oxalis
SIZE: 4 inches
Full sun to partial shade
Sandy to gritty, well-drained soil
Bears three-leaflet purple-tinged leaves and purple flowers from summer to fall
Zones 9 to 10
P. 366

▲ *Oxalis regnellii*
var. *triangularis*
Wood Sorrel, Oxalis

SIZE: 4 to 10 inches

Full sun to partial shade

Sandy to gritty, well-drained soil

Bears leaves with three triangular green leaflets, burgundy on the undersides, and clusters of white or pale pink summer flowers

Zones 7 to 10

P. 366

▼ *Oxalis tetraphylla*
'Iron Cross'
Wood Sorrel, Oxalis, Good Luck Plant

SIZE: 6 inches

Full sun to partial shade

Sandy to gritty, well-drained soil

Bears four-leaflet leaves with burgundy blotches at the bases and hot pink flowers in summer

Zones 7 to 10

P. 366

Pancratium maritimum
Sea Lily
SIZE: 12 inches

Full sun or partial shade

Rich, evenly moist, well-drained soil

Bears umbels of fragrant white 4-inch-wide
flowers in late summer

Zones 8 to 11

P. 367

Pleione formosana
SIZE: 3 to 6 inches

Partial to full shade

Very well drained soil rich in organic matter

Bears pleated leaves and solitary rose-pink
flowers in spring that have a white lip mottled with red-brown to purplish pink on the
inside

Zones 8 to 10

P. 368

Polianthes tuberosa

Tuberose

SIZE: 2 to 4 feet

Full sun

Light, evenly moist soil rich in organic matter

From summer to fall bears erect spikes of waxy white intensely fragrant flowers

Zones 8 to 10; to Zone 7 with winter protection

P. 370

Puschkinia scilloides (inset, close-up)

Striped Squill

SIZE: 6 to 8 inches

Full sun or partial shade

Average, well-drained soil

In spring, bears erect racemes of bell-shaped, very pale bluish white flowers that have a darker stripe on each tepal

Zones 3 to 9

P. 370

Ranunculus asiaticus
Persian Buttercup

SIZE: 8 to 18 inches

Full sun

Light, rich, moist, well-drained soil; dry in
summer when dormant

Bears branched stems of one to four cup-
shaped, single or double flowers in late
spring and early summer in yellow, red,
pink, or white

Zones 7 to 11

P. 372

Ranunculus ficaria
Lesser Celandine

SIZE: 2 to 6 inches

Partial to full shade

Rich, moist soil

Bears handsome, heart-shaped leaves and solitary, cup-shaped golden yellow flowers with
shiny petals in early spring

Zones 4 to 8

P. 372

Ranunculus ficaria 'Brazen Hussy'

Lesser Celandine

SIZE: 2 to 6 inches

Partial to full shade

Rich, moist soil

Bears handsome, heart-shaped black-purple
  leaves and golden yellow flowers in early
  spring

Zones 4 to 8

P. 372

Rhodophiala bifida

SIZE: 12 inches

Full sun to partial shade

Deeply prepared, rich, well-drained soil

Produces umbels of two to six funnel-shaped
  deep red flowers in summer

Zones 9 to 10

P. 374

▲ *Sandersonia aurantiaca*

SIZE: Climbs to 2 or 3 feet

Full sun

Rich, well-drained soil

Bears nodding, lanternlike orange flowers in summer

Zones 7 to 10

P. 375

▼ *Sanguinaria canadensis* (inset, *S. canadensis* 'Flore Pleno')

Bloodroot, Red Puccoon

SIZE: 4 to 6 inches

Partial to full shade

Rich, evenly moist, well-drained soil

Native North American wildflower with cup-shaped white flowers in spring and scalloped, kidney-shaped leaves

Zones 3 to 9

P. 375

Sauromatum venosum (inset, flower)
Voodoo Lily, Monarch of the East
SIZE: 1 to 1½ feet

Partial to full shade

Rich, evenly moist, well-drained soil

In spring or early summer produces foul-smelling flowers consisting of a yellowish spathe surrounding a purple spadix

Zones 8 to 10; to Zone 7 with winter protection

P. 376

Scadoxus multiflorus
Blood Lily
SIZE: 1½ to 2 feet

Full sun or partial shade

Rich, well-drained soil

Bears round 4- to 6-inch-wide red flower heads followed by orange berries in summer

Zones 9 to 11; to Zone 8 with winter protection

P. 378

Scadoxus puniceus
Royal Paint Brush, Giant Stove Brush
SIZE: 20 inches

Full sun or partial shade

Rich, well-drained soil

From spring to early summer, bears 4-inch-
wide cone-shaped pink or red flower heads
surrounded by conspicuous red bracts

Zones 9 to 11

P. 378

Schizostylis coccinea
Crimson Flag
SIZE: 1½ to 2 feet

Full sun or partial shade

Average to rich, moist, well-drained soil

Bears showy spikes of cup-shaped red flowers
in late summer or fall

Zones 7 to 9; to Zones 5 or 6 with winter protection

P. 379

▲ *Scilla bifolia*
Twin-leaf Squill

SIZE: 3 to 6 inches

Full sun or partial shade

Average, well-drained soil

Bears loose, one-sided racemes of starry purple-blue flowers in early spring

Zones 4 to 8

P. 380

▼ *Scilla mischtschenkoana*
Squill

SIZE: 4 to 6 inches

Full sun or partial shade

Average, well-drained soil

In late winter or early spring produces racemes
of starry silvery blue flowers with darker
stripes

Zones 4 to 8

P. 380

▲ *Scilla peruviana*

Cuban Lily, Peruvian Jacinth

SIZE: 6 to 18 inches

Full sun or partial shade

Average, well-drained soil

Bears rounded racemes of star-shaped white or purplish blue flowers in early summer

Zones 8 to 9

P. 380

▼ *Scilla siberica*

Siberian Squill, Spring Squill

SIZE: 4 to 8 inches

Full sun or partial shade

Average, well-drained soil

In spring bears loose clusters of deep blue bell- to bowl-shaped nodding flowers

Zones 4 to 8

P. 380

Sparaxis elegans
Wand Flower, Harlequin Flower
SIZE: 4 to 12 inches

Full sun

Average to rich, well-drained soil

Bears loose clusters of funnel-shaped flowers in spring or summer in shades of red, orange, or white marked with yellow or violet

Zones 9 to 11; to Zones 7 or 8 with winter protection

P. 382

Sparaxis tricolor
Wand Flower, Harlequin Flower
SIZE: 4 to 16 inches

Full sun

Average to rich, well-drained soil

Bears loose clusters of red, orange, or purple flowers with dark red or black central blotches in late spring to early summer

Zones 9 to 11; to Zones 7 or 8 with winter protection

P. 382

Sprekelia formosissima
Aztec Lily, Jacobean Lily, St. James Lily

SIZE: 4 to 14 inches

Full sun

Deeply prepared, rich, well-drained soil

Bears solitary bright red 5-inch-wide orchidlike
  flowers in spring

Zones 9 to 11; to Zone 7 or 8 with winter protection

P. 383

Stenanthium gramineum
Featherfleece

Size: 3 to 6 feet

Partial shade

Deeply prepared, moist, rich, well-drained soil

Native North American wildflower bearing
  arching panicles of fragrant starry white,
  greenish white, or purple flowers in summer.

Zones 7 to 9

P. 384

▲ *Stenomesson variegatum*

SIZE: 1½ to 2 feet

Full sun

Rich, well-drained soil

Bears umbels of up to six pendent, tubular, white, pink, yellow, or red flowers that have green-marked tepals

Zones 10 to 11

P. 385

▼ *Sternbergia candida*

SIZE: 4 to 8 inches

Full sun to partial shade

Very well drained, average to rich soil

A late winter– to spring-blooming species bearing fragrant, funnel- to goblet-shaped white flowers

Zones 8 to 10

P. 386

Sternbergia lutea
Autumn Daffodil, Winter Daffodil
SIZE: 6 inches

Full sun to partial shade

Very well drained, average to rich soil

A fall-blooming species bearing golden yellow goblet-shaped flowers that resemble crocuses

Zones 6 to 9

P. 386

Tecophilaea cyanocrocus
Chilean Blue Crocus
SIZE: 3 to 4 inches

Full sun

Sandy, very well drained soil rich in organic matter

Bears funnel-shaped flowers in spring that are rich gentian blue with white striping at the throat

Zones 7 to 9

P. 387

▲ *Tigridia pavonia*

Peacock Flower, Tiger Flower

SIZE: 1½ to 2 feet

Full sun

Light, evenly moist soil rich in organic matter

Bears spotted, somewhat irislike flowers in summer in a range of colors, including red, pink, orange, yellow, and white

Zones 8 to 10

P. 388

▼ *Tigridia pavonia* 'Aurea'

Peacock Flower, Tiger Flower

SIZE: 1½ to 2 feet

Full sun

Light, evenly moist soil rich in organic matter

Bears yellow somewhat irislike flowers in summer speckled with red

Zones 8 to 10

P. 388

Trillium grandiflorum
Great White Trillium, Wood Lily, Wake-robin

SIZE: 1 to 1½ feet

Partial to full shade

Moist, well-drained soil rich in organic matter

Native North American wildflower bearing short-stalked white flowers that fade to pink

Zones 4 to 8

P. 389

Triteleia ixioides
(inset, close-up)
Pretty Face, Golden Star

SIZE: 2 feet

Full sun or partial shade

Rich, well-drained soil

In early summer bears many-flowered umbels of small yellow flowers with purple-striped tepals

Zones 7 to 10

P. 390

Triteleia laxa
Grass Nut, Triplet Lily, Ithuriel's Spear

SIZE: 2 feet

Full sun or partial shade

Rich, well-drained soil

Bears loose, many-flowered umbels of pale lavender to dark purple-blue flowers in early summer

Zones 6 to 10; to Zone 5 with winter protection

P. 390

Tritonia crocata

SIZE: 8 to 12 inches

Full sun

Rich, well-drained soil

Bears arching spikes of cup-shaped orange to pinkish red flowers in spring

Zones 8 to 10; to Zone 7 with winter protection

P. 391

Tropaeolum tricolorum

SIZE: climbs from 3 to 6 feet

Full sun

Average, well-drained, evenly moist soil

From winter to early summer bears flowers
with orange to yellow petals, orange-red
sepals with maroon tips, and yellow or purple spurs

Zones 8 to 10

P. 392

Tulbaghia violacea
(inset, close-up)

Society Garlic, Pink Agapanthus

SIZE: 1½ to 2 feet

Full sun

Average to rich, well-drained soil

Produces clumps of grassy leaves striped in
cream and gray-green and small umbels of
fragrant lilac flowers from midsummer to
fall

Zones 7 to 10

P. 393

▲ *Tulipa* 'Abba'

Triumph Tulip

SIZE: 14 to 24 inches

Full sun

Rich, well-drained soil

Mid- to late spring–blooming tulip bearing cup-shaped rose-red blooms with slight yellow edging

Zones 3 to 8

P. 397

▼ *Tulipa acuminata*

SIZE: 16 to 18 inches

Full sun

Rich, well-drained soil

Bears solitary red or yellow flowers streaked with red in midspring

Zones 3 to 8

P. 402

Tulipa 'Angélique'
Double Late Tulip, Peony-flowered Tulip

SIZE: 14 to 24 inches

Full sun

Rich, well-drained soil

Late-flowering tulip bearing large pale pink blooms blushed with darker pink and shading to cream at the tepal edges

Zones 3 to 8

P. 400

Tulipa 'Apeldoorn's Elite'
Darwin Hybrid Tulip

SIZE: 20 to 28 inches

Full sun

Rich, well-drained soil

Mid- to late spring–blooming tulip bearing brilliant red flowers feathered with yellow at the tepal edges

Zones 3 to 8

P. 397A

▲ *Tulipa* 'Aristocrat'

Single Late Tulip

SIZE: 18 to 30 inches

Full sun

Rich, well-drained soil

Bears purplish rose flowers with paler tepal
  edges in late spring

Zones 3 to 7

P. 398

▼ *Tulipa aucheriana*

SIZE: 6 to 8 inches

Full sun

Rich, well-drained soil

Midspring-blooming species with starry pink
  flowers that have a yellow to yellow-brown
  central blotch

Zones 4 to 8

P. 402

▲ *Tulipa batalinii*

SIZE: 4 to 8 inches

Full sun

Rich, well-drained soil

Bears bowl-shaped pale yellow flowers marked with bronze or dark yellow in mid- to late spring

Zones 3 to 8

P. 402

▼ *Tulipa batalinii*
'Bronze Charm'

SIZE: 4 to 8 inches

Full sun

Rich, well-drained soil

Bears bowl-shaped yellow flowers blushed with bronze in mid- to late spring

Zones 3 to 8

P. 402

Tulipa biflora

SIZE: 3 to 5 inches

Full sun

Rich, well-drained soil

Bears starry, fragrant white flowers that are yellow at the base in early spring

Zones 5 to 9

P. 403

Tulipa 'Black Parrot'

Parrot Tulip

SIZE: 14 to 26 inches

Full sun

Rich, well-drained soil

Late season–flowering tulips with dark burgundy, featherlike tepals

Zones 3 to 8

P. 399

Tulipa 'Christmas Marvel'
Single Early Tulip

SIZE: 10 to 18 inches

Full sun

Rich, well-drained soil

Bears reddish pink cup-shaped blooms in early to midspring

Zones 3 to 8

P. 396

Tulipa clusiana
Lady Tulip

SIZE: 10 to 12 inches

Full sun

Rich, well-drained soil

Early to midspring-blooming tulip with white flowers striped with dark pinkish red

Zones 3 to 8

P. 403

Tulipa clusiana 'Cynthia'
Lady Tulip
SIZE: 10 to 12 inches
Full sun
Rich, well-drained soil
Early to midspring-blooming tulip with red-
and-yellow-striped blooms
Zones 3 to 8
P. 403

Tulipa 'Crème Upstar'
Double Late Tulip, Peony-flowered Tulip
SIZE: 14 to 24 inches
Full sun
Rich, well-drained soil
Late-flowering tulip bearing yellow flowers with
pink edges and a white base
Zones 3 to 8
P. 400

Tulipa 'Esperanto'
Viridiflora Tulip

SIZE: 18 to 20 inches

Full sun

Rich, well-drained soil

Late spring–blooming tulip with pinkish red
  flowers feathered in green

Zones 3 to 8

P. 399

Tulipa 'Fringed Elegance'
Fringed Tulip

SIZE: 14 to 26 inches

Full sun

Rich, well-drained soil

Mid- to late spring–blooming tulip with yellow
  blooms that have fringed tepal edges

Zones 3 to 8

P. 399

▲ *Tulipa* 'Generaal de Wet'
Single Early Tulip

SIZE: 10 to 18 inches

Full sun

Rich, well-drained soil

An old cultivar bearing orange and yellow
blooms with a musky, sweet fragrance in
early to midspring

Zones 3 to 8

P. 396

▼ *Tulipa* 'Georgette'
Single Late Tulip

SIZE: 18 to 30 inches

Full sun

Rich, well-drained soil

Bears clusters of yellow blooms edged and
brushed with red in late spring

Zones 3 to 7

P. 398

Tulipa 'Hamilton'
Fringed Tulip
SIZE: 14 to 26 inches

Full sun

Rich, well-drained soil

Mid- to late spring–blooming tulip with buttercup yellow flowers that have fringed tepal
edges

Zones 3 to 8

P. 399

Tulipa 'Heart's Delight'
Kaufmanniana Tulip, Waterlily Tulip
SIZE: 6 to 12 inches

Full sun

Rich, well-drained soil

From very early to midspring, bears single red,
rose-pink, and yellow blooms plus handsomely mottled leaves

Zones 3 to 8

P. 400

▲ *Tulipa humilis*

SIZE: 4 to 6 inches

Full sun

Rich, well-drained soil

Bears starry, crocuslike rose-pink flowers with a
yellow base in early spring

Zones 4 to 8

P. 403

▼ *Tulipa humilis* 'Lilliput'

SIZE: 4 to 6 inches

Full sun

Rich, well-drained soil

Bears starry, crocuslike scarlet flowers that have
violet bases in early spring

Zones 4 to 8

P. 403

Tulipa humilis 'Persian Pearl'

SIZE: 4 to 6 inches

Full sun

Rich, well-drained soil

In early to midspring, bears starry, magenta-
to purple-pink blooms that are yellow at
the base

Zones 4 to 8

P. 403

Tulipa 'Ivory Floradale'

Darwin Hybrid Tulip

SIZE: 20 to 28 inches

Full sun

Rich, well-drained soil

Mid- to late spring–blooming cultivars bearing
large ivory white blooms

Zones 3 to 8

P. 397

Tulipa 'Maytime'
Lily-flowered Tulip
SIZE: 18 to 26 inches
Full sun
Rich, well-drained soil
Bears goblet-shaped reddish violet flowers with white-edged tepals in mid- to late spring
Zones 3 to 8
P. 398

Tulipa 'Mirella'
Kaufmanniana Tulip, Waterlily Tulip
SIZE: 6 to 12 inches
Full sun
Rich, well-drained soil
Bears single white blooms from very early to midspring
Zones 3 to 8
P. 400

Tulipa neustruevae

SIZE: 3 to 4 inches

Full sun

Rich, well-drained soil

In early spring, bears yellow, crocuslike flowers that have outer tepals marked with greenish brown

Zones 3 to 8

P. 404

Tulipa 'New Design'

Triumph Tulip

SIZE: 14 to 24 inches

Full sun

Rich, well-drained soil

Mid- to late spring–blooming tulip bearing cup-shaped pink flowers and leaves edged in pinkish white

Zones 3 to 8

P. 397

Tulipa 'Orange Emperor'
Fosteriana Tulip
SIZE: 8 to 26 inches

Full sun

Rich, well-drained soil

Bears solitary, bowl-shaped orange flowers with a yellow base in midspring

Zones 3 to 8

P. 401

Tulipa 'Orange Queen'
Darwin Hybrid Tulip
SIZE: 20 to 28 inches

Full sun

Rich, well-drained soil

Mid- to late spring–blooming tulip with orange-and-red flowers

Zones 3 to 8

P. 397

▲ *Tulipa* 'Oratorio'

Greigii Tulip

SIZE: 6 to 12 inches

Full sun

Rich, well-drained soil

In early to midspring, bears single, bowl-shaped
watermelon to coral-pink flowers and
purple-mottled leaves

Zones 3 to 8

P. 401

▼ *Tulipa orphanidea* 'Flava'

SIZE: 8 to 10 inches

Full sun

Rich, well-drained soil

Bears brilliant yellow flowers that shade to red
at the tops of the tepals in early to midspring

Zones 5 to 8

P. 404

Tulipa 'Parade'
Darwin Hybrid Tulip
SIZE: 20 to 28 inches

Full sun

Rich, well-drained soil

Mid- to late spring–blooming tulip bearing red
flowers with a yellow base and a black yellow-edged central eye

Zones 3 to 8

P. 397

Tulipa 'Peach Blossom'
Double Early Tulip
SIZE: 12 to 16 inches

Full sun

Rich, well-drained soil

An old cultivar bearing showy, fragrant, peony-
like rose-pink flowers in midspring

Zones 3 to 8

P. 396

▲ *Tulipa praestans* 'Fusilier'

SIZE: 8 to 12 inches

Full sun

Rich, well-drained soil

Bears bowl-shaped brilliant red blooms in early
spring

Zones 4 to 8

P. 404

▼ *Tulipa* 'Purissima'

Fosteriana Tulip

SIZE: 8 to 26 inches

Full sun

Rich, well-drained soil

Bears solitary, fragrant, bowl-shaped white
flowers in midspring

Zones 3 to 8

P. 401

▲ *Tulipa* 'Red Emperor'

Fosteriana Tulip

SIZE: 8 to 26 inches

Full sun

Rich, well-drained soil

Bears solitary, bowl-shaped red flowers with a black heart in midspring

Zones 3 to 8

P. 401

▼ *Tulipa* 'Salmon Parrot'

Parrot Tulip

SIZE: 14 to 26 inches

Full sun

Rich, well-drained soil

Late season–flowering tulip bearing creamy yellow flowers with pinkish red featherlike tepals

Zones 3 to 8

P. 399

Tulipa saxatilis 'Lilac Wonder'

SIZE: 8 to 10 inches

Full sun

Rich, well-drained soil

Bears fragrant, star-shaped lilac-pink to rose-purple flowers with yellow centers in mid- to late spring

Zones 5 to 10

P. 405

Tulipa 'Sorbet'

Single Late Tulip

SIZE: 18 to 30 inches

Full sun

Rich, well-drained soil

Bears cup- or goblet-shaped white blooms striped with red in late spring

Zones 3 to 7

P. 398

Tulipa 'Spring Green'
Viridiflora Tulip
SIZE: 18 to 20 inches

Full sun

Rich, well-drained soil

Late spring tulip with single creamy white flowers that are feathered in green

Zones 3 to 8

P. 399

Tulipa 'Stresa'
Kaufmanniana Tulip, Waterlily Tulip
SIZE: 6 to 12 inches

Full sun

Rich, well-drained soil

From very early to midspring, bears red-and-yellow blooms that open during the day and close at night

Zones 3 to 8

P. 400

Tulipa 'Sweet Lady'
Greigii Tulip
SIZE: 6 to 12 inches

Full sun

Rich, well-drained soil

In early to midspring, bears single pink flowers
blushed with apricot-pink and leaves
striped with dark maroon

Zones 3 to 8

P. 401

Tulipa tarda
SIZE: 4 to 6 inches

Full sun

Rich, well-drained soil

Bears clusters of star-shaped golden yellow
flowers with white tips in midspring

Zones 3 to 8

P. 405

Tulipa turkestanica

SIZE: 6 to 10 inches

Full sun

Rich, well-drained soil

Bears clusters of up to 12 starry white flowers
with yellow or orange at the center in early
to midspring

Zones 4 to 8

P. 405

Tulipa vvedenskyi

SIZE: 10 to 12 inches

Full sun

Rich, well-drained soil

In early to midspring, bears red blooms that
have black or red blotches at the base

Zones 5 to 8

P. 406

Tulipa 'West Point'
Lily-flowered Tulip
SIZE: 18 to 26 inches
Full sun
Rich, well-drained soil
Bears goblet-shaped brilliant yellow flowers in mid- to late spring
Zones 3 to 8
P. 398

Urginea maritima
Sea Onion, Red Squill
SIZE: To 5 feet
Full sun
Poor to average, very well drained soil
Produces 1- to 3-foot-long racemes of tiny, densely packed white flowers in late summer or fall
Zones 9 to 11
P. 407

Veltheimia bracteata

SIZE: 1½ feet

Full sun

Average, well-drained soil

Bears rosettes of handsome, glossy leaves and
dense, rounded racemes of pinkish purple
flowers in spring

Zones 10 to 11; to Zone 9 with winter protection

P. 408

Watsonia borbonica
(inset, plant habit)

SIZE: 3 to 5 feet

Full sun

Light, evenly moist soil rich in organic matter

Bears branched spikes of up to 20 pink flowers
in summer

Zones 9 to 10

P. 409

Zantedeschia aethiopica
Calla Lily
SIZE: 2 to 3 feet

Full sun or partial shade

Rich, moist soil

Bears glossy, arrowhead-shaped leaves and showy white flowers from late spring to midsummer

Zones 8 to 11; to Zone 7 or 6 with winter protection

P. 410

Zantedeschia elliottiana
Golden Calla, Yellow Calla
SIZE: 2 to 3 feet

Full sun or partial shade

Rich, moist soil

Bears dark green heart-shaped leaves spotted with white, and yellow flowers in summer

Zones 9 to 11

P. 411

Zantedeschia hybrid 'Black Magic'
Hybrid Calla Lily

SIZE: 2 to 2½ feet

Full sun or partial shade

Rich, moist soil

Bears heavily mottled white leaves and creamy white-yellow flowers that have a black throat in summer

Zones 9 to 10; to Zone 8 with winter protection

P. 411

Zantedeschia hybrid 'Carmine Red'
Hybrid Calla Lily

SIZE: 1½ to 2 feet

Full sun or partial shade

Rich, moist soil

Bears carmine-colored flowers in summer

Zones 9 to 10; to Zone 8 with winter protection

P. 411

Zantedeschia hybrid 'Pacific Pink'

Hybrid Calla Lily

SIZE: 1½ to 2 feet
Full sun or partial shade
Rich, moist soil
Bears pink blooms in summer
Zones 9 to 10; to Zone 8 with winter protection
P. 411

Zantedeschia rehmannii

Pink Calla

SIZE: 12 to 16 inches
Full sun or partial shade
Rich, moist soil
Bears dark green leaves and pink, white, or purple flowers in summer
Zones 9 to 11
P. 411

Zephyranthes atamasco (inset, close-up)
Atamasco Lily
SIZE: 8 to 12 inches

Full sun

Rich, moist, very well drained soil

Native southeastern wildflower bearing white funnel-shaped flowers in spring or summer

Zones 10 to 11

P. 412

Zephyranthes grandiflora
Rain Lily, Rain Flower, Zephyr Lily, Fairy Lily
SIZE: 8 to 10 inches

Full sun

Rich, moist, very well drained soil

Bears funnel-shaped pink flowers from late summer to fall

Zones 9 to 11

P. 413

Zephyranthes rosea

Rain Lily, Rain Flower, Zephyr Lily,
Fairy Lily

SIZE: 6 to 8 inches

Full sun

Rich, moist, very well drained soil

Bears funnel-shaped pink flowers with white
throats in fall

Zones 10 to 11

P. 413

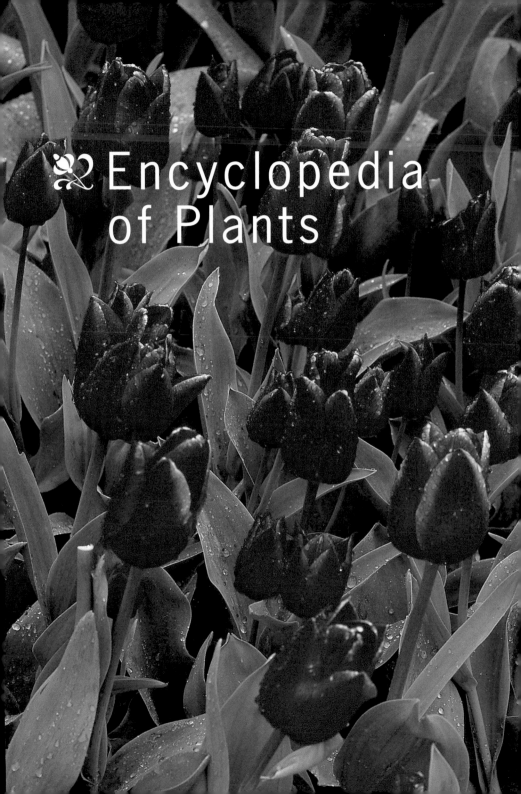

Encyclopedia
of Plants

🥀 Encyclopedia of Plants

🌱 *Achimenes*

ah-KIM-eh-neez. Gesneriad family, Gesneriaceae.

Relatives of popular houseplants such as African violets and Cape prim-roses (*Streptocarpus* spp.), achimenes are tender perennials primarily native to Central America. About 25 species belong to the genus, all of which grow from scaly rhizomes that somewhat resemble caterpillars. They bear showy salverform flowers, meaning each bloom has a tubular base and an abruptly flared and flattened face that has five prominent lobes. Blooms are borne singly, in pairs, or in clusters from summer to fall above ovate, often hairy, dark green leaves with toothed margins. The plants are dormant in winter. In the garden, achimenes are primarily used in containers and hanging baskets, although they also can be grown in shade gardens.

HOW TO GROW

Grow achimenes in pots set in a bright, shaded area protected from direct sun, which will scorch the leaves. They require rich, evenly moist soil and high humidity for best growth. Pot sections of dormant rhizomes in damp peat moss or vermiculite any time from late winter to late spring, covering to a depth of ½ to 1 inch. Start them in a humid, warm (65° to 70°F) spot. Water very sparingly until they begin to grow; otherwise the rhizomes will rot. When plants are 2 inches tall, move them to pots or baskets filled with a light, loose medium rich in organic matter such as compost or leaf mold. (Don't pack the medium into the pots.) Continue watering moderately until they are growing actively, then keep them evenly moist. Plants that dry out may enter dormancy prematurely. Pinch

to encourage branching. Move containers outdoors when night temperatures remain above 60° to 65°F. Plants may require staking. Feed every
two weeks with a dilute fertilizer. In late summer, gradually reduce watering, then dry the containers out completely. Store the rhizomes, still in
their containers, in a cool (50° to 55°F), dry spot. Divide and repot in late
winter or spring to repeat the cycle. Propagate by dividing the rhizomes.

A. hybrids
P. 30

Achimenes, Monkey-faced Pansy, Orchid Pansy. Cultivars are much more
commonly grown than the species and are available in white, pink, red,
blue, purple-blue, and violet. Blooms are 1½ to 3 inches wide and are
borne from summer to fall on arching 1- to 2-foot-long stems. Cultivars
include 'Peach Blossom', with rosy salmon flowers; 'Little Beauty', dark
pink; 'Ambroise Vershaffelt', white flowers with purple veins at the throat;
'Blue Sparks', blue flowers; 'Harry Williams', red; 'Purple King', red-purple. Tender; survives outdoors in Zones 10 and 11.

☙ *Acidanthera* see *Gladiolus*

☙ *Agapanthus*

ag-ah-PAN-thus. Lily family, Liliaceae.

Although commonly called lilies-of-the-Nile, the ten species of *Agapanthus* hail from southern Africa, not along the Nile. They are tender perennials, some evergreen, that produce thick, fleshy roots and bold clumps of
basal, strap-shaped leaves. Striking, rounded umbels of trumpet-shaped
blue, blue-violet, or white flowers appear on erect, leafless stalks above
the foliage in summer. The individual flowers may be tubular, bell, or
trumpet shaped and consist of six petal-like tepals.

HOW TO GROW

Give agapanthus full sun and fertile, well-drained, evenly moist soil. *Agapanthus* species are hardy perennials from at least Zone 9 south; some hybrids, especially deciduous ones, are hardy to Zone 6 with protection. For
plants overwintered outdoors, well-drained soil (sandy soil is ideal) and a
consistent cover of mulch are essential. Where they are not hardy, grow
these striking plants in large containers or tubs either set on terraces or
sunk to the rim in the soil. Or plant clumps in the ground and dig them

each fall for overwintering. They bloom best when the roots are slightly crowded. Feed pot-grown plants monthly in early summer until flower buds appear. Water regularly when plants are growing and flowering actively, but gradually withhold water in fall and keep them nearly dry over winter. Overwinter them in a bright, cool (40° to 50°F) spot and water sparingly until active growth resumes in spring. Propagate by dividing the clumps, removing offsets, or sowing seeds. Repot or divide in late winter or early spring as necessary.

A. africanus   P. 30
a. af-rih-KAH-nus. African Lily. Evergreen, clump-forming 2- to 3-foot-tall species that spreads from 1½ to 2 feet. Bears rounded 6- to 12-inch-wide umbels of dark purple-blue flowers in late summer. Individual blooms are trumpet shaped and 1 to 2 inches long. Zones 9 to 11.

A. campanulatus
a. cam-pah-nue-LAY-tus. Deciduous, clump-forming 2- to 4-foot-tall species that spreads from 1½ to 2 feet. Bears rounded 4- to 8-inch-wide umbels of bell-shaped flowers that are pale to dark purplish blue and ¾ to 1½ inches long. 'Albovittatus' bears white-striped leaves. Zones 7 to 10.

A. hybrids   P. 31
Species and hybrids ranging from 1 to 4 feet in height are available. 'Peter Pan' is a heavy-blooming dwarf cultivar that reaches 18 inches. 'Bressingham White' and 'Snowy Owl' bear white flowers. 'Headbourne Hybrids' have pale blue to violet flowers and are reportedly hardy to Zone 6. 'Storm Cloud' bears especially dark purple-blue flowers. Tender perennials, hardy from Zones 6 to 10, depending on the selection.

❦ Allium
AL-ee-um. Lily family, Liliaceae

While the best-known members of this genus undoubtedly are onions, garlic, leeks, and shallots, *Allium* also contains a wealth of ornamental plants suitable for the flower garden. Commonly called ornamental onions or simply alliums, these bulbs bear showy, rounded flower clusters called umbels atop hollow, unbranched stems. The umbels range from 1-inch pompons to huge 5-inch balls and are carried above the leaves. They can consist of many densely packed flowers that form a round inflorescence or may have fewer, more loosely arranged, blooms. The individual flowers are small and starry or bell shaped and have six petal-like tepals. Leaves, which are grassy or straplike and onion scented when bruised, are borne at the base of the plant and often fade as or just after the flowers open. Alliums grow from tunicate bulbs, although many species have very small bulbs or ones that are barely developed and are borne on a horizontal rhizome. Other species produce bulbs clustered on slender rhizomes. Dig up a clump of chives *(A. schoenoprasum)*, and you'll find a tight clump of bulbs on slender rhizomes that really look more like fleshy stems with hairlike roots attached at the bottom. The species with poorly developed bulbs are sold in pots and grown like herbaceous perennials rather than like typical bulbs. Ornamental species with both well- and poorly developed bulbs are listed here. About 700 species belong to this large genus.

HOW TO GROW

A site in full sun with well-drained soil is the rule for most alliums. They grow well in a range of soils—from poor soil to rich, fertile loam—provided it is well drained. They also tolerate relatively dry soil. Plant dormant bulbs in fall with the tops at a depth of about three times the diameter of the bulb. Plant pot-grown clumps of alliums in spring or fall, setting the plants at the same depth they were growing in the pot. Tall, nonspreading species look best when planted in clumps with the bulbs fairly close together—space *A. aflatunense* bulbs about 6 inches apart; *A. giganteum*, 1 foot apart. *A. christophii* also is best spaced 1 foot apart. Space smaller species about 3 to 6 inches apart and container-grown plants a distance of about half their height. Many species have foliage that dies back just before or after flowering, and the dying foliage can be very unattractive—plus the plants leave a hole to fill in the garden. Solve this problem by either interspersing the alliums among clumps of annuals or low-growing perennials, shrubs, or ground covers, or simply plant the alliums behind their companions. Don't cut the foliage back before it yellows completely—it is making food for next year's blooms. Divide plants in spring or fall if clumps become overcrowded. Propagate by removing offsets from the parent bulbs or dividing the clumps just after they finish flowering. Some species produce bulbils in the flower heads. These are small bulbs that can be planted like seeds and will yield blooming-sized plants sooner than seeds would. Bulbils are genetically identical to their parents and can be used to propagate cultivars. Species alliums can be grown from fresh seeds sown outdoors in summer or fall as soon as they are ripe, and some species, including *A. christophii*, self-sow. Seeds yield blooming-sized plants in about 3 years.

A. acuminatum
a. ah-kew-mih-NAY-tum. Dwarf species native to western North America with very small egg-shaped bulbs. Plants bear loose, domed 1½- to 2½-inch-wide umbels of about 25 starry pinkish purple flowers on 4- to 12-inch-tall stems in early summer. The leaves just wither as the flowers open. Zones 4 to 9.

A. aflatunense   P. 32
a. ah-fla-too-NEN-see. Persian Onion. Asian species with rounded 1- to 2½-inch-wide bulbs. Bears round 4½-inch-wide umbels of many densely packed red-violet flowers on 2- to 3-foot-tall stems in early summer. Leaves wither as the flowers open. Seed heads are ornamental. The hybrid 'Purple Sensation', with violet blooms, is usually listed here. Zones 4 to 8.

A. atropurpureum
a. ah-tro-pur-PUR-ee-um. Medium-size species with small round bulbs and 2½-inch-wide umbels of densely packed, starry dark purple to purple-maroon flowers on 20-inch-tall stems in summer. Zones 3 to 8.

A. caeruleum   P. 32
a. see-ROO-lee-um. Blue Globe Onion, Nodding Onion. Siberian species with small rounded bulbs and 2-inch-wide umbels of 30 to 50 densely packed, starry dark blue flowers on 1- to 2-foot stems in early summer. Requires very well drained soil and a hot site for best results. Zones 3 to 8.

A. carinatum   P. 33
a. kare-in-AY-tum. Keeled Garlic. Medium-size species with very small egg-shaped bulbs. Bears loose 2-inch-wide umbels of 25 or 30 bell-shaped purple flowers on 1- to 2-foot-tall stems in midsummer. Usually produces bulbils in the flower clusters. *A. carinatum* ssp. *pulchellum* (also listed as *A. pulchellum*) bears 2½-inch-wide umbels of reddish violet blooms on 1- to 1½-foot-tall stalks that lack bulbils. Zones 5 to 8.

A. cernuum   P. 33
a. SIR-new-um. Nodding Onion, Wild Onion. Native North American species with clusters of very small oval bulbs on short rhizomes. Bears 2½-inch-wide umbels of from 25 to 40 rose-purple, pink, or white flowers on 1½-

to 2-foot stems in early summer. Both the umbel and the individual flowers are nodding. Foliage remains green until late summer. Grows in shade or sun and tolerates heavy (but not wet) soil or dry sandy conditions. Forms large handsome clumps and naturalizes easily. Self-sows. Zones 4 to 9.

A. cristophii   P. 34
a. krih-STOF-ee-eye. Star of Persia. Formerly *A. albopilosum.* Striking species with small round bulbs and attractive gray-green leaves that wither as the flowers open. Bears huge ball-like 8- to 12-inch-wide umbels of about 100 starry silvery purple flowers on 1- to 2-foot stalks in summer. Seed heads are showy, and plants self-sow. Zones 4 to 8.

A. cyaneum   P. 34
a. sy-AH-nee-um. Dwarf species bearing clusters of small bulbs on short rhizomes. Bears ¾-inch-wide umbels of 6 to 18 blue flowers in summer on 4- to 10-inch-tall stems. Zones 5 to 9.

A. cyathophorum var. farreri
a. sy-eh-tho-FOR-rum var. FAR-rer-eye. Dwarf plant producing clusters of small bulbs on short rhizomes. Bears loose ½-inch-wide umbels on 6- to 12-inch-tall stalks. Umbels consist of from 6 to about 30 pendent, bell-shaped violet-purple flowers. Zones 4 to 9.

A. denudatum
a. deh-nue-DAH-tum. Formerly *A. albidum.* Dwarf species with very small rounded bulbs clustered on branching rhizomes. Bears clusters of very short, strap-shaped leaves and round ½-inch-wide umbels of white flowers atop 4- to 10-inch stems in early summer. Zones 4 to 9.

A. flavum
a. FLAY-vum. Small Yellow Onion. Dwarf species with small rounded bulbs and loose ½-inch-wide umbels of 10 to as many as 60 yellow flowers in summer on 4- to 14-inch-tall stalks. Zones 4 to 10.

A. giganteum   P. 35
a. jy-GAN-tee-um. Giant Onion. Striking, tall species with rounded 2- to 3-inch-wide bulbs. Produces dense, round 4- to 5-inch-wide umbels of 50 to 100 starry rosy purple flowers in summer on 3- to 5-foot-tall stalks. Leaves wither as the flowers open. Bulbs tend to be short-lived in the garden. 'White Giant' bears white flowers. Zones 4 to 8.

A. hybrids   P. 36

Many excellent hybrid ornamental onions have been developed. All of the following grow from fully developed bulbs and bear round or nearly round umbels and bloom in early summer: 'Gladiator' *(A. aflatunense × A. macleanii)*, which bears 6- to 8-inch-wide umbels of many rose-violet flowers on 4- to 5-foot-tall stems; 'Globemaster' *(A. christophii × A. macleanii)*, with very long-lasting 10-inch-wide umbels of rich violet flowers on 2- to 3-foot-tall stems and handsome ornamental seed heads; 'Lucy Ball' *(A. aflatunense × A. macleanii)*, bearing 5-inch-wide umbels of 50 or more starry dark lilac-purple blooms on 3-foot-stems; 'Mars' *(A. stipitatum × A. aflatunense)*, bearing 6-inch umbels of red-purple flowers on 3-foot-tall stems; 'Mount Everest', with 6-inch-wide umbels of white flowers on 2- to 3-foot stems; and 'Rien Poortvliet', which bears 6- to 8-inch-wide umbels of rich purple flowers. Zones 4 or 5 to 8.

A. karataviense   P. 36

a. kare-ah-tah-vee-EN-see. Turkistan Onion. A dwarf species with 1- to 2-inch-wide bulbs. The 6- to 10-inch-tall plants are grown as much for their foliage as for their flowers. The 4-inch-wide leaves are gray-green to gray-purple and reach 6 to 9 inches long. In early summer, it bears up to 50 starry pale pink flowers in umbels that range from 3 to 5 or more inches across. Leaves remain attractive for a few weeks after the flowers fade. Zones 5 to 9.

A. macleanii

a. mak-leh-AH-nee-eye. Formerly *A. elatum.* Bulbous species similar to *A. giganteum* with ¾- to 2-inch-wide bulbs. Bears 5- to 6-inch-wide umbels of about 50 violet flowers in summer on 3-foot-tall stems. Attractive green leaves. Zones 5 to 8.

A. moly   P. 37

a. MOL-ee. Lily Leek, Golden Garlic. Charming medium-size species with 1-inch-wide bulbs and showy, loose 2-inch-wide umbels of 20 to 30 star-shaped golden yellow flowers in early summer on ½- to 1-foot-tall stalks. Needs very well drained soil that is nearly dry after flowering. Tolerates partial shade. Bulbs produce abundant offsets where happy and are good for naturalizing. 'Jeannine' bears 3-inch-wide umbels in early summer on 12- to 16-inch-stalks. Zones 3 to 9.

A. narcissiflorum
a. nar-sih-sih-FLOR-um. Narcissus Onion. Dwarf species that grows from very small bulbs clustered on a thickened rhizome. Produces pendent 1-inch-wide umbels of six to ten flowers in summer on 6- to 12-inch-tall stalks. Individual blooms are bell shaped and pinkish purple. Bears blue-green leaves that last through the season. Zones 4 to 8.

A. neapolitanum
a. nee-ah-pol-ih-TAH-num. Naples Onion, Daffodil Garlic. Formerly *A. cowanii.* Dwarf species that grows from ¾-inch-wide bulbs. Bears loose 2-inch-wide umbels of 20 to 30 fragrant white flowers in spring on 6- to 12-inch-tall stems. Leaves wither as the flowers open. Zones 6 to 10.

A. nigrum
a. NYE-grum. Black Onion. Formerly *A. multibulbosum.* Medium-size species growing from 2-inch-wide bulbs. Produces somewhat flattened 3- to 4-inch-wide umbels of 20 to 30 or more cup-shaped creamy white flowers on 1½- to 3-foot-tall stems in early summer. Each flower has a dark green to black ovary in its center, and umbels sometimes contain bulbils. Seed heads are ornamental. Zones 6 to 10.

A. oreophilum   P. 37
a. or-ee-OFF-ih-lum. Formerly *A. ostrowskianum.* Dwarf species growing from very small bulbs that produce loose 1½-inch-wide umbels of 10 to 15 bell-shaped pinkish purple flowers in early summer on 2- to 8-inch stalks. Leaves wither as the flowers open. Zones 4 to 9.

A. rosenbachianum
a. ro-sen-bak-ee-AH-num. A tall species growing from round bulbs under 1 inch wide. Produces 4-inch-wide umbels of more than 50 star-shaped purple flowers in early summer on 3- to 4-foot-tall stalks. Leaves wither as the flowers open. Seed heads are ornamental. 'Album' bears white flowers. Zones 4 to 10.

A. roseum
a. RO-zee-um. Rosy Garlic. Medium-size species growing from very small bulbs. Bears loose 1- to 3-inch-wide umbels of 5 to as many as 30 rose-pink flowers on 1- to 1½-foot-tall stems in late spring. 'Grandiflorum' bears 4-inch-wide umbels. Zones 5 to 8.

A. schoenoprasum
P. 38

a. sho-no-PRAZ-um. Chives. Mounding species producing clumps of long, very narrow, poorly developed bulbs on short rhizomes. Has edible round leaves that remain green through the summer and are evergreen in warm climates. Bears dense 1-inch-wide cloverlike umbels of 30 or more rosy pink flowers in summer. Clumps reach 1 to 2 feet and spread as far. Tolerates light shade. Cut plants—foliage and all—to the ground after flowering to encourage reblooming and fresh foliage and to discourage reseeding. Zones 3 to 9.

A. schubertii
P. 38

a. shu-BER-tee-eye. Striking species that grows from a 1¼- to 1½-inch-wide bulb. Bears huge round umbels that range from 9 to 12 inches in diameter on 1- to 2-foot-tall stems. Pale purple individual flowers are loosely arranged on stalks of different lengths and ½ inch wide. Leaves wither as the flowers open. Zones 5 to 10.

A. senescens
P. 39

a. seh-NESS-ens. Dwarf species bearing small bulbs clustered on short stout rhizomes. Bears strap-shaped leaves that are evergreen to 25°F and 1-inch-wide umbels of 20 to 30 mauve-pink flowers in mid- to late summer. Plants reach 6 to 12 inches in height and spread slowly into clumps. *A. senescens* ssp. *montanum* var. *glaucum* is grown for its clumps of attractive, twisted silver-blue leaves and pink flowers. Zones 5 to 9.

A. sikkimense

a. sik-ih-MEN-see. Formerly *A. tibeticum, A. kansuense.* Dwarf species bearing very small bulbs clustered on short rhizomes. Produces nodding 1-inch-wide umbels of about 10 blue bell-shaped flowers in early summer. Zones 6 to 10.

A. sphaerocephalon
P. 39

a. spare-ro-SEF-ah-lon. Drumstick Chives, Drumstick Allium, Round-headed Leek. Taller species, reaching 2 to 3 feet, that grows from small bulbs. Produces very dense (nearly solid) 1-inch-wide umbels of 30 to as many as 100 bell-shaped flowers in midsummer that vary from green to purple or purplish maroon. Umbels may contain bulbils. Zones 4 to 8.

A. stellatum

a. steh-LAH-tum. Prairie Onion. Native North American wildflower growing from rounded bulbs and producing leaves that die back before the flowers appear. Bears rounded 1- to 2-inch-wide umbels of cup-shaped rose-pink flowers from midsummer to fall. Zones 5 to 9.

A. tanguticum   P. 40

a. tan-GOO-tih-cum. Lavender Globe Lily. Clumping species with small rounded bulbs on branching rhizomes. Bears lavender-blue 2-inch-wide umbels on 2-foot-tall stalks in midsummer. Foliage remains attractive all season. 'Summer Beauty' bears dark lavender-blue umbels on 1½-foot stems. 'Blue Skies' produces light lavender-blue umbels over a long season. Zones 4 to 9.

A. thunbergii   P. 40

a. thun-BER-jee-eye. A dwarf species with clumps of very small bulbs on branched rhizomes. Bears 1- to 1½-inch-wide umbels of rose-purple flowers in fall. Plants reach about 8 inches in height, spread slowly to form small clumps, and have grassy foliage that remains green all season. 'Ozawa' bears rosy violet flowers. Zones 4 to 8.

A. triquetrum   P. 41

a. tri-KEH-trum. Three-cornered Leek. Medium-size 8- to 15-inch-tall species growing from small bulbs and producing three-cornered stems and linear leaves. In late spring or early summer it bears nodding 1- to 3-inch-wide umbels of 5 to 15 bell-shaped, lightly scented white flowers striped with green. Spreads quickly and is good for naturalizing. Zones 5 to 9.

A. tuberosum   P. 41

a. too-ber-O-sum. Garlic Chives. A species popular in herb and flower gardens alike that grows from poorly developed bulbs clustered on branched rhizomes and forms good-sized clumps. Bears rounded 2-inch-wide umbels of fragrant, starry white flowers on 2-foot plants from late summer to fall. Foliage is edible and remains green all season. Best planted in rich, evenly moist soil. Self-sows with abandon. Deadheading prevents excessive self-seeding; plants can become troublesome weeds. Zones 4 to 8.

A. unifolium   P. 42

a. yoo-nih-FO-lee-um. Formerly A. murrayanum. Wildflower native to the Pacific Northwest with small bulbs that are not on rhizomes, but that produces bulblets on short rhizomes. Bears rounded 2- to 2½-inch-wide umbels of about 20 bell-shaped pink to purplish pink flowers in late spring or early summer on 1- to 1½-foot-tall stalks. Grassy gray-green leaves wither as the flowers open. Best in moist soil. Zones 5 to 9.

A. ursinum   P. 42

a. ur-SYE-num. Ramsons, Bear's Garlic, Wood Garlic. Fairly dwarf species producing small rounded bulbs on branched rhizomes. Bears flattened 2-inch-wide umbels of 15 to 20 white flowers on 6- to 18-inch-tall stalks in spring. Thrives in partial shade. Zones 5 to 8.

❦ Alocasia

al-o-KASE-ee-uh. Arum family, Araceae.

Commonly called elephant's ears, *Alocasia* species are tender perennials that either are rhizomatous or grow from tuberous roots. About 70 species belong to the genus, all native to southern and Southeast Asia. Plants are grown for their large, showy, arrowhead-shaped leaves that have prominent veins and often are marked with bronze, black, or violet-black. The flowers are relatively insignificant: like those of closely related *Colocasia* species as well as Jack-in-the-pulpits (*Arisaema* spp.), they consist of an inflorescence made up of many tiny flowers clustered on a central stalk, called a spadix, that is surrounded by a modified leaf, called a spathe. Contact with the sap may cause skin irritation, and all parts of the plant cause stomach upset if eaten. *Alocasia* species usually are grown in tropical climates or as greenhouse plants, but a few selections have begun to find their way into more northern gardens, where they add a lush, tropical effect during the warm summer months.

HOW TO GROW

Select a site in partial shade with deep, rich, evenly moist soil that is well drained. A sheltered spot is best, and protection from hot sun is essential. Plants thrive in heat and humidity and can be grown outdoors year-round in Zones 10 and 11. In the North, start small plants or tubers indoors before the last frost date, and keep in a warm (70° to 75°F) spot. Move the plants outdoors only after the weather is warm and settled and night temperatures do not dip below 60°F. Sink them into the soil, still in their pots. Keep the soil evenly moist during the growing season. To overwinter, bring the pots indoors and keep the plants in a warm (60°F minimum), humid spot. Keep the soil somewhat drier in winter when plants are resting; mist the foliage to maintain high humidity. Repot, as necessary, in spring. Propagate by dividing the fleshy rhizomes or separating the offsets in spring.

A. hybrids   P. 43

A variety of hybrids with showy leaves are available. 'Hilo Beauty' bears green leaves mottled with cream (or light green). 'Black Velvet' has black leaves with silver veins. Zones 10 to 11.

A. macrorrhiza   P. 43

a. mak-row-RYE-zuh. Giant Taro. A tropical species that can reach 15 feet high and spread to 8 feet or more but is smaller in the North. Bears glossy, arrow-shaped green leaves with leaf blades that range from 2 to 4 feet long. Flowers have a yellow-green spathe. Widely grown in the tropics for its edible rhizomes. 'Variegata' bears leaves blotched with cream, gray-green, and dark green. Plants remain evergreen if temperatures briefly dip to 29°F, and they are killed to the ground but return if exposed to cooler temperatures only for short stretches. Zones 10 to 11.

❧ Alstroemeria

al-stro-MAIR-ee-uh. Lily family, Liliaceae.

Commonly known as Peruvian lily or lily-of-the-Incas, *Alstroemeria* species hail from mountainous regions and grasslands in South America. About 50 species belong here, all of which produce clumps of tubers or fleshy rhizomes and have thick, fleshy roots. The leaves are linear to lance shaped. Plants produce loose clusters of showy funnel-shaped flowers in summer. Each bloom has six petal-like tepals. Blooms are about 1½ inches long and range from 1½ to 4 inches wide.

HOW TO GROW

Give alstroemerias rich, moist, well-drained soil. In the North (Zones 5 and 6), plant them in full sun, preferably in a protected site such as at the base of a south-facing wall. From Zone 7 south, plant them in light shade. They do not tolerate the extremes of heat and cold characteristic of most gardens in North America and are best in areas with Mediterranean climates — with mild summers and winters. (They are commonly grown as cut flowers in California, for example.) When planting, set the tubers about 8 inches deep, and handle them carefully as they are brittle and can break. Mulch annually in early summer with compost to keep the soil rich. In areas with hot summers, mulch also helps keep the soil cool and moist and prolongs bloom. Water regularly in dry weather. Deadheading prevents seed formation and directs the plant's energy toward the formation of next year's flowers. Plants resent being disturbed, so do not transplant or divide them unless absolutely necessary, or for propagation. New divisions can be very slow to establish. In the North, protect clumps over winter with a thick layer of coarse mulch such as evergreen boughs, coarse leaves, pine needles, or salt hay. Clumps can be dug for overwintering indoors: pack them in moist peat moss and store them in boxes or paper bags in a cool (32° to 40°F), frost-free spot. Container-grown plants can be overwintered dry in their containers.

A. aurea   P. 44
a. AUR-ee-uh. Peruvian Lily, Lily-of-the-Incas. Formerly *A. aurantiaca*. A 2- to 3-foot-tall species, spreading to 1½ feet. Bears clusters of orange or yellow flowers with red-striped tepals in summer. 'Lutea' bears yellow blooms spotted with brown. Zones 7 to 10; to Zone 5 with winter protection.

A. ligtu   P. 44
a. LIG-too. Peruvian Lily, Lily-of-the-Incas. A 1½- to 2-foot-tall species forming 2½-foot-wide clumps. Bears clusters of yellow flowers spotted and streaked with yellow, white, red, or purple in summer. Ligtu Hybrids come in a wide range of pastel shades, with blooms often marked with dark red or black. Zones 7 to 10; to Zone 5 with winter protection.

✿× *Amarcrinum*
ah-mar-KRY-num. Amaryllis family, Amaryllidaceae.

This hybrid genus, the result of a cross between *Amaryllis belladonna* and *Crinum moorei*, contains a single species grown for its fragrant rose-pink trumpet-shaped flowers. The long-lived blooms are borne in late summer to early fall atop thick, leafless stems and are arranged in clusters, called umbels. Individual flowers have six petal-like tepals. The strap-shaped 1½- to 3-inch-wide leaves can reach 2 feet in length and are evergreen from about Zone 8 south. Plants grow from long-necked tunicate bulbs that are poisonous to rodents. Foliage and flowers also resist deer for the same reason. Plants divide to form clumps with time.

HOW TO GROW

Give plants full sun or partial shade with rich, well-drained soil. They require evenly moist conditions when actively growing from spring to fall and drier conditions when dormant in winter. In the North, grow them in large containers or tubs, where they can be planted with just the base of the bulb (about one-third of it) in the soil. Give container-grown plants partial shade in summer and feed them weekly during the growing season. Overwinter the bulbs in their containers indoors in a cool (45° to 50° nights), frost-free spot. While the plants are not growing actively, either keep the soil on the dry side (letting the leaves remain evergreen) or let the soil dry out completely and let the leaves wither away. Where hardy, they can be grown outdoors year-round: plant either in late summer or in spring, setting the bulbs with the noses just at the soil surface. Where marginally hardy, mulch them in late fall with evergreen boughs, salt hay, pine needles, or another coarse mulch. Propagate by separating offsets that appear at the base of the bulbs in early spring.

A. memoria-corsii
P. 45

a. mem-OR-ee-uh-COR-see-eye. Also listed as × *Crinodonna*. Vigorous hybrid bearing umbels of 10 to as many as 16 fragrant 3- to 4-inch-wide flowers on 2- to 3-foot-tall stems. Zones 8 to 10, to Zone 7 with winter protection.

❦ Amaryllis

am-ah-RILL-iss. Amaryllis family, Amaryllidaceae.

Amaryllis contains a single species, native to South Africa, that is grown for its showy, funnel-shaped blooms, which are borne in late summer and fall. The blooms are produced in umbels of 6 to 12 fragrant pink flowers atop fleshy, leafless stems. The individual flowers, which resemble lilies, have six petal-like tepals, or perianth lobes, that curve backward at the tips. Plants, which grow from a 2- to 4-inch-diameter tunicate bulb, have strap-shaped leaves that appear either in late fall or in late spring and die back in early summer. Like many other members of the amaryllis family, these plants are rodent- and deer-proof because the bulbs and other plant parts are poisonous. *Amaryllis* species are often confused with the bulbs sold for winter forcing and commonly called amaryllis: see *Hippeastrum* for information on those plants.

HOW TO GROW

Plant *Amaryllis* in full sun or partial shade with average, deeply prepared, well-drained soil. They are quite drought tolerant and happiest in Mediterranean climates where warm, dry summers prevail. Plant in late spring or early summer with the tops of the bulbs just under the soil surface. Where they are marginally hardy (Zones 7 and 8), plant them in a warm, protected site, such as against a south-facing wall, and set the bulbs 4 to 6 inches deep. Cover them over in winter (especially outdoors in Zone 7) with a coarse mulch such as evergreen boughs, coarse leaves, or salt hay. Where they are not hardy, grow them in large containers or tubs: gradually dry off the soil and overwinter plants indoors by setting the containers in a cool (40° to 50° nights), dry place. Or, dig the bulbs in fall and store them in dry peat moss or vermiculite over winter. Bulbs are happiest when left undisturbed—both in the ground and in containers. Dig and divide plants when they are dormant for propagation or if they become too crowded.

A. belladonna   P. 45
a. bel-uh-DON-uh. Belladonna Lily, Magic Lily, Naked Ladies, Resurrection Lily. A deciduous bulb that produces umbels of 2½- to 4-inch-long trumpets in late summer or early fall atop 1½- to 2-foot-tall stalks. Blooms come in shades from pale to dark pink, and white-flowered cultivars are also available. Clumps spread to several feet with time. Zones 8 to 10; to Zone 7 with winter protection.

Amorphophallus

ah-mor-fo-FAL-us. Arum family, Araceae.

With common names such as devil's tongue, snake palm, and voodoo lily, it isn't surprising that *Amorphophallus* species make an unusual addition to the garden. Between 90 and 100 species belong here, all native to the warm, moist tropics of Africa and Asia. All grow from cormlike rhizomes that in some cases reach immense proportions: an *A. titanum* corm that bloomed at the New York Botanical Garden weighed in at over 113 pounds. While the exotic blooms certainly are a curiosity, the single, deeply lobed leaf that each corm produces is extremely ornamental and can add an exotic, tropical flair to shady summer beds and borders. Corms that have reached flowering size (this may take several years) produce a single inflorescence before the leaf appears. The inflorescence consists of many tiny flowers clustered on a central stalk, called a spadix. The spadix is surrounded by a modified leaf, called a spathe. The exotic-looking blooms somewhat resemble those of calla lilies (*Zantedeschia* spp.) and Jack-in-the-pulpits (*Arisaema* spp.), both close relatives. The fact that *Amorphophallus* blooms are pollinated by flies and other insects attracted to carrion gives a hint to the foul odor emitted by some species. Fortunately the odor is released for a relatively short period — commonly only a few days.

HOW TO GROW

Give these plants a spot in partial to full shade with very rich, evenly moist soil. Roots form on the top of the corm. Where they are hardy, set the corms with the tops at least 4 to 6 inches below the soil surface — deeper in areas where they are only marginally hardy. In northern zones where they are not hardy, grow these plants in containers (set corms with the tops at least 2 to 3 inches deep) for overwintering indoors or plant directly in the soil and dig the corms in early fall after the foliage fades. Corms develop cup-shaped tops: in areas with wet winters, set them on their sides to prevent water from collecting. Mark the locations of corms, as plants are very late to emerge in spring. Keep the soil evenly moist while the plants are in leaf, but gradually withhold water later in the summer as they enter dormancy. To overwinter corms indoors, store them in a cool (55° to 60°F) place. Pack the corms in barely moist peat; corms of *A. konjac* can be stored on a shelf without any packing. Propagate by seeds or by separating offsets when corms are dormant.

A. konjac   P. 46

a. KON-jak. Devil's Tongue, Snake Palm, Voodoo Lily, Umbrella Arum. Formerly *A. rivieri*. A 3- to 6-foot-tall perennial bearing a leathery 12- to 16-inch-long red-purple spathe surrounding a dark brown spadix. A deeply lobed, brown-green leaf mottled with white follows the flowers. Leaves can reach 3 to 4½ feet in length. Zones 7 to 10; to Zone 6 with protection.

❦ *Anemone*

ah-NEM-oh-nee. Buttercup family, Ranunculaceae.

Anemone is a diverse genus of about 120 species that bear saucer- to cup-shaped flowers with a boss, or tuft, of showy yellow stamens in the center. The showy portion of the flowers actually are petal-like sepals instead of true petals, and flowers come in shades of pink, rose-red, scarlet, white, lavender, and violet-blue. Blooms are borne one per stem or in branched clusters and may be single, semidouble, or double. Also called wind-flowers (the botanical name is from the Greek word *anemos,* wind), anemones have attractive, deeply cut, fernlike leaves. Most produce a cluster of leaves at the base of the plant, but some species also have leaves along the wiry flower stems. Root systems are diverse: while many species grow from rhizomes or fleshy or fibrous roots, others produce woody tubers and are planted and treated like bulbs. Species treated like bulbs generally bloom from spring into early summer.

HOW TO GROW

Select a site in partial or half-day shade in light, rich, evenly moist soil. Although they tolerate full sun provided the soil remains moist, all the species listed here are ideal for woodland gardens. They go dormant after flowering, and once dormant, tolerate drier conditions. With the exception of *A. coronaria,* plant in fall; see the species listing below for details on planting *A. coronaria.* Soak tubers in water for at least 12 hours before planting. *A. canadensis* doesn't have woody tubers and *A. sylvestris* has a woody base but fibrous roots; treat these two species as you would ordinary perennials. Since it's hard to tell top from bottom, set the tubers on their sides, and plant them 2 to 3 inches deep — 4 to 6 inches deep at the northern limit of their hardiness. Propagate by dividing the clumps immediately after the foliage turns yellow in late spring or early summer.

A. apennina

a. ah-pen-NYE-nuh. Apennine Windflower. An 8-inch-tall species growing from short creeping rhizomes and spreading to about 1 foot. Bears toothed, lobed, dark green leaves and solitary 1- to 1¼-inch-wide flowers in spring that are blue with yellow stamens. Zones 6 to 9.

A. blanda   P. 46

a. BLAN-duh. Grecian Windflower. A 6- to 8-inch-tall species growing from woody, knobby tuberous rhizomes. Bears fernlike leaves and white, pink, or blue 2-inch-wide daisylike flowers in spring. Cultivars include 'White Splendour' with large white flowers; 'Radar', with magenta blooms; 'Blue Star', with large blue blooms; and 'Pink Star', with pink flowers. Zones 4 to 8.

A. canadensis

a. can-ah-DEN-sis. Meadow Anemone. Vigorous 6- to 8-inch-tall native North American wildflower spreading by rhizomes to 2 feet or more. Bears single 2-inch-wide white flowers from late spring to early summer. Zones 3 to 7.

A. coronaria   P. 47

a. cor-o-NAIR-ee-uh. Florist's Anemone, Poppy Anemone. A tender, short-lived 1 to 1½-foot-tall species that grows from stem tubers. In spring, bears very showy 2- to 3-inch single or double blooms with black centers in shades of scarlet and violet-blue, as well as white. Plant the woody tubers 2 inches deep. Plant outdoors in fall in Zones 8 to 10, but in pots or in the spring in the North. (Tubers are sold in fall with spring-blooming bulbs such as daffodils and tulips even in areas where plants are not hardy.) Give them full sun or partial shade in well-drained, rich, somewhat sandy soil. When planting outdoors in fall, cover the beds with mulch over winter, but remove it in late winter. In the North, treat florist's anemones as annuals: they can be planted in spring, but for best flowering, plant tubers in pots in fall (several tubers per 6- to 8-inch-pot), then overwinter them in a greenhouse, cold frame, sun porch, or other cool, freeze-free spot. Water sparingly at planting time and until foliage appears. Once buds appear, feed each time you water with a dilute liquid fertilizer and keep the soil evenly moist. Cultivars include the De Caen Hybrids, which are single-flowered types, and St. Brigid Hybrids, which are double flowered. Zones 8 to 10.

A. nemorosa   P. 47

a. neh-moh-RO-suh. Wood Anemone. Vigorous 4- to 10-inch-tall species that spreads by heavily branching rhizomes. Bears leaves with narrow, deeply toothed lobes and white, pale pink, or lavender-blue ½- to ¾-inch flowers in spring. Cultivars include 'Robinsoniana', with pale lavender-blue flowers; 'Rosea', with rose-pink blooms; and 'Flore Plena', with double white flowers. Zones 4 to 8.

A. pavonina

a. pah-VO-nee-na. Tender 8- to 10-inch-tall species growing from a tuber. Bears deeply lobed leaves and showy, solitary 1¼- to 4-inch-wide flowers in spring in shades of red, pink, and purple. Grow as you would *A. coronaria*. Zones 8 to 10.

A. ranunculoides   P. 48

a. rah-nun-kew-LOY-deez. Buttercup Anemone, Yellow Windflower. Vigorous, fast-spreading 2- to 4-inch-tall species that spreads by rhizomes to 1½ feet or more. Bears deeply lobed leaves and solitary ¾- to 1¼-inch-wide blooms with five or six tepals in spring. 'Superba' has bronze-green leaves. Zones 4 to 8.

A. sylvestris   P. 48

a. sil-VES-tris. Snowdrop Anemone. Vigorous 1- to 1½-foot-tall species that
has fibrous roots with a woody base and spreads via root suckers to about
2 feet. Bears single white 2-inch-wide flowers in spring. Zones 3 to 8.

❦ *Anemonella*

an-nem-oh-NEL-uh. Buttercup family, Ranunculaceae.

This genus contains a single species native to woodlands in eastern North
America—*Anemonella thalictroides,* commonly called rue anemone. It
bears cup-shaped flowers that very closely resemble those of its relatives,
the true anemones (*Anemone* spp.). Flowers of the two genera both lack
true petals; the showy structures called "petals" actually are petal-like
sepals surrounding a dainty cluster of stamens in the center of the
blooms. The structure of their pistils, the female portion of the flower,
differs. While the pistils in *Anemone* flowers consist of three parts—
stigma, style, and ovary—*Anemonella* flowers have knoblike stigmas set
directly atop the ovary, without a connecting style. Plants grow from
tuberous roots and bear dainty dark blue-green leaves that are divided
two or three times into rounded, toothed leaflets.

HOW TO GROW

Select a site in partial shade with average to rich, evenly moist soil. The
tubers will rot in constantly wet conditions. Plants thrive in woodland
gardens, shady rock gardens, and similar sites provided they do not have
to compete with aggressive neighbors. Propagate by seed or divide
clumps in early spring. When adding this plant to your garden, be sure to
purchase nursery-propagated plants—or ones purchased at a native
plant society or botanical garden sale—not ones collected from the wild.

A. thalictroides   P. 49

a. thal-ick-TROY-deez. Rue Anemone. A native 4- to 8-inch-tall wildflower
with ¾-inch-wide flowers that are white or pale pink and appear from
spring to early summer above fernlike blue-green leaves. Plants form 1-
foot-wide clumps with time. 'Oscar Schoaf' is a double pink cultivar
sometimes sold as 'Rosea Flore Pleno' or 'Schoaf's Pink'. Zones 4 to 8.

❦ *Anomatheca*

ah-nom-ah-THEE-kuh. Iris family, Iridaceae

Anomatheca species are cormous perennials native to grasslands of central and southern Africa. They bear lance-shaped leaves and racemes of small trumpet- to funnel-shaped flowers in late spring and early summer. The individual flowers have six petal-like tepals. Brown capsules with bright red seeds follow the flowers in fall. All of the six species in the genus die back after flowering and require a dry dormant period.

HOW TO GROW

Select a site in full sun with average, sandy soil. Plant the corms in spring at a depth of about 2 inches. Where hardy, the plants can be left in the ground year-round, but they require dry soil after their foliage dies back and they go dormant. In the North, dig the corms after the first light fall frost, dry them off, cut off the tops, and dust off excess soil, then overwinter them in barely damp vermiculite or peat as you would gladiolus—in a cool (45° to 50°F), dry place. Check periodically for signs of rot, and if corms begin to shrivel, mist the vermiculite with water. *Anomatheca* species also are good choices for growing in containers. To overwinter them, dry off the pots gradually and either remove the corms from the pots or store them, pot and all, until the following spring.

A. laxa   P. 49

a. LAX-uh. Formerly *A. cruenta*, *Lapeirousia cruenta*, *L. laxa*. A 6- to 12-inch-tall species with somewhat grassy leaves. Bears clusters of five or six trumpet-shaped ¾-inch-long red flowers in early summer. Zones 8 to 10.

❦ *Anthericum*

an-THEER-ih-kum. Lily family, Liliaceae.

Anthericum species are grown for their loose, erect panicles or racemes of small white flowers borne in spring or summer. The flowers consist of six petal-like tepals and are carried on erect stalks above clumps of long, narrow, basal, grasslike leaves. Unlike many other lily-family plants, these plants grow from fleshy or tuberous roots. About 50 species belong to the genus, all of which are native to Europe, Turkey, and Africa.

HOW TO GROW

Select a site in full sun with rich, well-drained soil. Plant the roots in spring, amending the soil with sand and plenty of organic matter. Water regularly when plants are actively growing; they tolerate drier conditions when dormant. Protect clumps from fluctuating winter temperatures by covering them in late fall with a coarse mulch such as evergreen boughs, salt hay, pine needles, or coarse hay. These plants thrive for years without needing to be divided. Dig them in early spring if they become over-crowded or for propagation, or propagate by seeds.

A. liliago   P. 50
a. lil-ee-AH-go. Saint Bernard's Lily. A 2- to 3-foot-tall perennial with clumps of arching gray-green 1½-foot-long grassy leaves. Bears slender 2-foot-long racemes of starry white 1½-inch-wide flowers in late spring or early summer. Zones 4 to 7.

A. ramosum
a. rah-MO-sum. A 2½- to 3-foot-tall perennial producing clumps of arching gray-green 1½-foot-long grassy leaves. Bears slender, branched 2-foot-long panicles of starry white 1½-inch-wide flowers in late spring or early summer. Somewhat more heat tolerant than *A. liliago.* Zones 4 to 8.

❦ Arisaema
air-ih-SEE-muh. Arum family, Araceae.

The best-known member of this genus is a native North American wild-flower commonly called Jack-in-the-pulpit, *Arisaema triphyllum.* About 150 species belong here—they are native to North America as well as Japan, China, and the Himalayas. The plants are either tuberous or grow from rhizomes, and they produce their unusual flowers in spring or sum-mer. The inflorescence consists of many tiny flowers clustered on a cen-tral stalk—the "Jack," which is more correctly called a spadix. The spadix is surrounded by a modified leaf—the "pulpit," which is more correctly called a spathe. In most species, the spathe bends over at the tip to shelter and partially enclose the spadix. The flowers are followed by round red berries in fall. Plants bear attractive leaves that are divided or lobed in a palmate (handlike) fashion.

HOW TO GROW
Select a site in partial shade with rich, moist, well-drained soil. Plant tu-bers or purchased plants in either fall or spring. For best results, work plenty of compost or other organic matter into the soil at planting time, and mulch to keep the soil moist. Once planted, they require little care.

Where they are not hardy, grow *Arisaema* species in containers and over-winter them indoors while still in their pots in a cool (40° to 45°F) spot and keep the soil just barely moist. Propagate the plants by separating off-sets in late summer or fall, before the foliage dies back. Or sow fresh seeds as soon as they are ripe.

A. candidissimum   P. 50
a. can-dih-DIS-sih-mum. A 14- to 16-inch-tall species with hooded 3- to 6-inch-long spathes that are greenish at the base and white with pink stripes at the top. Blooms have a sweet scent and appear in early summer. After the flowers appear, plants bear a single leaf with three ovate leaflets. Zones 6 to 9.

A. consanguineum
a. con-san-GWIH-nee-um. Summer-blooming 2- to 3-foot-tall species bearing hooded 4- to 8-inch-long spathes striped with white and greenish brown. Plants have a single leaf with 10 to 20 leaflets above the inflorescence. Zones 7 to 9.

A. dracontium
a. dra-CON-tee-um. Green Dragon, Dragon Root. A wildflower native to eastern North America that bears green 2- to 3-inch-long spathes in spring. The spathes surround a 4- to 8-inch-long whiplike spadix that extends far beyond the spathe. Plants produce a single leaf divided into 5 to as many as 17 segments that is only about 1 to 1½ feet tall at blooming time but reaches 2 to 3 feet as the season progresses. Zones 4 to 9.

A. ringens   P. 51
a. RIN-jenz. An early summer–blooming 10- to 12-inch-tall species with hooded 4- to 6-inch-long green spathes striped and tipped with purple. Bears a pair of three-leaflet leaves above the spathes. Zones 6 to 9.

A. sikokianum   P. 51
a. sih-ko-kee-AH-num. A 1- to 1½-foot-tall species that in late spring produces a hooded 6- to 8-inch-long purple-brown spathe that surrounds a white club-shaped spadix. Bears two leaves with three or five leaflets. Zones 5 to 9.

A. triphyllum   P. 52
a. tri-FIL-lum. Native North American wildflower bearing hooded 4- to 6-inch-long green spathes, often striped with dark purple, in spring and early summer. Bears one or two three-leaflet leaves and reaches 1 foot. Zones 4 to 9.

❦ Arum

AIR-um. Arum family, Araceae.

Closely related to Jack-in-the-pulpits (*Arisaema* spp.), arums—or lords and ladies as they are sometimes called—are tuberous, deciduous perennials native to southern Europe, northern Africa, and Asia. About 26 species belong to the genus, most of which bloom in spring or early summer. Most species produce new leaves in fall or early winter that last until about the time the plants bloom, then go dormant. The exotic-looking "flowers" somewhat resemble those of calla lilies (*Zantedeschia* spp.), another close relative, and may have a sweet or unpleasant scent. They are actually an inflorescence consisting of many tiny flowers clustered on a central stalk, called a spadix. The spadix is surrounded by a modified leaf, called a spathe. Showy spikes of red or orange berries follow the flowers in late summer and fall. Leaves may be spear, arrow, or heart shaped and are often attractively marbled. In areas with mild winters, the leaves remain attractive until late spring and add interest to shade and woodland gardens at that time of year. All parts of the plants are poisonous if ingested, and the sap can cause skin irritation.

HOW TO GROW
Select a site in sun or partial shade with deeply prepared, rich, moist, well-drained soil. A sheltered site is best, especially because it helps protect the foliage in winter. Set tubers with the tops 4 to 6 inches below the soil surface (roots develop from the tops of the tubers). Mark the locations of the plants to avoid digging into them by mistake when they are dormant. Mulch with compost in spring to keep the soil rich and help retain moisture. In areas where plants are marginally hardy, cover them with a coarse mulch such as evergreen boughs in late fall. In areas where arums are not hardy, grow them in pots and overwinter them in a cool (40° to 50°F) spot. Propagate by separating offsets or by sowing fresh seeds.

A. creticum   P. 52
a. KREH-tih-kum. Tuberous, spring-flowering species with arrow-shaped dark green leaves and fragrant flowers. Spathes are yellow or creamy white and are 6 to 10 inches long. Plants range from 1 to 2½ feet in height. Zones 8 to 10.

A. dioscoridis
a. dye-oss-KOR-ih-dis. Tuberous 8- to 12-inch-tall species with spring flowers featuring 6- to 14-inch-long spathes that are deep purple or green and

blushed or spotted with maroon. Bears narrow, arrow-shaped leaves. Flowers have an unpleasant scent. Zones 7 to 9.

A. italicum   P. 53

a. ih-TAL-ih-kum. Italian Arum. Tuberous perennial primarily grown for its handsome, leathery, arrow-shaped leaves that range from 10 to 14 inches long. Bears flowers with pale greenish white 6- to 16-inch-long spathes in early summer and showy, erect spikes of orange-red berries that are attractive until fall, when the new leaves appear. 'Marmoratum', also sold as 'Pictum', is more commonly grown than the species: it bears leaves netted with pale green or cream veins. Zones 6 to 9; to Zone 5 with protection.

A. maculatum   P. 53

a. mak-yoo-LAY-tum. Lords and Ladies, Cuckoo-pint, Adam-and-Eve. A 12- to 15-inch-tall species that is similar to *A. italicum* but bears glossy, arrow-shaped leaves that usually have black or purple spots and appear in spring with the flowers. Blooms have yellow-green 6- to 10-inch-long spathes usually edged and spotted with purple. Berries are bright red. Zones 6 to 9.

❧ Asphodeline

as-FO-deh-line. Lily family, Liliaceae.

Commonly known as Jacob's rods or simply asphodels, *Asphodeline* species are Mediterranean natives grown for their narrow, erect, unbranched racemes of starry yellow or white flowers. About 20 species, both biennials and perennials, belong to the genus. They form clumps of rhizomes that are fleshy or fibrous and produce grassy basal leaves. *Asphodeline* species, which once were classified in *Asphodelus,* also have smaller leaves up the flower stalks, and this is one characteristic that distinguishes plants in the two genera. Like other lily-family plants, Jacob's rods bear flowers with six petal-like tepals. The racemes bloom from bottom to top, and individual flowers generally open for only a day.

HOW TO GROW

Select a site in full sun with average, well-drained soil that is deeply prepared. Plants are best in areas with cool summers, and flowers are very short-lived in areas with hot summer weather. Established clumps can thrive for years without requiring division or other care. Propagate by dividing the clumps in spring or fall or by sowing seeds.

A. liburnica

a. lye-BUR-nih-kuh. A 2- to sometimes 3-foot-tall species with fleshy roots and blue-green leaves. Produces slender 6- to 9-inch-long racemes of starry pale yellow 2-inch-wide flowers in midsummer. Zones 6 to 8; to Zone 5 with winter protection.

A. lutea
P. 54

a. LOO-tee-uh. King's Spear, Yellow Asphodel. Fleshy-rooted perennial, from 3 to 5 feet tall in bloom, that forms clumps of blue- or gray-green leaves. Bears dense, erect ½- to 1½-foot-long racemes of starry bright yellow flowers in late spring or early summer. Blooms are fragrant and 1 inch wide. Zones 6 to 8; to Zone 5 with winter protection.

❦ Asphodelus

ah-sfoe-DEL-us. Lily family, Liliaceae.

Native from the Mediterranean and central Europe to Asia, *Asphodelus* species are grown for their dense, erect racemes of starry, funnel-shaped flowers. The flowers are white or pink and have six petal-like tepals. The leafless flower stalks are borne above clumps of grassy basal leaves. (Species in the closely related genus *Asphodeline* bear flower stalks that have leaves on them.) The genus contains 12 species, including perennials growing from clumps of congested, fleshy rhizomes as well as annuals, biennials, and short-lived perennials with fibrous roots.

HOW TO GROW

Select a site in full sun with average, well-drained soil that is deeply prepared. Established clumps can thrive for years without requiring division or other care. Propagate by dividing the clumps in spring or fall or by sowing seeds.

A. aestivus

a. ESS-tih-vus. A 3-foot-tall species with leathery 1- to 1½-foot-long linear leaves and racemes of 2- to 3-inch-wide flowers in spring that are white or white flushed with pink. Zones 7 to 10.

A. albus
P. 54

a. AL-bus. A 2½- to 3-foot-tall species with linear 1- to 2-foot-long leaves and starry white ¾- to 1½-inch flowers with pink veins in early summer. Zones 7 to 10.

❦ Babiana

bah-bee-AH-nuh. Iris family, Iridaceae.

Both the common and botanical names for this genus of 50 to 60 species of South African plants have an unusual derivation. The corms of these plants are a favorite food of baboons, thus the common name baboon flower. The botanical name comes from the Dutch and Anglicized names for these African primates: *bobbejane* and *babianer*. *Babiana* species bear pleated, lance-shaped leaves and freesialike spikes of funnel-shaped flowers that come in shades of purple, blue, violet, red, pink, yellow, cream, and white. Flowers appear in spring and often are very fragrant. They are made up of six petal-like tepals.

HOW TO GROW

Select a site in full sun with light, rich, well-drained soil. Plants tolerate poor soil, provided it is well drained. A spot with light shade during the hottest part of the day provides beneficial heat protection, however. These plants are best in frost-free regions with dry summers, such as California, where they grow during the winter months and are dormant during the hot, dry summers. However, they can grow in areas with rainy summers provided they are in very well drained soil; a spot in a raised bed or rock garden also is beneficial. In the North, grow babianas in containers or treat the corms as you would gladiolus: plant in spring, dig them after they have entered dormancy in summer or fall, and store them dry over winter in a cool (50° to 60°F), dry, frost-free place. Where hardy, plant corms in late summer or early fall for bloom the following spring, setting them with the tops 4 to 6 inches deep. Where plants are marginally hardy, try deeper planting—from 8 to 10 inches provided the soil is deeply prepared and well drained. (In the wild, they are found at depths up to 1 foot, and corms planted shallowly will gradually move deeper into the soil.) Pots of corms planted in fall and overwintered in a cool greenhouse or sunroom with nighttime temperatures between 40° and 50°F will bloom in early spring. Water regularly when plants are growing actively, and gradually withhold water once the leaves begin to turn yellow. Propagate by separating the offsets.

B. rubrocyanea
P. 55

b. roo-broh-sye-AN-ee-uh. Low-growing 2- to 8-inch-tall species that bears spikes of five to ten ¾- to 1½-inch-wide red-and-blue flowers in spring. Zones 8 to 10.

B. stricta

P. 55

b. STRIK-tuh. A 5- to 12-inch-tall species with four- to eight-flowered spikes of ¾- to 1½-inch-long flowers in spring in shades of blue, purple, mauve, and yellow. Kew Hybrids bear blooms in a range of pastel colors. Zones 8 to 10.

❦ Begonia

beh-GOAN-yah. Begonia family, Begoniaceae.

The vast *Begonia* clan contains some 1,300 species—tuberous plants as well as annuals, perennials, shrubs, climbers, succulents, and epiphytes. They are native to tropical and subtropical regions worldwide. Begonias have fleshy leaves and stems and grow from rhizomes, fibrous roots, or tubers. Male and female flowers are borne separately, usually on the same plant. (Female flowers have a swollen, winged seed capsule directly behind the petals; males don't.) The fleshy leaves vary in shape, size, and color. Rounded and wing-shaped foliage is common. North of Zone 10, most begonias are suitable only for house or greenhouse culture, but a few tuberous species are popular for summer bedding displays and pot culture. One hardy species is grown in shade gardens.

HOW TO GROW

Culture depends on the species you are growing. Tuberous begonias are a bit demanding but aren't difficult if you have the right site. They grow best in areas with cool summers (60° to 65°F nights) that are somewhat humid, and they are disappointing in areas with hot, dry summers. Grow them in partial shade and loose, well-drained soil rich in organic matter. A site protected from wind is best. Start with firm, solid tubers that do not have soft spots or cuts. (These plants actually grow from stem tubers; see page 4 for more information on these structures.) Small pink buds may be evident; avoid tubers that have already sprouted. Start tubers indoors 8 to 10 weeks before the last spring frost date in flats filled with loose, free-draining potting medium that is barely moist. If buds are not visible on the top of the tubers (the concave side), place them upside down on the surface of the medium and set them in a warm (70° to 80°F), humid place for about a week. After that, check for buds every few days. Once ½-inch pink buds appear, plant the tubers with the medium barely covering the tops. Water sparingly until they are growing actively—too much moisture causes rot. Once the tubers are actively growing, keep them evenly moist and set them in a bright spot protected from direct sun. Move started tubers to individual 4- to 5-inch pots when the shoots are about 1½ inches tall. Move plants to the containers where they will bloom or to shady spots in the garden once the shoots are several inches tall, but keep them indoors until all danger of frost has passed and the soil has warmed. Insert stakes at planting time, otherwise it's easy to damage the tubers. Loosely tie the brittle stems to the stakes with soft yarn or strips of nylon stocking. Propagate from seeds or cuttings of young shoots with a small "heel" of the tuber attached. To overwinter tuberous begonias, dig the tubers after the first light frost in fall and spread them out, tops and all, in a shady, dry, well-ventilated spot protected from further frosts. Let the tops dry, then shake the soil from the tubers. Store them in a cool (40° to 50°F), well-ventilated, dry place in shallow trays filled with dry peat moss. Or, hang them in net bags or pantyhose filled with peat. Check regularly for signs of rot, and discard rotted tubers. Replant as you would new tubers in spring.

Plant *B. grandis* ssp. *evansiana* and *B. sutherlandii* in partial to full shade in rich, evenly moist, well-drained soil. To propagate, collect the tiny tubers that appear in the leaf axils in late summer or fall and plant them outdoors where they are to grow. Or plant them indoors in late winter in pots. Either way, barely cover them with loose soil. Or start from seeds. Plants also self-sow.

B. grandis ssp. *evansiana* P. 56

b. GRAN-diss ssp. eh-van-see-AH-nuh. Hardy Begonia. A 2- to 2½-foot perennial that grows from a small tuber and spreads to 1 foot. Bears arching clusters of pink flowers in late summer or fall above wing-shaped 4-inch-long leaves that are olive green above and usually red beneath. The variety *alba* bears white flowers. Zones 6 to 10; to Zone 5 with winter protection.

B. sutherlandii P. 56

b. suh-ther-LAN-dee-eye. Sutherland Begonia. A tuberous species bearing pendent clusters of orange 1-inch flowers all summer atop 1- to 2-foot mounds of bright green lance-shaped leaves. Overwinter indoors as houseplants (they are ideal for containers and hanging baskets, as well as shady sites with rich soil) or let plants go dormant and keep them relatively dry and cool, as for conventional tuberous begonias. Zones 8 to 10; to Zone 7 with winter protection.

B. tuberhybrida hybrids

P. 57

b. × too-ber-HI-brih-duh. Tuberous Begonia. Upright to pendent perennial plants with tuberous roots, fleshy stems reaching 8 to 12 inches, glossy bright to dark green leaves, and showy flowers in shades of yellow, orange, pink, red, salmon, and white. Flowers are single or double and can be 3 inches or more across. 'Non-Stop' and 'Clips' mixes are two strains that come true from seeds. Zones 10 to 11.

❦ *Bellevalia*

bel-leh-VAH-lee-uh. Lily family, Liliaceae

Native from the Mediterranean to western Asia, *Bellevalia* species are spring-blooming bulbs bearing flowers that resemble those of their close relatives the grape hyacinths (*Muscari* spp.) and hyacinths (*Hyacinthus* spp.). Plants grow from tunicate bulbs and have long strap-shaped green to gray-green leaves that are basal and can extend from 1 to 1½ feet in length. The small bell-shaped flowers have six lobes and are carried in erect, densely packed racemes. They come in violet-blue, lavender, and white.

HOW TO GROW

Select a site in full sun or light shade with rich, well-drained soil. These are spring-blooming plants that disappear by midsummer, so spots under deciduous trees, which offer full sun before the trees leaf out, are fine. These bulbs are ideal for rock gardens or sunny beds and borders: they prefer dry soil once they enter dormancy in summer. Plant the bulbs in fall with the tops 2 inches below the soil surface. If clumps become crowded or begin to bloom less, divide them in summer just as the leaves die back. Propagate by separating offsets, by division, or by seeds.

B. hyacinthoides

b. hi-ah-sin-THOY-deez. Formerly *Strangweja spicata*. Produces long strap-shaped leaves through fall and winter and loose, few-flowered racemes of ¼- to ½-inch-wide pale blue flowers in spring on 2- to 6-inch-tall stalks. Zones 7 to 9.

B. pycnantha

P. 57

b. pik-NAN-tha. Also listed as *Muscari paradoxum*. Bears gray-green leaves topped by dense 1-foot-tall clusters of violet-blue flowers edged in yellow. Individual flowers are ¼ inch long and appear in spring. Zones 5 to 8.

B. romana

b. ro-MAH-nuh. Formerly *Hyacinthus romana*. A 12-inch-tall species with loose racemes of 3/8-inch-long white flowers in spring. Zones 7 to 9.

❦ Bessera

BESS-er-uh. Lily family, Liliaceae.

Two species of wildflowers native to Mexico belong to the genus *Bessera*. Both are tender perennials that grow from corms and produce narrow, grasslike, basal leaves and loose umbels of nodding, somewhat bell-shaped flowers. The individual flowers, which are carried on very thin stems, have six petal-like tepals. Each flower has six stamens that are united for about half their length to form a daffodil-like corona or cup (called a staminal cup) in the center.

HOW TO GROW

Select a site in full sun with average, well-drained soil. Plant the bulbs in spring at a depth of 2½ to 3 inches. Where hardy, they can be left in the ground year-round and require very little care. Where they are marginally hardy, look for a protected spot such as at the base of a south-facing wall, and protect plants in fall with a heavy layer of coarse mulch such as evergreen boughs, pine needles, salt hay, or coarse leaves. In the North, dig the corms after the first light frosts of fall (earlier if the foliage dies back), dry them off, brush off excess soil, and store them in a cool (40°F to 50°F), dry place over winter, as you would gladiolus corms. *Bessera* species also will grow in pots. Propagate by removing the offsets in fall or by seeds.

B. elegans   P. 58

b. EL-eh-ganz. Coral Drops. A 2-foot-tall species with grassy 2- to 2½-foot-long leaves. Bears 1½-inch-wide umbels of three to nine scarlet flowers in late summer or early fall. Zones 9 to 11; to Zone 8 with winter protection.

❦ Bletilla

bleh-TIL-uh. Orchid family, Orchidaceae

Bletilla species are deciduous, terrestrial orchids that have pleated, linear to rounded leaves and bear loose racemes of small bell-shaped flowers in spring to early summer. They spread by short rhizomes and produce tuber- or cormlike underground pseudobulbs. About 9 or 10 species belong to the genus, all native to Asia—China, Japan, and Taiwan.

HOW TO GROW

Select a site in partial shade—shelter from hot sun is essential in summer—with rich, evenly moist, well-drained soil. A protected spot is best. Work in plenty of compost or leaf mold at planting time to ensure rich, moisture-retentive soil. Keep the soil evenly moist in summer when plants are actively growing. Plants also thrive in containers, and container culture is a good option in areas where these orchids are not hardy. Crowded clumps bloom best, so leave plants undisturbed as long as possible—either in the ground or in pots. Where not hardy, overwinter them indoors. In pots, let the soil dry out and the leaves die back, then store them in a cool (50° to 60°F), dry place. Or pack rhizomes in dry peat moss or vermiculite over winter and replant in spring. Propagate by dividing the clumps in early spring.

B. striata   P. 58

b. stry-AY-tuh. Chinese Ground Orchid, Hyacinth Bletilla. Formerly *B. hyacinthina*. A 1- to 2-foot-tall species that spreads as far. Bears 1- to 1½-foot-long lance-shaped leaves. From spring to early summer it produces loose clusters of up to 12 flowers that are 1 inch wide and magenta-pink. *B. striata* f. *alba* bears white flowers. Zones 7 to 9; to Zone 5 or 6 with winter protection.

❦ Bloomeria

bloo-MEER-ee-uh. Lily family, Liliaceae.

Three species belong to the genus *Bloomeria*, all perennials that grow from corms and are native to California and Mexico. They are closely related to ornamental onions (*Allium* spp.) and brodiaeas (*Brodiaea* spp.). Plants bear linear, basal leaves and loose, long-stemmed umbels of yellow star- or wheel-shaped flowers that have six petal-like tepals.

HOW TO GROW

Select a site in full sun or partial shade with light, sandy soil with plenty of organic matter. Plant the corms in fall at a depth of 2 to 3 inches. For best effect, arrange them in drifts. Where they are marginally hardy, protect the plants over winter with a coarse mulch such as evergreen boughs, salt hay, or pine needles. Once the plants begin actively growing in spring, keep the soil evenly moist. Like many plants native to the Southwest, bloomerias require dry soil in summer after they go dormant; the corms rot in soil that remains too wet. In the East, where summers are too rainy, and in the North, where winters are too cold, grow these plants in containers. Either plant in the fall and keep them in a cold frame or cool greenhouse (40° to 50°F) over winter and keep the soil just barely moist, or plant in spring. To overwinter container-grown plants, once they have bloomed and the foliage has died back, set the pots in a dry, well-ventilated spot until fall, then move them to a cool, dry spot. Or dig the corms and store them in dry peat or vermiculite in a cool, dry spot. Propagate by removing offsets in summer as soon as the foliage dies back or in fall.

B. crocea   P. 59

b. KRO-see-uh. Golden Stars. California native wildflower with a single ½-inch-wide linear leaf that dies down about the time plants flower. Bears loose umbels of showy orangy yellow flowers with darker stripes atop 6- to 12-inch-tall stems in late spring or early summer. Individual blooms are ¾ to 1 inch wide and borne on long individual stems. Zones 9 to 10; to Zone 8 with winter protection.

❦ *Brimeura*

brih-mee-YOUR-uh. Lily family, Liliaceae.

Two species belong to this genus in the lily family, both bulbous, spring-blooming perennials native to southeastern Europe. They bear loose racemes of dainty, bell-shaped flowers on leafless stalks. The individual flowers are tubular and have six fairly short lobes at the tips. The linear, grasslike leaves are borne at the base of the plant.

HOW TO GROW

Select a site in full sun or light shade with rich, well-drained soil. These are spring-blooming plants that disappear by midsummer, so spots under deciduous trees, which offer full sun before the trees leaf out, are fine. Plant the bulbs in fall with the tops 2 inches below the soil surface. Propagate by dividing the clumps in summer, after the leaves begin to turn yellow but before they disappear completely. Or sow seeds.

B. amethystina
P. 59

b. am-eh-thiss-TYE-nuh. Formerly *Hyacinthus amethystinus*. Spring-bloom-ing bulbs with 8- to 10-inch-tall racemes of between 6 and 12 pale blue flowers that are tubular to bell shaped and ½ inch long. *B. amethystina* var. *alba* bears white flowers. Zones 5 to 9.

❦ *Brodiaea* see *Dichelostemma, Triteleia*

❦ *Bulbine*

BUL-bean. Lily family, Liliaceae.

Sometimes grown for their showy racemes of spring or summer flowers, *Bulbine* species are native to South Africa and eastern Africa, as well as Australia. About 30 species belong to the genus, some of which grow from bulbous or tuberous roots. Most are tender perennials, although one species is an annual. Plants produce clumps of linear to lance-shaped leaves topped by lacy racemes of small star-shaped flowers. The individual flowers, which are arranged in fairly dense racemes, consist of six petal-like tepals. Most species bear yellow flowers.

HOW TO GROW
Select a site in full sun with sandy, well-drained soil. Plants tolerate poor, dry soil. In areas with dry, mild climates, such as Southern California, they can be grown outdoors year-round: plant them in rock gardens or even flower gardens. Elsewhere, grow them in containers. When plants are growing actively, water regularly, but let the soil almost dry out between waterings. Where plants are not hardy, bring containers indoors in fall and overwinter in a cool (40° to 50°F), dry, well-ventilated place. Propagate by rooting offsets produced around the clump or by seeds. Divide plants as necessary in spring.

B. alooides

b. al-oh-OY-deez. A native South African species reaching 1 foot in height and forming clumps of fleshy, lance-shaped leaves. Bears 8- to 12-inch-long racemes of starry yellow ⅛-inch-wide flowers in late spring. Zones 10 to 11.

B. frutescens
P. 60

b. fru-TESS-ens. Formerly *B. caulescens*. A 1- to 1½-foot-tall South African species with succulent, lance-shaped leaves and 6- to 12-inch-long racemes of starry ¼- to ½-inch-wide flowers in summer. Zones 10 to 11.

❦ Bulbinella

bul-bih-NEL-uh. Lily family, Liliaceae.

Bulbinella species are fleshy-rooted perennials native to South Africa as well as New Zealand that are closely related to *Bulbine*. About 20 species belong here, all producing clumps of succulent, grasslike leaves topped by racemes of flowers in late winter, spring, or summer, depending on the species. Individual flowers are small — usually about ½ inch across — and starry or cup shaped. They are packed very densely into cylindrical racemes. Each flower consists of six petal-like tepals.

HOW TO GROW

Select a site in full sun or partial shade with moist, well-drained soil that has a neutral to acid pH. These are suitable plants for areas with mild winters, such as southern California. *B. hookeri* grows naturally in moist, peaty soil, but also tolerates drier conditions. Where plants are marginally hardy, look for a protected, south-facing site and protect them over winter with a thick, coarse mulch such as evergreen boughs, pine needles, or salt hay. Where not hardy, grow them in containers overwintered indoors in a cool (40° to 50°F) spot. Amend the soil or potting mix with peat moss to ensure an acid pH and good moisture retention. Propagate by dividing the clumps in fall or by seeds.

B. hookeri

b. HOOK-er-eye. New Zealand native with sword-shaped leaves that reaches 1½ to 2 feet in height. Bears 1-foot-long racemes of yellow flowers from spring to summer. Best in areas with somewhat cool summers. Zones 8 to 9.

B. rossii

P. 60

b. ROSS-ee-eye. New Zealand native reaching 4 feet in height that bears racemes of yellow flowers in spring. Zones 8 to 9.

❦ Bulbocodium

bul-bo-CO-dee-um. Lily family, Liliaceae.

Two species belong to the genus *Bulbocodium*, both perennials that grow from corms and are native to dry grasslands and meadows in eastern and southern Europe. They are closely related to autumn crocuses (*Colchi-*

cum species) and bear their showy flowers quite near the ground. Blooms appear in spring and are borne either singly or in twos or threes. The lance- to strap-shaped leaves appear slightly after the flowers and lengthen after the blooms disappear. Like other lily-family plants, these plants produce flowers that consist of six petal-like tepals.

HOW TO GROW

Select a site in full sun or very light shade with rich, well-drained soil. These plants can be finicky: give them rich soil amended with both leaf mold and grit to ensure good drainage and moisture retention. The soil should remain evenly moist in spring when plants are growing actively. Plant the corms in fall at a depth of 3 inches. Some gardeners replant them in fresh soil every 2 to 3 years to keep plants vigorous. Propagate by division in early summer, as the plants go dormant, by separating offsets, or by seeds.

B. vernum P. 61

b. VER-num. Spring Meadow Saffron. A 1½- to 3-inch-tall species with showy rosy purple blooms in spring. Blooms are somewhat crocuslike and have 1½- to 3-inch-long petals. Zones 3 to 9.

ꙮ *Caladium*

cah-LAY-dee-um. Arum family, Araceae.

These tender, tuberous perennials from the South American tropics are grown for their large, showy, arrowhead-shaped leaves rather than their flowers. The common names angel wings and elephant ears refer to the striking foliage, but these plants are more often simply called caladiums. The species are seldom grown, although they do feature leaves marked with various amounts of white or other colors. Plant breeders have developed a wide variety of hybrids treasured for their brightly patterned foliage variegated in various shades of green as well as pinks, rose-reds, maroon, and white. Like other arum-family plants, caladiums bear flowers that are actually an inflorescence consisting of many tiny flowers clustered on a central stalk, called a spadix. The spadix is surrounded by a modified leaf, called a spathe. The blooms somewhat resemble those of calla lilies (*Zantedeschia* spp.) but have a greenish white spathe that isn't showy. While seven species belong to this genus, all of the commonly grown cultivars belong to a single genus, *Caladium bicolor*.

HOW TO GROW

Select a site in partial to full shade with evenly moist, well-drained soil that is very rich in organic matter. Slightly acid pH is best. In all but the very warmest climates (Zones 10 and 11), start the tubers indoors 8 to 10 weeks before the last spring frost date. To start tubers, set them close together in flats filled with barely moist vermiculite, and cover the tops with 1 inch of vermiculite. Set the flats in a warm (70° to 85°F), humid place until leaves and roots sprout. Then plant the tubers in individual bulb pans (shallow pots) or group them in large pots. Keep the soil evenly moist, and set them in a bright spot, such as a north or east window. Move the plants outdoors in early summer, once soil and air temperatures have moderated (nighttime temperatures remain above 55°F, and the soil has warmed to 60°F at a depth of several inches). Either keep them in pots or transplant to a shady spot with rich, moist soil. Bright, dappled shade is best; be sure to shelter plants from direct sun, which will scorch the leaves. Water regularly and feed monthly to encourage large leaves. Remove the flowers as they appear. These plants can be grown as annuals, but overwintering the tubers isn't difficult. Let the soil dry gradually in fall, dig the tubers before frost, and set them in a warm, dry spot. Clean off soil and remove roots and tops before storing them in sand or vermiculite in a warm (60° to 70°F) place. Pot-grown plants can be stored under similar conditions—just turn the containers on their sides. To propagate, cut the tubers into parts with a knife in spring, then dust the cut pieces with sulfur before potting them up.

C. bicolor
P. 61

c. BI-kuh-lor. Caladium, Angel Wings, Elephant Ears. A 1½- to 2-foot-tall species that can spread to 2 feet. Bears arrow-shaped 8- to 12-inch-long leaves and greenish white flowers in spring. Cultivars include 'Candidum', with white leaves netted in green; 'Fanny Munson', with pale pink leaves edged in green and netted with dark pink; 'White Christmas', with white leaves with green midribs and veins; 'Little Miss Muffet', an 8- to 12-inch-tall selection with chartreuse leaves spotted with burgundy; and 'Carolyn Whorton', with pink leaves edged with green and netted with dark pink veins. Florida Series cultivars bear leaves that are thicker and more sun tolerant than older cultivars. These include 'Florida Cardinal', with green-edged burgundy leaves; 'Florida Fantasy', with white leaves with red veins that are netted with green; and 'Florida Sunrise', with rose leaves with red main veins and white smaller veins. Tender perennial, hardy in Zones 10 to 11.

❦ *Calochortus*

kal-o-KOR-tus. Lily family, Liliaceae.

Charming wildflowers native to western North America as well as Central America, *Calochortus* species have a variety of common names that refer to their tuliplike flowers: they have been called butterfly tulips, mariposa lilies, globe tulips, fairy lanterns, and sego lilies. The botanical name is from the Greek, *kalos,* beautiful, and *chortus,* grass. About 60 species belong to the genus, all of which are herbaceous perennials that grow from edible, tunicate bulbs, which once were used as food by Native Americans. Plants bear linear- to lance-shaped leaves that are most often grassy and basal. Flowers, which are borne singly or in clusters, face up, out, or are nodding. They can be cup shaped and tuliplike, rounded and lantern shaped, or bell shaped. Each bloom has three showy petals that usually have prominent markings and/or showy, irislike beards in a contrasting color at the base. These, in nearly all cases, mark the location of a specialized gland called a nectary located near the base of the petal on the inside of the bloom.

HOW TO GROW

Give these plants full sun and very well drained soil. They are happiest and easiest to grow in the West, because warm, dry summers and mild winters suit their tastes. There, they can be naturalized or used in beds and borders or in rock gardens. Plant the bulbs in fall at a depth of 4 to 6 inches. Site selection is the secret to success from the Midwest eastward, where summer rainfall, winter wet, and alternate cycles of freezing and thawing do not suit the plants' natural preferences. (Gardeners in these regions may want to buy new bulbs annually, much like tulips, to ensure an annual display.) Give *Calochortus* species perfectly drained soil—amend with coarse sand or grit as well as organic matter at planting time to ensure both good drainage and moisture retention—and combine them with plants that do not need supplemental watering in the summer. A south-facing site at the base of a rock in a rock garden or next to a rock wall helps provide winter protection. In early winter, once the ground has frozen, mulch with evergreen boughs, salt hay, or dry, coarse leaves (oak leaves are suitable) to protect the plants from alternate cycles of freezing and thawing. Top the mulch with a weighted-down sheet of plastic mulch to keep the site dry over winter. Propagate by separating offsets in summer or by seeds. Some species produce bulbils in the leaf axils, which also can be planted.

C. albus

c. AL-bus. Fairy Lantern, Globe Lily. A wildflower, native to California, that ranges from 4 to 20 inches tall. Bears loose clusters of nodding 1-inch-long rounded to bell-shaped white flowers in spring and early summer. Zones 6 to 10.

C. amabilis

c. ah-MAB-ih-liss. Golden Fairy Lantern, Golden Globe Tulip. California native wildflower featuring loose clusters of nodding deep yellow blooms with 1- to 1¼-inch-long petals and prominent green-tinged sepals in spring and early summer. Zones 6 to 10.

C. macrocarpus

c. mak-ro-KAR-pus. Green-banded Mariposa. Summer-blooming 8- to 20-inch-tall species native to the West that bears one to three upward-facing, cup-shaped blooms per stem in summer. Blooms are 2½ to 3½ inches wide and purple with a darker purple ring near the base of the petals. Zones 6 to 10.

C. superbus   P. 62

c. soo-PER-bus. California native wildflower ranging from 1½ to 2 feet tall and bearing small loose clusters of upward-facing, cup-shaped 2- to 3-inch-wide blooms in late spring. Flowers are cream, lavender-blue, or yellow with yellow and maroon at the base of the petals. Zones 5 to 10.

C. venustus   P. 62

c. veh-NOO-stus. White Mariposa. A ½ to 2-foot-tall native California wildflower with clusters of one to three upward-facing, cup-shaped flowers from late spring to early summer. Blooms are 2 to 3 inches across and come in white or yellow as well as red or purple. Petals are marked with yellow and maroon at the base. Zones 6 to 10.

C. vestae

c. VES-tye. Native California wildflower ranging from 1 to 2 feet tall and bearing small clusters of cup-shaped, upward-facing blooms from late spring to summer. Individual blooms are 2 to 3 inches wide and white with yellow and maroon markings at the base of the petals. Zones 5 to 10.

❦ *Camassia*

kah-MASS-ee-uh. Lily family, Liliaceae.

Handsome and easy to grow, camassias are native North American plants that are underused in gardens. The botanical name is derived from Native American words for these plants—camass or quamash. The boiled bulbs, which can reach half a pound or more, were extremely important food plants. Plants grow from rounded, tunicate bulbs and produce grassy clumps of narrow, lance-shaped, basal leaves that are erect and generally 1 to 2 feet long. They produce erect racemes of small starry flowers in spring or early summer that extend well above the foliage. (Heights given below are for plants in bloom.) Like other lily-family plants, their individual flowers consist of six petal-like tepals. Blooms come in shades of blue, violet-blue, cream, and white.

HOW TO GROW

Give camassias a site in full sun or partial shade and rich, well-drained soil. In the wild, most species grow naturally in moist meadows that may be under water for periods of time in spring but that are dry during the summer months. When plants are actively growing in spring, evenly moist conditions are essential, but dry soil in summer after the foliage dies back suits them just fine. Wet, waterlogged soil when plants are dormant—especially in winter—is generally fatal. Plant the bulbs in fall, setting the tops of the bulbs 4 inches below the soil surface. For best effect, arrange them in drifts of a dozen or more, spacing bulbs 6 to 8 inches apart. *Camassias* produce offsets, which can be used for propagation, but offset production is slow, and clumps are best left undisturbed. Dig and divide in summer just as the foliage dies back for propagation or if clumps show signs of overcrowding such as reduced flowering. Or propagate by seeds. Plants self-sow, and seedlings take 3 to 4 years to bloom.

C. cusickii   P. 63

c. kew-SIK-ee-eye. Camass, Cusick Quamash. A 2- to 3-foot-tall species native to northeastern Oregon. Bears erect, showy ½- to 1½-foot-long racemes of 30 to as many as 100 starry blue 2-inch-wide flowers in late spring. Zones 3 to 10.

C. leichtlinii   P. 63

c. lekt-LIN-ee-eye. Leichtlin Quamash. A 2- to 4-foot-tall species native to the Pacific Northwest. Bears erect ½- to 1-foot-long racemes of creamy white flowers in late spring. Individual blooms are 2 to 3 inches wide and 1 to 2 inches long; the petals twist together as they wither. 'Blue Danube' (also listed as 'Balu Donau') bears violet-blue flowers. 'Semiplena' features semidouble creamy white flowers on 2½- to 3-foot plants. 'Alba' bears single white blooms. Zones 4 to 10.

C. quamash

c. KWAH-mash. Quamash, Common Quamash. Formerly *C. esculenta*. A 1- to 2½-foot-tall species from the Pacific Northwest with 1-foot-long racemes of 10 to 30 flowers in late spring in blue, violet-purple, and white. Individual blooms are 1 to 2 inches wide and are slightly irregular in form—one tepal curves downward and the other five point up. This species produces offsets more quickly than other camassias. 'Orion' and 'Blue Melody' produce dark blue flowers. Zones 4 to 10.

C. scilloides   P. 64

c. sil-OY-deez. Wild Hyacinth, Western Camassia. Formerly *C. fraseri*, *C. hyacinthina*. A 1- to 2½-foot-tall species native from Pennsylvania and Minnesota south to Georgia and Texas. Bears 3- to 6-inch-long racemes of 10 to 40 1-inch-wide flowers in early summer in blue, violet-blue, and white. Zones 4 to 9.

❦ Canna

CAN-uh. Canna family, Cannaceae.

Once grown primarily for their showy, hot-colored flowers, cannas today are just as likely to be treasured for their enormous, often boldly colored leaves. There are about 50 species in the genus *Canna*—the only genus in the canna family—all tender perennials native to Asia and tropical and subtropical portions of North and South America. Plants have fleshy, branching rhizomes and thick roots. They bear large paddle-shaped leaves that generally are 1 to 2 feet long and have a sheath at the base that wraps around the stem. The flowers, which are borne in panicles or racemes, are asymmetrical and come in shades of red, orange, red-orange, pink, and sometimes white. Each bloom has three showy petals as well as a petal-like stamen and petal-like staminodes. Gardeners primarily grow cultivars to add dramatic color to gardens. All cannas lend tropical flair to summer plantings.

HOW TO GROW

Cannas thrive in full sun and well-drained, evenly moist soil rich in organic matter. Constantly wet soil—especially if it is cold in spring—rots the fleshy rhizomes, although there are cannas that can be grown in pots set in a pond or water garden. From Zone 8 south, grow cannas outdoors year-round (they may survive Zone 7 winters in a protected site with a heavy layer of mulch). In the North, either replace them annually or overwinter the rhizomes indoors; overwintered rhizomes give the best show simply because the clumps are bigger.

Cannas can be started from seeds, but purchasing rhizomes is faster and the only way to get most of the improved cultivars. Purchased rhizomes should have at least one or two pointed growing tips and be thick, fleshy, and firm with no soft spots. From Zone 7 south, plant them outdoors, in soil amended with organic matter, after the last spring frost date. In the North, pot up the rhizomes indoors with the growing tips just under the soil surface. Keep them warm (75°F) and barely moist until they begin to grow, then move them to a sunny spot, keep them evenly moist, and fertilize weekly. Transplant to the garden after the last frost date, once the soil has warmed to about 65°F. Mulch, water regularly, and feed monthly in summer. Deadhead to keep the plants neat looking and encourage rebloom.

To overwinter, dig them after a light frost and cut back the tops. Store the rhizomes in barely damp vermiculite or peat in a cool (40° to 50°F), dry place. Pot-grown plants can be stored in their containers—keep the soil dry or nearly dry. Inspect stored rhizomes ocassionally in winter: discard rotted pieces or cut away rotted portions and dust cuts with sulfur; sprinkle the vermiculite or other packing medium with water occasionally during winter to keep the roots from shriveling. In spring, cut the rhizomes into pieces with at least two growing points each—or plant the clumps whole—and start them as you would new rhizomes. (Do not divide the rhizomes in fall before storage, because the cut surfaces tend to rot over winter.) Dig and divide in-ground plants every 3 to 5 years. To start from seeds, sow in midwinter. Nick the hard seed coats with a file and soak the seeds in warm water for 48 hours. Then place the seeds in a plastic bag filled with moist peat moss and set it in a warm (75°F) place. Inspect the bag every few days and pot up seedlings as they appear. Seed-grown plants produce rhizomes that can be overwintered in subsequent years.

C. × generalis

PP. 64, 65

c. × jen-er-AL-iss. Canna, Canna Lily. Bold 5- to 6-foot-tall perennials with 1- to 2-foot-long leaves that can be green or are variegated. Showy 1-foot-tall clusters of 3- to 5-inch flowers bloom from midsummer to frost. Many cultivars with solid green leaves and flowers in shades of red, orange, yellow, and pink are available, as well as bicolored ones. Cultivars described as "self-cleaning" drop their blooms naturally as they fade, keeping the plants attractive looking without deadheading. Standard-size cannas range from 4 to 6 feet or more in height by the end of the summer. 'City of Portland' features green leaves and pink flowers, while 'Cleopatra' has green, purple, or purple-and-green-blotched leaves and blooms in various combinations of red, white, and yellow. Standard-size cultivars featuring variegated or burgundy foliage as well as showy flowers include 'Pretoria' (also called 'Bengal Tiger'), with orange-yellow blooms and yellow-and-green-striped leaves edged in maroon; 'Roi Humbert' or 'Red King Humbert', with bronze-purple leaves and red flowers; and 'Durban', with red flowers and leaves striped with orange, yellow, red, and green. 'Phaison' (also sold as 'Tropicana') bears orange flowers and purple leaves striped with yellow and red. 'Wyoming' has burnt orange flowers and burgundy leaves. 'Yellow King Humbert' has deep yellow flowers and burgundy leaves. Dwarf cultivars include 2-foot-tall 'Tropical Rose', with rose-pink flowers, and 2½- to 3-foot-tall Pfitzer series cultivars, both of which can be grown from seeds. Other dwarf cultivars include 'Apricot Dream', with gray-green leaves and soft salmon flowers with rose throats; 'China Doll', a 3-foot-tall self-cleaning selection with pink blooms and green leaves; and 'Orange Punch', a self-cleaning selection with green leaves and tangerine orange blossoms with yellow throats. 'Red Futurity' is a self-cleaning dwarf with bronze-green to black leaves and deep red flowers; 'Rose Futurity', also self-cleaning, bears dark burgundy leaves and rich coral-pink and rose flowers. 'Pink Sunburst' is a 3-foot-tall selection with salmon-pink flowers and green-and-yellow-striped leaves that have a pink cast. 'Striped Beauty' is a 2- to 3-foot-tall selection with yellow-and-green-striped leaves and red buds opening into yellow flowers with white stripes. Tender perennial, hardy in Zones 7 or 8 to 11.

C. glauca

c. GLAW-kuh. A 4- to 6-foot-tall species with narrow, rounded gray-green leaves that are 1 to 6 inches wide and 1 to 1½ feet long. Bears small pale yellow flowers with 3-inch-long petals in summer. Tender perennial hardy in Zones 7 or 8 to 11.

❧ *Cardiocrinum*

kar-dee-o-KRY-num. Lily family, Liliaceae.

Three species of bulbs from China, Japan, and the Himalayas belong to this genus, all once classified with the true lilies, or *Lilium* species. They grow from scaly bulbs, as do true lilies, and bear erect stalks of showy, lily-like, trumpet-shaped flowers that are followed by attractive brown seed capsules. The leaves do not resemble those of true lilies, however: they are handsome and broadly heart shaped. The botanical name is taken from the Greek *kardia,* heart, and *krinon,* a type of lily. *Cardiocrinum* species grow from very large bulbs that are monocarpic, meaning they die after they flower, but the bulbs generally leave plenty of offsets after flowering to replace themselves.

HOW TO GROW
Select a site in partial shade with rich, deeply prepared, moist soil that is well drained. Plants are happiest in the Pacific Northwest, where summers are cool and wet and winters are mild. In the East, look for a cool site that offers protection from winds. Plant the bulbs in fall, setting the tops just under the soil surface. Work plenty of well-rotted manure, compost, or other organic matter deeply into the soil at planting time. Mulch with compost or chopped leaves to keep the soil moist and cool. Water regularly in dry weather. Mulch heavily in late fall to protect bulbs over winter. Propagate by separating offsets, which take 3 to 5 years to reach flowering size, or by seeds.

C. cathayanum

c. kah-THAY-ah-num. Formerly *Lilium cathayanum.* A 4½-foot-tall species native to China bearing heart-shaped, 8-inch-long leaves. In summer, it produces racemes of 4½-inch-long flowers that are greenish on the outside and creamy white inside with a few purple dots. Zones 7 to 9.

C. giganteum   P. 66

c. jy-GAN-tee-um. Formerly *Lilium giganteum.* A 5- to 12-foot-tall species from China and the Himalayas bearing 1½-foot-long heart-shaped leaves. Produces erect racemes of up to 20 nodding 6- to 8-inch-long white trumpets that are striped with maroon inside. Blooms are very fragrant. Zones 7 to 9; to Zone 6 in a protected site.

❦ *Chamaelirium*

kah-mee-LEER-ee-um. Lily family, Liliaceae.

The genus *Chamaelirium* contains a single species of tuberous perennial that is native to eastern North America. It grows naturally in bogs and moist woodlands and produces rosettes of rounded to spoon-shaped glossy green leaves that last well into winter. The botanical name comes from the Greek *chamai,* on the ground, and *lirion,* lily. While the foliage is primarily basal, the flowers are produced in erect, feathery spikes in summer that can reach 1 to 3 feet. Spikes are cylindrical and densely packed with tiny creamy white flowers that have six narrow petal-like tepals. The species is dioecious, meaning male and female flowers are borne on separate plants.

HOW TO GROW

Select a site in partial shade with rich, moist—even boggy—soil. An acid soil pH is best. Plants withstand considerable sun with consistent moisture. Use this wildflower in moist shade gardens, bog gardens, and natural areas. Propagate by dividing plants in spring or sowing seeds in fall; both male and female plants are required for seed production.

C. luteum P. 66

c. LOO-tee-um. Devil's Bit, Blazing Star, Fairy Wand. A native 1- to 3-foot-tall wildflower that bears cylindrical racemes of creamy white ¼-inch-wide flowers from early to midsummer. Female plants bear 1-foot-long racemes. Male plants bear 2- to 5-inch-long racemes that are often pendent toward the tip and have somewhat yellower flowers that are more densely packed than those of the female. Zones 3 to 8.

❦ *Chasmanthe*

chaz-MAN-thee. Iris family, Iridaceae.

Closely related to *Gladiolus* and *Crocosmia, Chasmanthe* species produce fans of erect, sword-shaped leaves and showy, spikelike racemes of flowers in summer. Three species belong to the genus, all native South African perennials that grow from corms. They produce flowers that have curved, tubular to funnel-shaped bases and open into six lobes, or petal-like tepals. The upper tepal is longer than the other five and projects out to form a hood.

HOW TO GROW
Select a site in full sun to partial shade with rich, moist, well-drained soil. *Chasmanthe* species are grown much like gladiolus: plant the corms in spring after the soil has warmed up, setting them 3 to 4 inches deep. For best effect, arrange them in drifts, with corms spaced 3 to 4 inches apart. Water regularly in dry weather. Dig the corms in fall after the first light frost—dig them earlier if the leaves die back. Let them dry for a few hours, brush off excess soil, and store them in paper bags in a cool (40° to 50°F), dry place over winter. Where hardy, the corms can be left in the ground year-round. In this case, cut back the leaves in late winter. Propagate by separating and planting the offsets in spring or fall or by sowing seeds.

C. aethiopica   P. 67
c. ee-thee-O-pih-kuh. A 2-foot-tall species forming clumps of sword-shaped leaves. In spring to early summer, plants produce 6- to 7-inch-long racemes of 3-inch-long red or orange flowers with maroon throats. Zones 8 to 10.

C. floribunda   P. 67
c. flor-ih-BUN-duh. A 2- to 4-foot-tall species producing clumps of sword-shaped leaves and branched 1-foot-long racemes of 3-inch-long yellow or orange flowers in summer. Zones 9 to 10.

❦ Chionodoxa

ky-on-o-DOX-uh. Lily family, Liliaceae.

Both the common and the botanical names of this genus of easy-to-grow bulbs celebrate their dainty, early-season blooms. They are commonly known as glory-of-the-snow, because the flowers appear in late winter or early spring as snows recede. The botanical name is from the Greek *chion,* snow, and *doxa,* glory. Six species belong to the genus, all small bulbous perennials that have tunicate bulbs and produce two or three narrow, linear to strappy leaves. They bear racemes of six-lobed, upward-facing, star-shaped flowers. Blooms often have a white eye and come in shades of rich, true blue as well as pink and white. Individual flowers have six petal-like tepals. The tepals are united at the base to form a short tube: *Scilla,* to which these plants are closely related and with which they are often confused, has tepals that are split all the way to the base of the flower.

HOW TO GROW

Select a site with average, well-drained soil that is in full sun or in partial to full shade under deciduous trees so that plants receive full sun in spring when they are actively growing. Plant the bulbs in fall with the bases at a depth of about 3 inches. For best effect, arrange them in drifts—a plant or two here and there will be lost in the spring garden, while plantings of 20 to 50 or more bulbs are stunning. Plants produce offsets freely and also self-sow with enthusiasm: they are ideal for naturalizing and when left undisturbed will form large showy colonies. Propagate by digging and dividing the clumps and/or separating the offsets and seedlings in early summer just as the foliage dies back.

C. forbesii   P. 68

c. FORBS-ee-eye. Glory-of-the-snow. A 4- to 8-inch-tall species producing loose racemes of 4 to 12 flowers in early spring. Individual flowers are blue with white eyes and ½ to ¾ inch wide. 'Alba' bears white flowers. 'Pink Giant' produces pink flowers with white centers. Zones 3 to 9.

C. luciliae   P. 68

c. loo-SIL-ee-ee. Glory-of-the-snow. A 4- to 6-inch-tall species with racemes of three to six ½- to 1-inch-wide blue flowers with white centers in early spring. Zones 3 to 9.

C. nana

c. NAY-nuh. Glory-of-the-snow. A 4- to 6-inch-tall species with racemes of two to three ¼- to ½-inch-wide blue flowers with white centers in early spring. Zones 7 to 9.

C. sardensis   P. 69

c. sar-DEN-sis. Sardenian Glory-of-the-snow. A 4- to 6-inch-tall species bearing racemes of 8 to 12 ½-inch-wide flowers in early spring. Individual blooms are bluish purple and lack white centers. Zones 5 to 9.

❦ Chlidanthus

klih-DAN-thuss. Amaryllis family, Amaryllidaceae.

A single species native to Peru beongs to the genus *Childanthus*, a bulb sometimes grown for its fragrant yellow flowers. The botanical name is from the Greek *chlide*, a luxury or costly ornament, and *anthos*, flower. The lilylike flowers are borne in summer in small clusters of one to four.

Individual blooms have a long slender tube at the base and open into six flaring lobes, or petal-like tepals. Plants grow from small tunicate bulbs and produce strap-shaped gray-green leaves that resemble those of daffodils and appear in midsummer either with the flowers or slightly after the flowers open.

HOW TO GROW

Select a site in full sun with moist, well-drained, somewhat sandy soil. In Zones 9 to 11, these plants can be grown outdoors year-round: plant them in spring with about 2 inches of soil over the tops of the bulbs. From Zone 8 north, grow them in pots or plant them outdoors in spring after the last frost date, setting the bulbs with their noses just above the soil surface. Keep the soil barely moist until flowers appear, then water regularly to keep it evenly moist. Pot-grown plants can be kept on a deck or terrace or grown with pots sunk to the rim in the garden. To overwinter, bring the pots indoors after the first light frost of fall, dry them off, and store them in a cool (50° to 55°F), dry place over winter. Repot in spring. Or dig bulbs as the foliage dies back in fall and store them in dry peat moss in a cool (50°F), dry spot. Propagate by separating the offsets in spring.

C. fragrans   P. 69
c. FRAY-grens. Delicate Lily, Fragrant Amaryllis, Peru Childanthus. A tender, bulbous perennial bearing lemon-scented, slender-tubed, golden yellow flowers atop 6- to 8-inch-tall stems in summer. Individual flowers are 3 inches wide and 4 to 5 inches long. Zones 9 to 11.

❦ Clivia

KLIH-vee-uh/KLY-vee-uh. Amaryllis family, Amaryllidaceae.

Clivias, also known as kaffir lilies, are tender perennials native to South Africa that have swollen, bulblike bases and fleshy roots. Plants bear handsome, evergreen, generally strap-shaped leaves and showy, tubular to trumpet-shaped flowers. Individual flowers, which are carried in umbels atop thick, leafless stalks, have a short tube at the base and six spreading lobes, or petal-like tepals. They come in shades from orange-red to nearly scarlet as well as yellow and are follwed by clusters of round, shiny red berries. Clivias are hardy in only the warmest climates, but make outstanding plants for large containers and tubs and also are easy-to-grow houseplants.

HOW TO GROW

Give clivias a site in partial shade with rich, well-drained soil. Where they are not hardy, grow them in tubs or large containers. For best results divide the clumps only when the plants show signs of overcrowding. (With time, the fleshy roots will fill up the containers, leaving little room for soil.) Root-bound plants tend to bloom best. Like many South African species, clivias need regular watering from late winter or early spring through summer when they are growing actively and drier conditions when dormant in winter. Gradually dry them off in late summer and fall, and overwinter pot-grown plants in a cool (45° to 50°F), sunny, well-ventilated room or greenhouse. Keep the soil barely moist until growth resumes in late winter or spring. Plants that do not receive a cool, dry dormancy may still flower, but the flower stalks generally fail to elongate, and the blooms are borne down in between the leaves. Propagate by dividing the clumps and potting up the offsets in late winter or early spring. Or sow seeds.

C. miniata   P. 70

c. min-ee-AH-tuh. Kaffir Lily. A tender, evergreen perennial with arching dark green 2-inch-wide leaves that reach 1½ to 2½ feet in length. Bears clusters of 10 to 20 trumpet-shaped 2- to 3-inch-long orange, red-orange, or yellow flowers in spring and early summer. Plants are about 1½ feet tall, with flower clusters extending above the leaves. 'Aurea', also sold as 'Citrina', bears yellow flowers. Zones 10 to 11.

❦ Colchicum

KOL-chih-kum. Lily family, Liliaceae.

Commonly known as colchicums or autumn crocuses, *Colchicum* species are grown for their crocuslike flowers that grace the garden in fall. About 45 species belong to the genus, all of which are perennials that grow from corms. Most, but not all, autumn crocuses (or colchicums) bloom from early to late fall and produce lush clumps of basal leaves in spring. The leaves range from strap or lance shaped to rounded and often are pleated or ribbed. The funnel- or goblet-shaped flowers consist of six petal-like tepals. Despite their crocuslike appearance, *Colchicum* species are not closely related to the true crocuses (*Crocus* spp.), which belong in the iris family. *Colchicum* species have six stamens (the male part of the flower), three styles and stigmas (female parts of the flower), and an ovary that is above where the petals are attached. *Crocus* species, on the other hand, have three stamens, one style with three stigmas, and an ovary that is borne beneath where the petals are attached. True crocuses also bear grassy leaves.

HOW TO GROW

For all the species listed here, select a site in full sun or light shade with average, deeply prepared, well-drained soil. Plant the corms in late summer or fall, as early as you can obtain them. Set them with no more than 2 to 3 inches of soil over the tops of the corms. (Have the soil already prepared, and work in plenty of organic matter such as compost, so you can plant as soon as the corms arrive; the corms can bloom even before they are planted.) Space corms 6 to 9 inches apart to accommodate their large leaves. When selecting a site, keep in mind that the large lush clumps of spring foliage these plants produce are quite unattractive when they begin to turn yellow and go dormant in early summer. For this reason, autumn crocuses are best used at the front of informal perennial plantings, mixed borders, shrub borders, and natural areas rather than in neat, formal plantings. Combining them with low perennials or ground covers also helps provide support for the flowers, which tend to flop over. Where happy, autumn crocuses produce an abundance of offsets and form handsome drifts with time. Divide the clumps every few years when they become crowded. Propagate by separating offsets in summer, just as the foliage dies back, or by seeds.

C. agrippinum

c. ah-grih-PYE-num. A 3- to 4-inch-tall species with clumps of narrow to strap-shaped 6-inch-long leaves. In early fall corms bear one or two funnel-shaped 2-inch-long purplish pink flowers checkered with darker pink. Zones 4 to 8.

C. autumnale   P. 70

c. aw-tum-NAL-ee. Autumn Crocus, Meadow Saffron. A 4- to 6-inch-tall species with lance-shaped leaves that can reach 12 to 14 inches in length. In midfall, corms bear one to six pale lavender-pink 1½- to 2½-inch-long flowers. Several cultivars are available, including 'Alboplenum', with double white flowers; 'Album', a single white; and 'Pleniflorum' (also listed as 'Roseum Plenum' and 'Plenum'), with large double 2- to 3-inch-long rose-pink flowers. Zones 4 to 8.

C. bornmuelleri

c. born-MULE-er-eye. A 4- to 5-inch-tall species with narrowly oval 6- to 10-inch-long leaves. In midfall, corms bear one to six fragrant, funnel-shaped 2- to 3-inch-long blooms that are rose-purple with purplish brown anthers. Zones 4 to 8.

C. byzantinum

c. bih-zan-TYE-num. A 4- to 6-inch-tall species with ribbed, rounded to lance-shaped leaves that reach 1 foot in length. In early to midfall, corms bear numerous (up to about 20) 2-inch-long funnel-shaped pale pink or lilac-pink flowers. Zones 4 to 8.

C. cilicicum

c. sih-LIH-sih-kum. A 4- to 6-inch-tall species with rounded to lance-shaped 1- to 1½-foot-long leaves. In fall, each corm produces from 3 or 4 to as many as 25 funnel-shaped 2- to 3-inch-long rose-purple flowers. Zones 4 to 8.

C. hybrids   P. 71

A variety of showy-flowered hybrids ranging from 5 to 10 inches tall or more have been developed. All produce leaves that can reach 10 inches in length. 'The Giant' is a free-flowering selection that produces 3-inch-long goblet-shaped rose-lilac blooms in early to midfall. 'Waterlily' produces double pinkish lilac blooms with 2- to 3-inch tepals. 'Violet Queen' produces fragrant, funnel-shaped 2- to 2½-inch long violet-purple blooms in early fall. 'Lilac Wonder' bears rose-purple 2-inch-long goblet-shaped flowers. Zones 4 to 8.

C. speciosum   P. 72

c. spee-see-O-sum Autumn Crocus. A 5- to 7-inch-tall species with 7- to 10-inch-long rounded to somewhat lance-shaped leaves. In fall, corms bear one to three 2- to 3-inch-long reddish violet tuliplike blooms with yellow anthers. Zones 4 to 8.

❧ Colocasia

kol-o-KAYE-see-uh. Arum family, Araceae.

Native to tropical Asia, the six species of *Colocasia* are tender perennials with thick, tuberous roots and large, generally shield- or arrow-shaped leaves. Flowers consist of a spathe and spadix, much like Jack-in-the-pulpits (*Arisaema* spp.) and calla lilies (*Zantedeschia* spp.), both close relatives. However, in cultivation these plants seldom bloom, and the one species found in gardens is grown for its huge ornamental leaves. All parts of the plant contain calcium oxalate crystals, which cause long-lasting pain and stomach upset if eaten. These plants are grown for their edible tubers — they are commonly known as taro and dasheen — but the tubers must be cooked thoroughly before they are edible.

HOW TO GROW

Colocasia species are native to swampy areas and require partial shade and deep, rich soil that is wet or at least constantly moist. A sheltered spot is best, because wind will damage the large leaves. Plants thrive in heat and humidity. They can be grown in containers set in a pond or water garden. In the North, start the tubers indoors in pots 8 to 10 weeks before the last frost date, grow them in a warm (70° to 75°F) spot, and transplant outdoors only after the weather is warm and settled. In areas with long growing seasons, plant them directly in the garden after the last frost. Add plenty of organic matter to the soil at planting time. To overwinter the tubers, dig them before the first fall frost, cut off the tops, then dry them for a few hours. Pack them in barely moist sand or peat moss and store them at 40° to 50°F. Use these plants to add a tropical flair to beds and borders, in the bog garden, or in containers.

C. esculenta   PP. 72, 73

c. es-kew-LEN-tuh. Elephant's Ear, Taro, Dasheen. Also listed as *C. antiquorum*. A tender 3- to 7-foot perennial with heart- or arrow-shaped 2-foot-long leaves. Insignificant flowers. 'Black Magic' bears purple-black leaves. 'Illustris' has purple leaf stalks and green leaves with black-purple veins. Zones 9 to 11; to Zone 8 with winter protection.

❧ *Commelina*

com-el-EYE-nuh. Spiderwort family, Commelinaceae.

Like their better-known relatives, the spiderworts (*Tradescantia* spp.), *Commelina* species bear three-petaled flowers that each last for less than one day. Unlike spiderworts, which have three similar-sized petals, *Commelina* species usually bear flowers that have two petals that are quite a bit larger than the third. About 100 species belong to the genus, which contains annuals as well as perennials that grow from either fibrous or tuberous roots. One species, common dayflower *(C. communis),* is a troublesome, fleshy-leaved weed with flowers that have two dark blue petals and one paler blue one. It thrives in shady sites with moist soil, where it self-sows with abandon and also roots at the leaf nodes, as do many other species in the genus. It does not produce tubers.

HOW TO GROW
Give the tuberous species listed here — *C. tuberosa* — a site with partial shade and rich, well-drained soil. Plant the tubers in spring. In the warmest climates, it can be grown outdoors year-round. In the North, dig the tubers after the first light frosts of fall and overwinter them indoors as you would dahlias — in barely moist peat moss or sand in a cool, dry spot. Propagate by dividing the tubers in spring or by seeds.

C. coelestis   P. 73
c. ko-LES-tis. Blue Spiderwort. A vigorous, tuberous-rooted species that forms 2- to 3-foot-tall 1½-foot-wide clumps. Bears fleshy leaves and blue ¾- to 1¼-inch-wide flowers from summer to fall. Zones 9 to 11.

C. tuberosa
c. too-ber-O-suh. Tuberous Day Flower. A mat-forming 8-inch-tall species native to Central and South America that spreads to several feet. Bears lance-shaped leaves and clusters of greenish flowers striped with blue-purple in summer. Zones 10 to 11.

❦ *Convallaria*
con-vah-LAIR-ee-uh. Lily family, Liliaceae.

Commonly known as lilies-of-the-valley, these lily-family plants bear arching racemes of small, sweetly scented, nodding, bell-shaped flowers. Plants have leaves ranging from ovate-lance shaped to rounded, and they spread by fleshy, freely branching rhizomes to form dense mats. Experts differ on whether *Convallaria* contains three species or a single, variable one.

HOW TO GROW
A site in partial shade with evenly moist, rich soil is ideal, although plants grow in full sun (with adequate moisture) to full shade. Established

clumps tolerate dry shade, but will not survive in wet, poorly drained sites. In the South, where plants struggle with the heat, a site in partial to full shade is best. In cooler zones, plants spread vigorously, so keep them away from other perennials or divide clumps frequently to keep them in check. Plant lily-of-the-valley pips—bare root pieces of the fleshy rhizome that have both growing buds and roots—in fall, late winter, or early spring, ideally before the leaves emerge. Cut the plants to the ground in late summer if the foliage becomes unattractive. Divide them in summer or fall if they encroach on other plantings, if flowering is reduced because of overcrowding, or for propagation.

C. majalis
P. 74

mah-JAH-liss. Lily-of-the-valley. Vigorous, ground-covering perennial that reaches 6 to 9 inches in height and spreads to several feet. Bears one-sided racemes of waxy white ¼-inch-wide bells in spring followed by round glossy red berries. 'Fortin's Giant' is a vigorous selection with ½-inch-wide flowers on 1-foot-tall plants. *C. majalis* var. *rosea* bears very pale mauve-pink flowers. Zones 2 to 8.

❦ Corydalis

co-RID-ah-liss. Poppy family, Papaveraceae.

Corydalis species produce handsome mounds of delicate-looking, ferny foliage and racemes of tubular, spurred flowers in spring. About 300 species, both biennials and perennials, belong to the genus, which was once classified in the fumitory family, Fumariaceae. *Corydalis* resemble bleeding hearts (*Dicentra* species), but while bleeding hearts have two spurs per flower, *Corydalis* blooms have only one. The species listed here grow from tubers and bloom in spring. All are spring ephemerals, meaning the foliage dies down by early summer after the plants flower.

HOW TO GROW
Unless otherwise noted below, grow tuberous corydalis in partial shade with rich, moist, well-drained soil. Plant the tubers in late summer or fall. Mark the locations of the clumps to avoid digging into them by mistake later in the season after they disappear. Transplant or divide clumps, if necessary, in early summer, just as the foliage dies down. Propagate by division in late spring or early summer just as the leaves die down, or by seeds.

C. cava

c. CAY-vuh. Fumewort. Often listed as *C. bulbosa*. Tuberous 4- to 8-inch-tall species forming 4-inch-wide mounds of lacy pale green leaves and dense racemes of 1-inch-long rich rosy purple or white flowers in early spring. Zones 5 to 8.

C. diphylla

c. dye-FIL-uh. Tuberous 4- to 6-inch-tall species that spreads to 4 inches. Bears lacy leaves and loose clusters of 6 to 10 1-inch-long white flowers with darker red-purple lips in spring. Grows in full sun, although plants tolerate partial shade. Requires very well drained soil and is best for a rock garden. Zones 5 to 8.

C. fumariifolia

c. few-mar-ee-ih-FO-lee-uh. Also listed as *C. ambigua*. A 4- to 6-inch-tall species, spreading to 4 inches, with lacy green leaves topped by spikelike racemes of 1-inch-long blue to purple-blue flowers from late spring to early summer. Zones 5 to 8.

C. solida   P. 74

c. SO-lee-duh. Also listed as *C. halleri, C. transsylvanica*. Vigorous 8- to 10-inch-tall tuberous species forming 8-inch-wide mounds of lacy gray-green leaves. In early spring it bears dense, spikelike racemes of mauve-pink ¾-inch-long flowers with spurs that curve downward. 'George Baker' (also listed as 'G.P. Baker') bears rich rose-pink flowers flushed with violet inside. 'Beth Evans' bears pink blooms. Zones 5 to 9.

❦ Crinum

KRY-num. Amaryllis family, Amaryllidaceae.

Crinums are tender perennial bulbs grown for their showy umbels of funnel- or bell-shaped flowers. Flower clusters, which are carried on leafless stalks, contain from 3 or 4 to as many as 20 or more blooms. The individual flowers, which are white or nearly white, often are fragrant. They have six petal-like lobes, or tepals. Shape varies: one common name for these plants is crinum lily, a reference to the lilylike shape of the blooms of some species. Another is spider lily: other species bear flowers with very narrow tepals that create a spidery effect. The plants grow from large tunicate bulbs and produce long (to 3 feet or more), narrow, strap- to sword-shaped leaves that may be deciduous, semievergreen, or evergreen. About 130 species belong to the genus, native to the tropics of both the Old and New Worlds, where they are found growing along streams and the edges of lakes—two other common names for these stunning plants are swamp lily and river lily.

HOW TO GROW

Select a site in full sun or partial shade with very deeply prepared, rich, moist, well-drained soil. Shade during the hottest part of the day is beneficial in areas with hot summers. Outdoors, plant the bulbs in spring with the tip of the bulbs just at the soil surface. Space plants 2 to 3 feet apart: where hardy, they can be grown outdoors year-round and left to establish large clumps. Where they're marginally hardy, select a warm, south-facing site and protect plants over winter with a coarse mulch such as evergreen boughs, pine needles, salt hay, or coarse leaves such as oak leaves. In the North, grow these plants in large containers or tubs. When planting in containers, set the bulbs with the long necks and even the top part of the bulb extending above the soil surface. In containers or in the ground, keep the soil evenly moist from spring through fall when plants are growing actively. For best results, feed in-ground plants two or three times during the season; feed container-grown plants weekly or every other week with a dilute, balanced fertilizer. To overwinter container-grown plants, move them to a cool (50°F), well-ventilated sunroom or greenhouse *before* the first fall frost. Keep the soil fairly dry while plants are dormant. Crinums resent root disturbance, so divide or transplant them only if absolutely necessary. Plants may refuse to bloom for several years after being disturbed. Move container-grown plants to larger pots only when they become quite crowded. Propagate by separating the offsets in spring or by sowing seeds.

C. americanum   P. 75

c. ah-mair-ih-KAH-num. Southern Swamp Lily, Florida Crinum. A native species found in boggy soils from Florida to Texas that spreads by stolons. Bears umbels of three to six fragrant flowers atop thick 1½- to 2-foot-tall stems from late spring to fall. Individual flowers are 4 to 5 inches long with narrow, wide-spreading tepals that are creamy white tinged with purple-brown on the backs. Zones 9 to 11.

C. asiaticum   P. 75

c. ay-see-AT-ih-kum. Poison Bulb, Grand Crinum. (Some varieties produce poisonous bulbs, other do not, thus the name poison bulb.) A variable 2-foot-tall species native to the tropics of Asia producing clumps of bulbs and large umbels of 20 or more fragrant white flowers in summer. Individual flowers are spidery, with narrow 3-inch-long tepals. Zones 8 to 11.

C. bulbispermum

c. bul-bih-SPER-mum. Jamaica Crinum. Formerly *C. longifolium.* A South African native bearing umbels of 8 to as many as 15 fragrant, funnel- to bell-shaped, lilylike flowers on 2- to 4-foot-tall stalks in late summer or early fall. Blooms are 3 inches wide, 3 to 4 inches long, and white or pink on the inside, blushed with red-purple on the outside. Zones 7 to 10.

C. hybrids

A variety of attractive hybrid crinums are avaliable. These include 'Carolina Beauty', with white flowers; 'Ellen Bosanquet', with spicy-scented wine red bell-shaped flowers; and 'Bradley', with fragrant rose-pink flowers that have white throats. Zones 7 to 10.

C. × powellii   P. 76

c. × pow-ELL-ee-eye. A hybrid species bearing showy umbels of 8 to 10 fragrant 4-inch-long flowers on 4- to 5-foot-tall stalks in late summer and fall. Blooms are trumpet-shaped, 3 to 4 inches long, and pink in color. 'Album' bears white flowers. Zones 7 to 10.

❧× *Crinodonna* see × Amarcrinum

❧ *Crocosmia*

kro-KOS-mee-uh. Iris family, Iridaceae.

Grown for their arching clusters of trumpet-shaped flowers, crocosmias are perennials native to the grasslands of South Africa. The flowers, which are borne in mid- to late summer, are carried in arching spikes or panicles. They are tubular to funnel shaped with six spreading lobes, or petal-like tepals. Blooms come in shades of orange, red-orange, and yellow. Plants grow from corms and produce 2- to 3-foot-tall clumps of ribbed, linear- to sword-shaped leaves. The botanical name *Crocosmia* is a reference to the fact that the flowers have a saffronlike fragrance when soaked in water: it is from the Greek *krokos,* saffron, and *osme,* smell. While seven species belong to the genus, gardeners primarily grow hybrids.

HOW TO GROW
Select a site in full sun with evenly moist soil that is rich in organic matter. Crocosmias tolerate partial shade in the South. Plant the corms in spring at a depth of 3 to 4 inches, spacing them 4 to 5 inches apart. Plants form dense, good-sized clumps with time. Where they are hardy, grow them outdoors year-round. Where they are marginally hardy, select a warm spot, such as one against a south-facing wall, and protect plants over winter by spreading a thick layer of a coarse mulch such as evergreen boughs, salt hay, pine needles, or coarse leaves after the ground has frozen in fall. (Mulch is especially important the first year; after that only plants in the coldest areas require winter protection.) Where these plants are not hardy, dig the clumps in fall, clean soil off the corms, pack them in dry sand, and overwinter them in a cool (35° to 40°F), dry place. It is best to avoid lifting the corms annually, however, because they will not flower as well. They also can be treated as annuals. Divide the clumps in spring if they become overcrowded and begin to bloom less or for propagation.

C. × *crocosmiiflora*   PP. 76, 77
c. × kro-kos-mih-FLOR-uh. Crocosmia, Montbretia. A vigorous 2- to 3-foot-tall hybrid bearing arching spikes, which may or may not be branched, of 1½- to 2-inch-long flowers in summer. Many cultivars have been selected, including 'Emberglow', with dark red blooms; 'Emily McKenzie', with orange flowers with red-brown throats; 'Lucifer', with bright red flowers and reportedly hardy to Zone 5; 'Venus' and 'Jackanapes' (also listed as 'Fire King'), with bicolored orange-red and yellow blooms; 'Jenny Bloom', with pale yellow flowers; and 'Citronella', with yellow blooms. Zones 6 to 9.

C. masoniorum
c. mah-so-nee-OR-um. A 3- to 4-foot-tall species with pleated leaves and 2-inch-long orange-red flowers in midsummer. Zones 7 to 9.

❦ *Crocus*
KRO-kus. Iris family, Iridaceae.

The cup-shaped blooms of crocuses are a familiar sight from late winter to early spring. Without doubt, hybrid crocuses are most widely planted, but this genus of 80 species offers gardeners a wealth of charming species that bloom in spring as well as fall. All grow from corms and produce grassy leaves that appear with or just after the flowers. Each corm produces from one to about four or five blooms that lack aboveground stems: the so-called stem that arises from the ground actually is the tubular base of the corolla (petals). The individual flowers, which range from cup to goblet shaped, consist of six petal-like tepals. Spring-blooming crocuses come in shades of yellow, white, purple, and lavender, with many selections bearing bicolored blooms. Autumn-blooming crocuses tend toward shades of rose-purple, purple, and violet. Many selections have showy stamens or styles in contrasting colors. True crocuses (*Crocus* spp.) are not to be confused with autumn crocuses (*Colchicum* spp.), which belong to the lily family. For more on the differences between these two genera, see *Colchicum*.

HOW TO GROW

Select a site in full sun with poor to average, sandy or gritty, well-drained soil. Spring-blooming selections tolerate light shade under deciduous trees, where they receive full spring sunshine when they are growing actively. The corms do not do well in clay soils or moist conditions. Most prefer dry soil in summer when they are dormant — some require dry conditions in summer and are best planted in very well drained sites in rock gardens or in containers that can be protected from summer rains. Plant the corms 3 to 4 inches deep. Spring-blooming crocuses are planted in fall, while fall-blooming selections are planted as soon as they are available in late summer or very early fall. For the longest display of bloom, plant a variety of species and cultivars. The earliest blooming crocuses include snow crocus *(Crocus chrysanthus)*, cloth-of-gold crocus *(C. angustifolius)*, and *C. tommasinianus*, which flower from late winter into early spring. Scotch crocuses *(C. biflorus)* and Dutch crocuses *(C. vernus)* bloom somewhat later, in early to midspring. Fall-blooming crocuses include *C. speciosus*, *C. kotschyanus*, *C. medius*, and *C. pulchellus*. Dutch crocuses *(C. vernus)* are one of the best species for naturalizing in a lawn, but they tend to die out after several years unless the turf is sparse. Replace them as necessary. Other species suitable for naturalizing include *C. biflorus* and *C. tommasinianus*. Do not mow the lawn until after the crocus foliage turns yellow and dies back. Naturalizing crocuses in wild gardens as well as beds and borders, rather than in grass, yields longer-lived stands. Propagate by separating the offsets just as the leaves turn yellow and the corms go dormant in early summer; most crocuses self-sow and produce abundant offsets where happy.

C. ancyrensis   P. 78

c. an-see-REN-sis. Golden Bunch Crocus. Late winter– to early spring-blooming species with 2-inch-tall bright yellow to orange-yellow flowers. Zones 3 to 8.

C. angustifolius

c. an-gus-tih-FO-lee-us. Cloth-of-gold Crocus. Formerly *C. susianus*. A spring-flowering 2-inch-tall species with orange-yellow flowers marked with maroon-brown on the outside. Zones 3 to 8.

C. biflorus   PP. 78, 79

c. bi-FLOR-us. Scotch Crocus. Late winter– to early spring–blooming species native from Italy, the Balkans, and the southern Ukraine to Iran, not Scotland. Bears white or lilac-blue flowers, usually in pairs, that have yellow throats. The outer petals are sometimes striped with brown-purple. Plants are 2 to 2½ inches tall in bloom. Vigorous and good for naturalizing. *C. biflorus* ssp. *alexandri* has white flowers striped with purple on the outside. *C. biflorus* ssp. *weldenii* 'Albus' has white flowers. 'Miss Vain' bears fragrant white flowers with pale lilac-blue bases and showy orange styles. *C. Biflorus* ssp. *weldenii* 'Fairy' bears white flowers dusted with lavender on the outside. Zones 3 to 8.

C. cartwrightianus   P. 79

c. cart-rite-ee-AH-nus. Fall Crocus. Fall- to early winter–blooming 2-inch-tall species bearing fragrant lilac to white flowers with brilliant orange styles on 2-inch plants. Requires very well drained soil and a dry summer dormancy. *C. cartwrightianus* f. *albus* bears white flowers. Zones 6 to 8.

C. chrysanthus   P. 80

c. krih-SAN-thus. Snow Crocus. Among the first crocuses to bloom in late winter to early spring. Bears lightly fragrant golden yellow flowers often marked with maroon on the outside and often featuring showy orange stamens. Plants reach 2 inches tall. Many cultivars are available, including 'Advance', with pale peach-yellow flowers that are white and bluish violet on the outside and feature orange stamens; 'Blue Bird', creamy white inside and violet-blue outside; 'Blue Pearl', soft blue on the outside with a bronze-yellow base and a yellow throat; 'Cream Beauty', creamy yellow on the outside, darker yellow inside, and featuring brilliant orange stamens; 'E.P. Bowles', lemon yellow with bronze-yellow at the base; 'Gipsy Girl', bright yellow striped with bronze-purple; 'Goldilocks', dark yellow with purple-brown at the base; 'Ladykiller', white striped with purple; 'Prins Claus', white flowers with oval blue-purple blotches on the outside of the tepals; 'Prinses Beatrix' (also listed as 'Princess Beatrix'), blue with rich yellow at the base; and 'Snow Bunting', white streaked with lilac on the outside. Zones 3 to 8.

C. etruscus

c. eh-TRUS-kus. Late winter– to early spring–blooming 3-inch-tall species with lilac flowers that have yellow throats. The outer tepals are buff to creamy colored on the outside, while the inner ones are lightly veined with purple. 'Zwanenburg' bears lilac-blue flowers. Zones 5 to 8.

C. flavus

c. FLAY-vus. Formerly *C. aureus.* Spring-blooming 3-inch-tall species with orange-yellow flowers. Zones 5 to 8.

C. goulimyi   P. 81

c. goo-LIM-ee-eye. Fall Crocus. Fall-blooming 3- to 4-inch-tall species with rosy lilac flowers. Zones 3 to 8.

C. imperati   P. 81

c. im-per-AH-tee. Italian Crocus. Late winter– to early spring–blooming species that reaches about 4 inches and bears purple flowers striped with tawny yellow on the outside. 'De Jager' bears flowers that are violet-purple with a yellow heart and tawny yellow-brown striped with purple outside. Zones 5 to 8.

C. korolkowii   P. 82

c. ko-rol-KO-vee-eye. Celandine Crocus. Late winter– to early spring–blooming species that reaches about 4 inches in bloom and bears golden yellow flowers feathered with brown on the outside. Requires completely dry conditions in summer once plants have gone dormant. Zones 3 to 8.

C. kotschyanus

c. kot-ski-AH-nus. Formerly *C. zonatus.* Fall-blooming 2- to 3-inch-tall species with pale violet flowers. Requires dry conditions in summer once plants have gone dormant. Zones 3 to 8.

C. laevigatus

c. lee-vih-GAH-tus. Fall- to early winter–blooming 1½- to 3-inch-tall species bearing white or lilac flowers that are yellow or tan on the outside and streaked with violet-purple. Zones 5 to 8.

C. longiflorus

C. lon-jih-FLOR-us. Fall-blooming 3- to 4-inch-tall species bearing fragrant pale to dark lilac flowers. Requires dry conditions in summer once plants have gone dormant. Zones 5 to 8.

C. medius

c. MEE-dee-us. Fall-blooming 3-inch-tall species with pale to dark purple flowers featuring brilliant orange styles. Zones 3 to 8.

C. minimus   P. 82

c. MIN-ih-mus. Late spring–blooming 3-inch-tall species with rich lilac-purple flowers and yellow-buff outer petals marked in dark purple. Zones 3 to 8.

C. niveus

c. NIV-ee-us. Fall-blooming 4- to 6-inch-tall species with white or pale lilac flowers featuring showy orange styles. Requires dry conditions in summer once plants have gone dormant. Zones 5 to 8.

C. ochroleucus

c. o-kro-LEW-kus. Fall-blooming 2-inch-tall species with creamy white flowers that have yellow throats. Zones 5 to 8.

C. pulchellus

c. pul-CHEL-us. Fall- to early winter–blooming 4- to 5-inch-tall species with pale lilac-blue flowers that have yellow throats. Zones 3 to 8.

C. sativus   P. 83

c. sah-TEE-vus. Saffron Crocus. Fall- to early winter–blooming 2-inch-tall species bearing lilac-purple flowers veined in dark purple. The showy red styles are the source of the spice saffron. Plants do not flower well in areas with cool, wet summers. Zones 5 to 8.

C. sieberi P. 83

c. SYE-ber-eye. Late winter– to early spring–blooming 2- to 3-inch-tall species bearing rose-purple flowers with yellow throats. 'Bowles White' bears white flowers; 'Firefly' has white blooms that are white on the outside and flushed with pale violet on the inside; 'Tricolor' features lilac-blue flowers and golden yellow centers edged in white. Zones 5 to 8.

C. speciosus P. 84

c. spee-see-O-sus. Fall Crocus. Vigorous, fall-blooming 4- to 6-inch-tall species with violet-blue flowers with darker purple-blue veins. Zones 3 to 8.

C. tommasinianus P. 84

c. tom-ah-sin-ee-AH-nus. Vigorous, late winter– to early spring–blooming species that reaches 3 to 4 inches and bears pale lilac to red-purple blooms. Good for naturalizing. 'Barr's Purple' bears violet flowers that are silvery on the outside. 'Ruby Giant' bears red-purple flowers. 'Whitewell Purple' bears red-purple blooms. Zones 3 to 8.

C. vernus P. 85

c. VER-nus. Dutch Crocus. Popular spring-blooming species reaching 4 to 5 inches and bearing white, pale lilac, or rich purple flowers. Many cultivars are available, including 'Flower Record', with dark purple blooms; 'Jeanne d'Arc', white with a purple base; 'Pickwick', white striped with purple; 'Mammoth Yellow', yellow; and 'Remembrance', violet-purple. Vigorous and good for naturalizing. Zones 3 to 8.

C. versicolor

c. VER-sih-kuh-lor. Late winter– to early spring–blooming 5- to 6-inch-tall species with white flowers sometimes striped with purple on the outside and lemon yellow throats. Zones 3 to 8.

❦ *Curcuma*

kur-KOO-muh. Ginger family, Zingiberaceae.

Curcuma species are tropical perennials native from India and Malay to Australia that grow from thick, fleshy, branching, aromatic rhizomes. Plants have reedlike stems and bear lance- or somewhat paddle-shaped leaf blades. Sometimes called pinecone gingers, they are grown for their large inflorescences that resemble colorful pinecones: showy, overlapping bracts often hide the true flowers, which are small and tubular, with three petals. The rhizomes of some species have been used as herbs, including *C. longa* (also listed as *C. domestica*), commonly known as turmeric and used both medicinally and in curries. True gingers belong to the genus *Zingiber*, and culinary ginger is *Z. officinale.*

HOW TO GROW

Give these plants partial shade and deeply prepared, moist soil rich in organic matter. They thrive in areas with warm summers and high humidity and are ideal for gardens in the tropics and subtropics or for adding an exotic touch to more northern gardens in summer. Where hardy, they can be grown outdoors year-round. In the North, plant the rhizomes out in spring after the soil has warmed up. To overwinter, dig the rhizomes after a light frost and cut back the tops. Store the rhizomes in barely damp vermiculite, peat, or sand in a cool (55° to 60°F), dry place. Inspect rhizomes ocassionally in winter: discard rotted pieces or cut away rotted portions and dust cuts with sulfur; sprinkle the vermiculite with water occasionally during winter to keep the roots from shriveling. Replant in spring. These plants also make excellent year-round container plants: keep them nearly dry in winter. Propagate by dividing the rhizomes in spring.

C. alismatifolia   P. 86
c. al-iss-mah-tih-FO-lee-uh. Pinecone Ginger, Siam Tulip. A 1½- to 2-foot-tall species with dark green leaves and small inflorescences of pink bracts. Zones 8 to 10.

C. petiolata
c. peh-tee-o-LAH-tuh. Queen Lily. A 2- to 3-foot-tall species with 10-inch-long leaves and 6-inch-long bloom spikes in summer that have tiny ½-inch-long yellow and white flowers surrounded by violet upper bracts and green lower bracts. Zones 8 to 10.

C. roscoeana
c. ros-ko-ee-AH-nuh. Jewel of Burma. A 2½- to 3-foot-tall species with oval leaves and erect 8-inch-long spikes in summer with yellow ½-inch-long flowers surrounded by showy orange bracts. Zones 8 to 10.

C. zedoaria   P. 86
c. zeh-do-AH-ree-uh. Pinecone Ginger. A 3-foot-tall species with handsome 1-foot-long rounded to lance-shaped leaves that have a maroon-brown

stripe down the center. In summer, it bears 4-inch-long bloom spikes with green bracts tinged with maroon-red or purple. Zones 8 to 10.

❦ *Cyclamen*

SYE-klah-men. Primrose family, Primulaceae.

Florist's cyclamen are fairly well known to gardeners and nongardeners alike, but this genus also contains several charming hardy species that deserve to be more widely grown. Hardy cyclamen are diminutive versions of the showy florist's pot plants: they grow from rounded tubers that actually are stem tubers rather than conventional tubers—see page 4 for more information on these structures. Plants have attractive, heart- to kidney-shaped dark green leaves usually handsomely marked with silver. Depending on the species, plants bloom in late winter to early spring or from late summer to fall. Their small pink or white blooms are carried on leafless stalks above the foliage and resemble shuttlecocks: they are solitary and nodding and have five reflexed (backward pointing) petals that are slightly twisted and are joined in a short tube at the base of the flower. In most species, once the flowers are pollinated the flower stalks (peduncles) coil down to the soil surface to release the seeds: the botanical name refers to this characteristic—it is from the Greek *kyklos*, circular. About 19 species belong to the genus, most native from Europe and the Mediterranean to Iran.

HOW TO GROW

For most species of hardy cyclamen, select a site in partial shade with loose soil that is well drained and rich in organic matter. Plant the tubers 1½ to 2 inches deep, spaced 3 to 4 inches apart. When the leaves fade each year, mulch the plants with compost or leaf mold, and mark their locations to avoid digging into them by mistake when plants are dormant. (Fall-blooming species are green from late summer or fall through spring and disappear in summer.) In areas where cyclamen are marginally hardy, mulch the plants in late fall with evergreen branches, oak leaves, or another coarse mulch to protect them from winter freezing and thawing cycles. Some species, including *C. creticum*, require dry soil when they are dormant. Grow them in a cold frame or cold greenhouse, or try them in pots sunk to the rim in the soil in summer in a spot that offers excellent drainage, then overwinter the pots in a cold frame or greenhouse where they can be protected from rain during their dormant season. Propagate by seeds: cyclamen tubers grow larger each year, but they do not produce offsets. Plants may self-sow.

C. cilicium

c. sih-LIH-see-um. A fall-blooming 2-inch-tall species with green ½- to 2-inch-long leaves heavily marked with silver. Bears pink or white ½- to ¾ inch-long flowers with dark red at the base of the petals. Can be grown as above or planted with the tubers at a depth of about 1 inch and given dry conditions after the foliage goes dormant in early summer. Flowers are produced with the leaves. Zones 5 to 9.

C. coum   P. 87

c. KOOM. Hardy Cyclamen. A late winter– to early spring–blooming 2- to 3-inch-tall species with attractive, rounded 1- to 2½-inch-long leaves that are either solid dark green or marked with silver; either way, they remain green over winter. Bears ½-inch-long flowers ranging from white to shades of pale to dark pink or pinkish red. Petals have dark reddish pink blotches at the base. Flowers appear with the leaves. Zones 5 to 9.

C. creticum

c. KREH-tih-kum. A spring-blooming 2- to 3-inch-tall species with 1½-inch-long gray-green leaves and white to pale pink ½- to 1-inch-long flowers. Plant tubers no more than 1 inch deep, or with the top of the tuber right at the soil surface, and give plants very well drained soil. They require dry soil conditions when dormant. Flowers appear with the leaves. Zones 7 to 9.

C. hederifolium   P. 87

c. heh-der-ih-FO-lee-um. Hardy Cyclamen. Formerly *C. neapolitanum*. Fall-blooming 4- to 5-inch-tall species bearing dark green 2- to 6-inch-long leaves that may be triangular or heart shaped and often are heavily patterned with silver. Bears 1-inch-long flowers in shades of pink with darker pink blotches at the base of the petals. Flowers appear before the leaves. Zones 6 or 7 to 9.

C. persicum

c. PER-sih-kum. Florist's Cyclamen. A tender species with 8-inch-tall mounds of dark green 1- to 5-inch-wide leaves often patterned in silver. Bears fragrant ½- to 1-inch-long flowers atop the foliage from late winter to early spring. Plant tubers no more than 1 inch deep, or with the top of the tuber right at the soil surface, and give plants very well drained soil.

They require cool (55° to 60°F), humid conditions when growing actively and dry soil conditions when dormant in summer. Zones 10 to 11.

C. purpurascens

c. pur-pur-AS-sens. Also listed as *C. europaeum, C. fatrense*. A mid- to late summer–blooming species that reaches about 4 inches. Bears 3-inch-long dark green leaves that are evergreen or sometimes deciduous and may have faint silver markings. Fragrant magenta-pink ¾-inch-long flowers appear with the leaves. Best in alkaline soil. Zones 5 to 9.

C. repandum   P. 88

c. reh-PAN-dum. Hardy Cyclamen. A spring-blooming 4- to 6-inch-tall species with dark green 5-inch-long leaves spotted or marked with gray-green. Bears fragrant magenta-pink ¾-inch-long flowers that appear with the leaves. Zones 7 to 9.

❦ Cypella

sih-PEL-uh. Iris family, Iridaceae.

Native to Central and South America, *Cypella* species are sometimes grown for their unusual-looking irislike flowers. The plants, which grow from elongated tunicate bulbs, bear pleated, lance-shaped leaves. The short-lived flowers are borne singly or in small clusters. The individual blooms consist of six petal-like tepals. The outer tepals are showy and spreading, while the much smaller inner tepals are erect and curve toward the center of the flowers. Although each flower lasts only a day, blooms in each cluster open in succession and plants produce new clusters from late summer to fall.

HOW TO GROW

Select a site in full sun with average to rich, well-drained soil. Sandy soil is ideal, and plants are best in a warm site. Plant the bulbs at a depth of 3 inches. Where they're hardy, grow them outdoors year-round: plant them in fall and protect the sites with mulch over winter. In the North, plant the bulbs in spring, and overwinter them indoors. To overwinter, dig the bulbs after the first frost in fall, cut off the tops, dry them off, and dust off excess soil. Or, keep them in pots year-round: gradually withhold water and keep the soil dry in winter. Either way, store them in a cool (40° to 45°F), dry place. Propagate by offsets in late winter or early spring or by seeds.

C. herbertii

P. 88

c. her-BER-tee-eye. A 1- to 3-foot-tall species native from Brazil south to Argentina. Bears loose clusters of 1½- to 3-inch-wide flowers with yellowish orange outer tepals and inner tepals spotted or lined with purple. Zones 9 to 10.

❦ Cyrtanthus

sir-TAN-thus. Amaryllis family, Amaryllidaceae.

Commonly known as fire lilies, *Cyrtanthus* species are bulbous plants native to Africa, primarily South Africa. The common name refers to the fact that these plants typically bloom most abundantly after fires sweep through their native habitat. Flowers, which may be fragrant, are borne in umbels atop leafless stalks and are either held horizontally or are pendulous. Individual blooms are tubular or funnel shaped, with a long, narrow, somewhat curved tube and six short petal-like tepals that usually flare out. Typically, the flowers come in shades of red and orange-red. Plants grow from tunicate bulbs that are either underground or partially exposed and bear strap-shaped or linear leaves that may be deciduous or evergreen.

HOW TO GROW

Select a site in full sun with average to rich, well-drained soil. Like many South African species, these plants need regular watering from late winter or early spring through summer when they are growing actively, and drier conditions when dormant in winter. In areas where they are hardy and that offer dry conditions in fall and winter, leave the corms in the ground year-round. In areas where they are marginally hardy, look for a protected, south-facing site and mulch plants over winter with evergreen boughs, salt hay, pine needles, or another coarse mulch. In the North and anywhere winters are wet, grow these plants in containers year-round or plant the bulbs in spring after the soil has warmed up and overwinter indoors. They bloom best when left undisturbed, so container culture is the best option in areas where they cannot be left outside year-round. Plant the bulbs in spring, setting them at a depth of 2 to 3 inches. Water regularly in dry weather. Gradually dry off the soil in containers in fall and store the pots in a cool (40° to 50°F), dry spot over winter. Or dig the bulbs in fall after the first light frost — earlier if the leaves die back — let them dry in a warm, shady spot for a few hours; brush off excess soil; and store them over winter in a cool, dry place. Propagate by separating and planting the offsets in spring or fall or by sowing seeds.

C. elatus
P. 89

c. eh-LAY-tus. Formerly *C. purpureus, Vallota speciosa.* A 1- to 2-foot-tall species with strap-shaped leaves and umbels of two to nine funnel-shaped 3- to 4-inch-long scarlet flowers in late summer. Zones 10 to 11.

❧ Dactylorhiza

dak-til-o-RYE-zuh. Orchid family, Orchidaceae.

This genus contains about 30 species of hardy terrestrial orchids that grow from fingerlike tubers: the botanical name, which refers to the roots, is from the Greek *daktylos,* finger, and *rhiza,* root. Commonly called marsh or spotted orchids, *Dactylorhiza* species bear fleshy leaves that are linear or lance shaped and sometimes spotted with purple. They produce showy, erect racemes of densely packed flowers in spring or summer. The individual flowers have showy lower lips and come in shades of rose-purple, violet-purple, red, pink, and white. Most species are native to Europe, northern Africa, and Asia, but one species is found in North America.

HOW TO GROW
Select a site in partial shade with moist, well-drained soil that is deeply prepared and rich in organic matter. These plants are happiest in areas with cool summers, such as the Pacific Northwest. They can be hard to establish: for best results look for a cool site protected from afternoon sun. Mulch the soil in spring with chopped leaves to keep it moist and cool. Plants resent root disturbance, so once established, transplant or divide them only if absolutely necessary. Propagate by division in spring.

D. maculata
P. 89

d. mak-yoo-LAH-tuh. Heath Spotted Orchid. A ½- to 2-foot-tall species with lance-shaped leaves that may be green or spotted with brown or purple. Bears racemes of rose-pink, mauve, reddish pink, or white flowers from spring to late summer. Zones 5 to 8.

❧ Dahlia

DAHL-ee-uh. Aster family, Asteraceae.

Dahlia contains some 30 species of tuberous-rooted, tender perennials from Central and South America, but gardeners are much more familiar with the hybrids of these popular plants. There are literally thousands to choose from with showy flowers in an array of shapes and sizes, from enormous doubles 10 inches or more wide to petite daisylike singles. Dahlias bloom from midsummer to frost, and flowers come in all colors except true blue. The plants have fleshy, pinnate leaves that are green or sometimes bronze or maroon.

HOW TO GROW

Give dahlias a site in full sun and rich, well-drained, evenly moist soil. Plants benefit from good air circulation but need protection from wind. They tolerate a site with only a half-day of sun but bloom less; in areas with very hot summers, shade during the hottest part of the day provides beneficial heat protection. Grow dahlias outdoors year-round from Zone 8 south. (In a protected site and heavily mulched over winter, they can survive in Zone 7.) In the North, grow them as tender perennials over-wintered indoors or as annuals.

Most gardeners start dahlias from pieces of the tuberous roots, commonly referred to as tubers, which are the only way to acquire most of the improved cultivars. Dahlias are fairly easy from seeds, too, and seeds offer the advantage of lots of plants for very little money. To start from tubers, start with thick, firm, fleshy tubers that each have a piece of stem attached: the eyes, or growing buds, are on the main stem, not on the tuber itself. Set tubers outdoors no more than 2 weeks before the last frost date (delay planting if the weather has been cold or wet), planting in a 6-inch-deep trench with the eyes, or buds, pointed up and about 2 inches below the soil surface (4 inches in hot climates). For a head start in areas with short seasons, pot up tubers indoors 4 to 6 weeks before the last frost date with the buds just above the soil surface, and keep in a warm (60° to 75°F), bright spot. Keep the soil barely moist until sprouts appear in 2 to 4 weeks. Move them to the garden after the last spring frost date, and plant them with the top of the tubers at the soil surface. Dahlias begin flowering about 2 to 2½ months after planting.

For cultivars that exceed 3 feet in height, install stakes *before* planting. For full-size plants, 6- to 7-foot stakes driven 1½ feet into the ground should suffice. Set the tubers with the eye nearest the stake. When planting individual tubers, pinch off all but two shoots; when planting small clumps of tubers, pinch off all but four to eight. Pinch shoots again when they have two to three sets of leaves to encourage branching and bushy growth. For full-size dahlias, when stems reach 2 feet, begin loosely tying them to their stakes with strips of cloth or nylon stockings. Mulch in early summer and water regularly. Feed plants first after thinning stems, again when buds first appear, and a third time about a month later. Deadhead-ing encourages new flowers to form. To pick dahlias for arrangements, cut them when the flowers are nearly open but still firm in the center.

To overwinter the roots, cut the stalks back to about 6 inches after frost and dig them up. Shake off the excess soil, and turn the clumps up-side down for a few hours to dry. (Some gardeners dig the clumps and re-tain as much soil around them as possible, dry them off, and store the clumps—soil and all—in dry sand over winter.) Attach labels to the clumps as you dig them, otherwise you won't be able to keep track of names or colors. Store them in a well-ventilated, relatively dry, cool (36° to 45°F), frost-free spot in boxes of barely moist vermiculite or sand, in paper bags or wrapped in newspaper, or in plastic bags punched with plenty of air holes. High humidity causes rot. Storing the clumps whole is best, but if you divide in fall, dust cuts with sulfur before storage. Inspect monthly for signs of rotting. Trim off rotted spots and dust the cuts with sulfur. Lightly mist the tubers if they begin to shrivel.

D. hybrids

PP. 90, 91

Dahlias come in a wealth of sizes, shapes, and heights. Enthusiasts recog-nize 16 different flower shapes, including cactus, waterlily, ball, anemone, collarette, and single dahlias. Size categories range from giant (or AA) blooms, which exceed 10 inches, to miniatures, which are 2 inches or less across. For dahlias that produce the most blooms per plant, stick to culti-vars with flowers under 6 inches across. If you prefer low-growing plants, look for the words "dwarf" or "bedding" in the description. These will generally range from 1 to 1½ feet tall. (With dahlias the term "miniature" refers to the flowers only, and miniatures are as large as other standard-size plants.) Standard-size plants range from 3½ to 6 feet. 'Bambino Mixed' and Coltness hybrids are dwarf plants that can be started from seeds. Seed mixes for full-size plants also are available. 'Bishop of Llandaff' bears orange-red flowers with maroon foliage. 'Ellen Houston' bears orange-red flowers and greenish black leaves. 'Fascination' bears pink flowers and green-black foliage. Zones 8 to 11.

❧ *Dichelostemma*

dye-keh-lo-STEM-uh. Lily family, Liliaceae.

Native to the western United States, *Dichelostemma* species are perennials closely related to *Brodiaea* as well as *Triteleia*. They are grown for their showy umbels or racemes of tubular- to bell-shaped flowers borne atop thin, leafless stalks. The flowers have tubular bases that extend at least half the length of the flowers and then separate into six petal-like tepals (often called petals). The leaves are basal and linear, and in most cases die back just as the flowers open. Like crocuses and glads, *Dichelostemma* species grow from corms. The individual corms last only one year, but are replaced annually as new ones develop during the growing season. Seven species belong to this genus, all once included in *Brodiaea*.

HOW TO GROW

Select a site in full sun or partial shade that has rich, well-drained soil. Plant corms in early fall, setting them 3 to 5 inches deep, depending on the size. They are most effective planted in drifts or clumps with fairly close spacing — 2 to 3 inches apart. Plants require even moisture when they are actively growing, but once the leaves die down and plants go dormant in summer, they require warm, dry conditions. In the West, where *Dichelostemma* species grow naturally in dry grasslands and woodlands, these plants are ideal for naturalizing. In areas where they are marginally hardy, plant them in a protected spot and cover the site over winter with a loose mulch of evergreen branches, pine needles, or salt hay. In the North and in areas with rainy summers, grow them in containers or try them in rock gardens or other sites that offer the excellent drainage and dry summer conditions they require. Container-grown plants are easy to move to a warm, dry site that is protected from rain to ensure a dry dormant period. Overwinter container-grown plants indoors in a cool (40° to 45°F), dry spot, then repeat the cycle in spring. Since the foliage often is dying back when the plants are flowering, underplant with shallow-rooted annuals such as sweet alyssum *(Lobularia maritima)* or Johnny-jump-ups *(Viola tricolor)* to fill in around the yellowing leaves. Propagate by separating offsets just as the plants go dormant or by seeds.

D. congestum   P. 92

d. con-JES-tum. Formerly *Brodiaea congesta*. A 1½- to 2-foot-tall species with dense, rounded 2-inch-wide racemes of purplish blue flowers in early summer. Individual flowers are tubular, ¾ inch long, and slightly constricted at the throat. *D. pulchellum,* commonly called blue dicks or wild hyacinth and formerly listed as *B. capitata* and *B. pulchella,* is a similar 1- to 2-foot-tall species with purple-blue flowers that are not constricted at the throat. Both are hardy in Zones 6 to 10.

D. ida-maia

P. 92

d. EYE-dah mah-EE-uh. Firecracker Plant. Formerly *Brodiaea ida-maia*. A 1- to 2½-foot-tall species bearing exotic-looking umbels of 10 to 12 or more nodding, tubular ¾- to 1-inch-long flowers in summer. The flowers are red with short (¼ inch long) yellow-green lobes at the tip that roll back. Zones 6 to 10.

❧ Dierama

dye-er-RAH-muh. Iris family, Iridaceae.

Commonly known as wand flowers or angel's fishing rods, *Dierama* species are grown for their graceful, arching spikes of pendent flowers that appear in late spring, where winters are mild, or in summer. The botanical name is from the Greek *dierama*, funnel, a reference to the flowers, which can be funnel or bell shaped. About 44 species belong to the genus, all native to Africa. They produce clumps of arching, grassy leaves that are green to gray-green in color and range from deciduous to nearly evergreen. The plants grow from corms, which last only one year but are replaced annually as new ones develop during the growing season.

HOW TO GROW

Select a site in full sun with rich, well-drained soil. A site sheltered from wind is best, and wand flowers are ideal for growing along ponds or streams where the soil is naturally moist. Plant the bulbs in fall at a depth of about 3 inches. Plants resent root disturbance and can be slow to reestablish, so once they are in the ground, they are best left undisturbed unless they become too crowded. Keep the soil evenly moist when the plants are growing actively in spring and summer; they require dry soil conditions when dormant. Where hardy, wand flowers can be grown outdoors year-round. In the North, grow them in containers. To overwinter container-grown plants, gradually withhold water as the foliage begins to die back, then store the pots in a cool (50°F), dry place over winter. Propagate by digging the clumps and separating the offsets in spring or by seeds.

D. pendulum

P. 93

d. PEN-dew-lum. Grassy Bells, Wand Flower. South African native reaching 3 to 6 feet in height and bearing arching stems of bell-shaped purple-pink 1½- to 2-inch-long flowers in summer. Zones 7 to 9.

❦ *Dodecatheon*

doe-dee-KATH-ee-on. Primrose family, Primulaceae.

Grown for their spring clusters of cyclamen- or shuttlecock-shaped flowers, *Dodecatheon* species are perennials primarily native to North America. About 14 species belong here, found in moist grasslands, alpine meadows, and sometimes woodlands. They grow from short rhizomes and either thick or fleshy roots; some species produce tiny bulblets. Commonly known as shooting stars (another common name is American cowslip), they produce a low basal rosette of lance-shaped, spoon-shaped, or rounded leaves topped in spring by umbels of 2 to 10 or more flowers held on leafless stalks high above the foliage. The small pendent flowers have five reflexed (backward pointing) petals and stamens united to form a beaklike projection. *Dodecatheon* flowers resemble those of cyclamen (*Cyclamen* spp.), which are close relatives, but cyclamen bear only solitary flowers that lack a beaklike projection, and they also grow from tubers. *Dodecatheon* plants go dormant shortly after they finish blooming.

HOW TO GROW

Select a site in full sun or partial shade with rich, moist, well-drained soil that is slightly acid to neutral in pH. In areas with warm summers, a spot with afternoon shade is best, since plants prefer cool conditions. Mulching helps keep the soil moist and cool. Since the plants go dormant and disappear completely in summer, mark their locations and combine them with other perennials that are not too vigorous or with annuals. Propagate by division in spring or by seeds.

D. clevelandii

d. cleve-LAN-dee-eye. California native ranging from 12 to 16 inches in height and forming a 6-inch-wide rosette of leaves. Bears umbels of 10 to 20 ¾-inch-long reddish purple flowers in early spring. Requires dry conditions during its summer dormancy. Zones 5 to 7.

D. dentatum

d. den-TAH-tum. An 8-inch-tall species native to western North America that forms an 8-inch-wide rosette of leaves. Bears small umbels of up to five ½- to ¾-inch-long white flowers in late spring. Best in a spot with moist soil in shade. Zones 5 to 7.

D. meadia P. 93

d. MEE-dee-uh. Common Shooting Star. A clump-forming wildflower native to the edges of woodlands and prairies from the eastern United States west to Texas. Forms low 1-foot-wide rosettes of leaves. Bears clusters of 12 to 15 magenta-pink ½- to ¾-inch-long flowers on 1½-foot-tall stalks in mid- and late spring. *D. meadia* f. *album* bears white flowers. Zones 4 to 8.

❧ *Dracunculus*

dra-KUNK-yew-lus. Arum family, Araceae.

Dracunculus species are tuberous perennials grown for their exotic, but foul-smelling, blooms. Three species belong to the genus, all native to the Mediterranean and the Canary Islands. As the common name dragon arum suggests, *Dracunculus* species are closely related to arums (*Arum* spp.). They also are kin to the more familiar Jack-in-the-pulpits (*Arisaema* spp.). The exotic-looking "flowers" actually are an inflorescence consisting of many tiny flowers clustered on a long thick central stalk, called a spadix. The spadix is surrounded by a large showy modified leaf, called a spathe. Leaves are divided into fingerlike lobes (those of arums are always arrow shaped) and may be marbled with white.

HOW TO GROW

Give these plants a spot in full sun or partial shade with rich, well-drained soil. Plants require soil that is moist in spring and early summer, when they are growing actively, and drier once they go dormant later in the season. Where they are hardy, plant the tubers 6 inches deep in fall; plant them in spring in areas where they are not hardy. In the North, grow these plants in containers or plant directly in the soil and dig the tubers in early fall after the foliage fades. Keep the soil evenly moist while the plants are in leaf, but gradually withhold water later in the summer as they enter dormancy. To overwinter them indoors, either dig the tubers and store them in dry peat or store them in pots with the soil kept dry. Either way, keep them in a cool (50° to 55°F), dry place. Propagate by seeds or by separating offsets when the tubers are dormant in spring or fall.

D. vulgaris P. 94

d. vul-GAIR-iss. Formerly *Arum dracunculus*. A spring- or summer-blooming species that normally is about 3 feet tall but can reach 5 feet. Plants spread to about 2 feet and bear 1-foot-long dark green leaves marked with white that have up to 15 lobes. The inflorescence consists of a dark maroon, velvety-textured 1½-foot-long spathe surrounding a nearly black 1-foot-long spadix. Zones 8 to 10.

❦ *Endymion* see *Hyacinthoides*

❦ *Eranthis*

eh-RAN-thiss. Buttercup family, Ranunculaceae.

Commonly known as winter aconites, *Eranthis* species are among the earliest flowers of spring. Their yellow cup-shaped flowers, each with a ruff of green beneath the blooms, appear in very early spring—the botanical name is from the Greek *er*, spring, and *anthos*, flower. Flowers, which are borne on leafless stems, consist of showy petal-like sepals that are yellow or white. The true petals are reduced to tubular nectaries. The leafy green collar under the blooms is a single, deeply divided leaf: all the other leaves are basal and also deeply divided. Plants grow from short rhizomes that have knobby tubers. About seven species belong to the genus.

HOW TO GROW

Select a site in full sun to partial shade with rich, moist, but not wet, soil. Winter aconites tolerate drier conditions in summer once the leaves have died back. They thrive on the edges of wooded areas under deciduous trees, where they receive full spring sunshine while they are growing actively but are in shade when dormant in summer. Like other vigorous, spring-blooming bulbs such as crocuses, they are ideal for naturalizing or using at the front of lightly shaded beds and borders. Plant tubers 2 inches deep and 3 inches apart in fall. Soak them overnight in warm water before planting. Old tubers that have dried out too much may not grow. Mulch in summer with well-rotted compost to keep the soil rich and moist. Clumps are best left undisturbed once established, and they form large drifts where happy. Dig and divide them in late spring, just as the leaves die down, if they become too crowded, outgrow their space, or for propagation. Plants also self-sow, and seedlings are easy to move.

E. cilicia

e. sil-IH-see-uh. Winter Aconite. A 2- to 3-inch-tall species bearing very finely lobed green leaves tinged with bronze and ¾- to 1½-inch-wide yellow flowers in early spring. Zones 4 to 9.

E. hyemalis P. 94

e. hi-MAL-iss. Winter Aconite. A 2- to 3-inch-tall species bearing lobed green leaves and ¾- to 1¼-inch-wide yellow flowers in late winter to early spring. Zones 4 to 9.

❧ *Eremurus*

air-eh-MURE-us. Lily family, Liliaceae.

Both the common and botanical names of *Eremurus* species make reference to the cylindrical racemes of these stately plants. They are commonly called foxtail lilies and desert candles, and the botanical name is from the Greek *eremos,* solitary, and *oura,* tail. About 40 to 50 species belong to the genus, all of which grow from fleshy roots that spread out around a central crown. They bear basal, usually strap-shaped, leaves that reach about 1 foot in length and die back after the plants flower. Each crown produces a single, tail-like bloom that consists of literally hundreds of small densely packed flowers that are starry in shape and have prominent, often showy, stamens. Blooms come in shades of pink, yellow, and white and have six petal-like tepals.

HOW TO GROW
Select a site in full sun that is protected from wind and has rich, well-drained soil. Sandy soil is ideal, and plants will not tolerate the poorly drained conditions offered by heavy clay soil. Plant the fleshy roots in fall. Handle them carefully, as they are brittle and easily broken. Prepare the site deeply (to about 2 feet) at planting time. The roots need to be planted at a depth of 4 to 6 inches and require a wide hole so their starfish-like arms can be spread out evenly. Set the roots on top of a layer of coarse sand or grit at the bottom of the hole to ensure excellent drainage. Mark their locations to avoid digging into them by accident when they are dormant either in winter or from late summer onward. Plants begin growing very early in spring, and late frosts can severely damage the top growth. To protect them, cover the site with a 3- to 4-inch-deep layer of compost, sand, or sawdust in late fall after the ground has frozen to a depth of 1 to 2 inches. In spring, if plants emerge above this layer before the danger of frost has passed, cover the new growth with evergreen branches or coarse leaves (such as oak leaves). Or protect them with large cardboard boxes overnight. Remove the mounds of mulch once danger of frost has passed.

Use foxtail lilies at the backs of perennial borders—they are especially effective when set against a dark background such as evergreens— and plant them in drifts to emphasize their bold, vertical lines. Leaves die down as the flowers fade, so plant them behind lower-growing perennials to hide the spaces they leave. Foxtail lilies are best left undisturbed once planted. Dig and divide them if necessary for propagation just as the leaves die down. Or start from seeds, which are slow to germinate.

E. himalaicus   P. 95

e. him-ah-LAY-ih-kus. Himalayan Foxtail Lily. A white-flowered species bearing 3-foot-long racemes of starry 1-inch-wide flowers in late spring and early summer. Plants reach 4 to 6 feet tall in bloom. Zones 5 to 8.

E. × isabellinus

e. × iss-ah-bell-EYE-nus. A hybrid species bearing ½- to 2-foot-long racemes of ¾- to 1½-inch-wide flowers in early summer in shades of pink, yellow, orange, and white. Plants are 6 to 8 feet tall in bloom. Many cultivars are available, including Reiter Hybrids, which come in a wide range of rich colors. 'Cleopatra' is a Reiter Hybrid with burnt orange flowers. Shelford Hybrids come in reds, pink, orange, yellow, and white. 'Pinokkio' ('Pinocchio') bears bright yellow flowers with orange anthers. 'White Beauty' bears white flowers. Zones 5 to 8.

E. robustus

e. ro-BUS-tus. Vigorous species, reaching 10 feet in bloom, that bears 4-foot-long leaves and 3- to 4-foot-long racemes of pale pink 1½-inch-wide flowers with yellow stamens from early to midsummer. Zones 5 to 8.

E. stenophyllus   P. 95

e. sten-o-FIL-us. Foxtail Lily. Fairly compact species, to 3 feet in bloom, bearing ½- to 1-foot-long racemes of dark yellow ¾-inch-wide flowers from early to midsummer. Flowers turn orange, then brown, as they fade. E. stenophyllus ssp. stenophyllus (sometimes listed as E. bungei) bears bright yellow flowers on 5-foot-tall plants. Zones 5 to 8.

❦ Erythronium

air-ih-THRO-nee-um. Lily family, Liliaceae.

These charming members of the lily family have a host of common names, including dogtooth violets, trout lilies, adder's tongues, and fawn lilies. They are grown for their nodding pink, white, yellow, or cream lily-like flowers that are borne in late spring to early summer. Unlike many bulbous plants, erythroniums also bear handsome leaves that are broad to oval in shape and often mottled with brown or cream. Each bulb bears two or sometimes three leaves. The yellowish white bulbs (which some sources describe as corms) have a membranous covering and are long and tooth or fang shaped. They are buried deep in the ground, with un-branched, subterranean stems leading up to the soil surface. Some species spread by offsets and stolons. Flowers are borne on leafless stalks, either singly or in small graceful racemes. Each individual bloom has six petal-like tepals. In some species they are strongly reflexed, meaning curved backward. About 22 species belong to the genus, native to North America, Asia, and Europe.

HOW TO GROW

Select a site in partial or dappled shade and deeply prepared, evenly moist soil rich in organic matter. Plant the bulbs in fall, setting the toothlike roots upright, not lengthwise, with 4 to 6 inches of soil over the tops. Do not let the bulbs dry out before planting; keep them packed in barely damp peat moss or vermiculite and keep them in a cool, shady place. Plant as soon as possible. Mulch plantings with chopped leaves, compost, or shredded bark to keep the soil rich, moist, and cool. Propagate by seeds, which are slow to germinate and reach blooming size, or by dividing clumps in summer immediately after they flower. Plants may self-sow.

E. americanum

e. ah-mair-ih-KAH-num. Yellow Adder's Tongue, Trout Lily. Wildflower native to eastern North America that reaches 3 to 6 inches in height. Bears 6-inch-long green leaves mottled with purple and solitary yellow flowers that are 1 to 2 inches across in spring. Zones 3 to 9.

E. californicum

e. kal-ih-FOR-nih-kum. Fawn Lily. A 6- to 14-inch-tall California native with rounded 3-inch-long green leaves lightly marked with brownish green. Bears creamy white 2- to 3-inch-wide flowers in spring, either singly or in racemes of up to three blooms. 'White Beauty' is a vigorous white-flow-ered selection. Zones 3 to 9.

E. dens-canis   P. 96

e. denz-KAY-niss. European Dogtooth Violet. A 4- to 6-inch-tall species with elliptic 4- to 6-inch-long green leaves marked with purple-brown. Bears solitary 1½-inch-wide flowers in spring in shades of pink, lilac, and white. Many cultivars are available, including 'Lilac Wonder', with purple flowers that have a single brown spot at the base of each petal; 'Pink Perfection', with pink flowers; 'Purple King', with rich purple flowers striped with pale brown and cream in the center; and 'Rose Queen', with rich, deep pink flowers. Zones 3 to 9.

E. grandiflorum
e. gran-dih-FLOR-um. A species native to western North America that reaches 6 to 12 inches in height and has solid green 4- to 8-inch-long rounded leaves. Bears yellow 2-inch-wide flowers in spring, either singly or in racemes of up to three. Zones 4 to 9.

E. hendersonii   P. 96
e. hen-der-SO-nee-eye. Dogtooth Violet. Wildflower native to the Pacific Northwest ranging from 6 to 14 inches in height and bearing 4- to 8-inch-long green leaves marked with pale brownish green bands. In spring, bears 2-inch-wide pale lilac flowers in racemes of up to 10 flowers. Plants prefer a spot that dries out during the summer (when they are dormant). Zones 3 to 9.

E. 'Pagoda'
A showy, vigorous hybrid ranging from 6 to 14 inches in height and bearing rounded green leaves heavily marked with bronze. In spring, produces rich sulphur yellow blooms in clusters of 2 to as many as 10 flowers. Zones 4 to 9.

E. revolutum   P. 97
e. rev-oh-LOO-tum. Western Trout Lily. An 8- to 12-inch-tall species native to the Pacific Northwest that has 6- to 8-inch-long green leaves heavily marked with brown. In spring, bears 1½- to 3-inch-wide lilac-pink flowers in racemes of up to four blooms. 'Pink Beauty' has deep lilac-pink blooms. Zones 5 to 9.

E. tuolumnense   P. 97
e. too-lum-NEN-see. An 8- to 14-inch-tall California native with rounded 8- to 12-inch-long green leaves. Bears racemes of four to seven yellow 1- to 2-inch-wide flowers in spring. Zones 3 to 9.

❦ *Eucharis*

YOO-kah-riss. Amaryllis family, Amaryllidaceae.

These handsome bulbs are grown for their clusters of sweetly fragrant white daffodil-like flowers. They grow from tunicate bulbs and also feature handsome, broad, hostalike leaves. The flowers have six spreading lobes surrounding a central cup that resembles the cup of a daffodil. The cup is formed by the filaments of the six stamens, which broaden and join at the base. Flowers are borne in umbels on leafless stalks well above the foliage. The genus contains 17 species of evergreen bulbs native to Central and South America. Despite the common name Amazon lily, they are not true lilies nor are they native to areas along the Amazon River. Instead they are found primarily in the Andes in Columbia and Peru—as well as in Central America.

HOW TO GROW

Give these tropical plants a spot in partial, dappled shade with average to rich soil that is well drained. They thrive in heat and humidity, but the large leaves burn if exposed to bright sunlight. While Amazon lilies can be grown outdoors year-round from Zone 9 south, in the North, plant them in containers or tubs. (Even in Zone 9, protect plants when temperatures threaten to dip below freezing.) They can be kept indoors year-round or moved outdoors during the summer months. Amazon lilies grow best, and are most effective, in large pots with several bulbs per pot—at least three or four per 8-inch-pot, for example. (Planting several bulbs per pot results in a mound of handsome foliage.) The bulbs resent being disturbed, so don't overcrowd when planting, and select containers large enough to allow for several years' growth. Keep the soil evenly moist when they are growing actively, but let the soil stay fairly dry in winter when plants are dormant and stop producing new leaves. (The plants are evergreen, so they never die back, just grow more slowly.) These are heavy feeders: feed weekly or biweekly with a dilute, balanced fertilizer when they are growing actively. Bring container-grown plants indoors before the first frost threatens. While the main flush of flowers comes in late summer, it is possible to induce a second blooming period in winter by keeping the plants fairly dry for about 6 weeks just after bringing them indoors—water only when the leaves begin to wilt—and then move plants to a warm, humid spot and resume watering and feeding more regularly.

E. × *grandiflora*   P. 98

e. × gran-dih-FLOR-uh. Amazon Lily, Eucharist Lily, Madonna Lily, Lily-of-the-Amazon. Plants grown in gardens as *E. amazonica* fall here. Bears glossy, dark green, elliptic to ovate leaves that have wavy margins and reach 12 inches in length. Umbels of 3-inch-wide white flowers with a sweet lemony scent appear on 20-inch-tall stems in summer. Foliage mounds are about 1½ feet tall, and plants reach 2 feet tall in bloom. Tender perennial hardy in Zones 9 to 11.

❦ *Eucomis*

yoo-CO-miss. Lily family, Liliaceae.

Grown for their unusual, long-lasting blooms that resemble pineapples, *Eucomis* species are primarily native to South Africa. Commonly called pineapple flowers or pineapple lilies, they bear cylindrical racemes of small densely packed flowers in late summer and early fall that are topped by a cluster of leafy bracts that resemble the leaves at the top of a pineapple. The individual flowers are star shaped and have six petal-like tepals that are fused at the base. The glossy green leaves, which usually range from 1 to 2 feet long, are strap to lance shaped and borne only at the base of the plant. About 15 species belong to the genus, all of which grow from large tunicate bulbs.

HOW TO GROW

Give pineapple lilies full sun or partial shade and rich, well-drained soil. Where hardy, plant the bulbs outdoors in fall at a depth of 5 to 6 inches. Like many South African natives, these bulbs require a dry dormant period, so in areas with rainy winters, mulch the plants with evergreen boughs, salt hay, pine needles, or coarse hay, and then top the site with heavy plastic to keep the soil dry. Where they are marginally hardy, look for a warm, south-facing site, such as at the base of a wall, and mulch heavily over winter. In the North, grow these bulbs in containers, setting the bulbs with the noses, or tips, slightly below or just emerging from the soil surface. To overwinter container-grown plants, gradually withhold water toward the end of the season and let the foliage die back, then store them—still in their containers—in a cool (40° to 50°F), frost-free, dry place. Whether outdoors or in containers, plants are happiest when left undisturbed and will thrive for years without needing division: dig and divide or pot on the bulbs only if they become overcrowded or for propagation. Bulbs can be stored over winter in dry peat in a cool (50°F) spot. Propagate by separating the offsets in early fall or just as the foliage dies down in early fall. Or sow seeds.

E. autumnalis   P. 98

e. aw-tum-NAL-iss. Formerly *E. undulata*. An 8- to 12-inch-tall species with wavy-margined leaves. In late summer and early fall, plants produce erect, cylindrical 2- to 6-inch-long racemes of greenish white 1-inch-wide flowers. Zones 8 to 10.

E. bicolor

e. BI-kuh-lor. A 1- to 2-foot-tall species with wavy-margined leaves. In late summer, bears erect 6-inch-long racemes of pale green 1-inch-wide flowers edged in purple. Zones 8 to 10.

E. comosa   P. 99

e. co-MO-suh. Pineapple Flower, Pineapple Lily. Formerly *E. punctata*. A 2- to 3-foot-tall species with wavy-margined leaves. Bears erect, cylindrical 1-foot-long racemes of white 1-inch-wide flowers in late summer that are edged in purple and have showy purple ovaries at the center of each flower. Zones 6 or 7 to 10.

E. pole-evansii

e. pole-ee-VAN-see-eye. Vigorous 3- to 6-foot-tall species with 2- to 4-foot-long wavy-margined leaves. Bears cylindrical 1½- to 3-foot-long racemes of greenish white flowers in late summer. Zones 8 to 10.

❦ Freesia

FREE-shuh. Iris family, Iridaceae.

Popular cut flowers, freesias are treasured for their fragrance as well as their graceful racemes of colorful, funnel-shaped blooms. About six species belong to the genus, all native South African tender perennials that grow from corms. Plants have narrow, sword-shaped or linear leaves that are mostly basal, although a few leaves are borne on the slender, branched flower stems. The flowers are tubular at the base and open to funnel shaped at the top, with six lobes (perianth segments). Hybrids are far more commonly grown than species, and double-flowered forms are available.

HOW TO GROW

Select a site in full sun with average to rich, moist, well-drained soil. Although freesias can be grown outdoors year-round in frost-free climates—southern California and the Deep South—they are grown primarily as container plants, especially in greenhouses. They require cool conditions and good air circulation to grow well. In winter, nighttime temperatures need to remain below 50°F, and plants tolerate temperatures to 40°F or lower. When growing freesias outdoors in Zones 10 and 11, schedule planting times so that they will be growing during seasons when temperatures remain cool at night. Plant the corms at a depth of 3 inches in the ground, from ½ to 1 inch deep in containers. Where hardy, plant in late summer or early fall for late winter or early spring bloom. When growing freesias in containers (to be kept indoors in a cool sunroom or greenhouse over winter) plant the corms in fall for bloom the following spring. Or plant them in spring after danger of frost has passed for summer bloom. Keep containers shaded and barely moist until shoots appear. Once they are growing actively, keep the soil evenly moist, but not wet, and gradually move them to full sun. Feed container-grown plants weekly. Plants require staking: install stakes and string or brushy twigs when plants are still fairly small. Replace the corms annually, or if you want to save them for next year, continue feeding the plants after the flowers fade, until the leaves turn yellow and die back. Then gradually dry off the plants and store the containers in a cool (40° to 50°F), dry, airy spot. Or clean the soil off the corms and store them in paper bags. Propagate by seeds or by separating offsets.

F. hybrids   P. 99

A wide variety of freesias have been selected for their fragrant 2-inch-long flowers. Hybrids range from 1 to 1½ feet in height and come in shades of pink, lavender, lilac-blue, red, yellow, creamy white, and orange-red. Many bear bicolor blooms, and double-flowered forms are available. Zones 10 to 11.

❦ Fritillaria

fri-tih-LAIR-ee-uh. Lily family, Liliaceae.

Fritillaria is a large diverse genus in the lily family that contains stately plants suitable for beds and borders as well as diminutive species for rock gardens. All of the 100 or so species that belong here grow from bulbs.

The bulbs consist of either fleshy, closely fitting scales (sometimes covered with a papery tunic) or of separate, overlapping scales (also thick and fleshy) arranged like those of lily bulbs. Plants produce lance-shaped to grassy leaves and nodding, bell- or funnel-shaped flowers in spring or early summer. Blooms are solitary or borne in erect, unbranched clusters. They consist of six petal-like tepals. Many species bear flowers that are marked with a tessellate, or checkered, pattern of contrasting colors.

HOW TO GROW

The culture of these fascinating plants varies by species, and the genus contains plants that are both easy and difficult to grow. Unless otherwise noted below, give fritillarias a site in full sun or light shade with moist, well-drained soil that is rich in organic matter. Among the easiest, most vigorous species are *F. acmopetala, F. imperialis, F. meleagris, F. persica, F. thunbergii,* and *F. verticillata.* Other species require perfect drainage and dry conditions when dormant. These include *F. affinis, F. aurea, F. hermonis, F. michailovskyi,* and *F. uva-vulpis*—all are good choices for rock gardens and raised beds. If in doubt about whether your garden offers the right conditions, start with a small number of bulbs and experiment to find a suitable site. Knowing the origins of the different species can help with site selection, and they are given in the species descriptions below. Whatever species you grow, keep in mind that the bulbs are fragile and should not be allowed to dry out before planting. Inspect bulbs carefully when you buy, because dried-out bulbs generally will not grow. If you can't plant bulbs immediately, store them in barely moist vermiculite or peat moss. Plant fritillaries fairly deeply—at least 4 times the height of the bulbs; plant *F. imperialis* with the tops of the bulbs 5 to 6 inches below the surface. Be sure to prepare the soil several inches *below* where the bulbs will sit to provide rich and well-drained conditions. Species with open-crowned, scaly bulbs, including *F. imperialis,* can catch moisture in the top of the bulbs, which causes rot. To prevent this, and also to provide excellent drainage for species that require it, place 2 to 3 inches of sharp sand (also called builder's sand) in the bottom of the planting holes and place the bulbs on their sides when planting. Space *F. imperialis* and *F. persica* about 1 foot apart, smaller species 3 to 4 inches apart. Mulch plantings with compost or feed with very well rotted manure in spring. For species intolerant of moist soil when they are dormant, plant in a raised bed and be sure to provide loose, gritty, well-drained soil. Divide established plantings only when they become too crowded. Plants of *F. imperialis* thrive for years without needing to be divided; other species produce good crops of offsets each year and need dividing every 3 or 4 years. Dig them in early summer after the foliage has ripened but before it disappears completely. Propagate by division or seeds.

F. acmopetala

f. ak-mo-PET-ah-luh. A 1- to 1½-foot-tall species from the eastern Mediterranean, including Lebanon and southern Turkey. Grows from 1½-inch bulbs often surrounded by bulblets at the base. Bears 1½-inch-long bell-shaped pale green flowers marked with red-brown in late spring. Although blooms are usually solitary they are sometimes borne in pairs or threes. Zones 6 to 8.

F. affinis   P. 100

f. af-FIN-iss. Rice-grain Fritillary. Formerly F. lanceolata. A 1- to 2-foot-tall native of western North America with ¾-inch-bulbs usually surrounded by many small bulblets at the base. Bears nodding, cup-shaped, greenish white flowers that are marked with red-purple from spring to early summer. Blooms are borne in racemes of 2 or 3 to 10 or more flowers. 'Limelight' bears green flowers with a few red-purple specks. 'Vancouver Island' bears maroon-brown blooms checked with green. Zones 6 to 9.

F. aurea

f. AW-ree-uh. A 6- to 8-inch-tall species from Turkey with ¾-inch bulbs often surrounded by small bulblets at the base. Bears solitary, bell-shaped yellow flowers checkered with orange or red-brown. 'Golden Flag' bears bright yellow flowers. Plants require very well drained soil and dry conditions when dormant. Zones 5 to 8.

F. biflora

f. bi-FLOR-uh. Black Fritillary, Mission Bells. A 6- to 12-inch-tall California native growing from ¾-inch-bulbs consisting of about three fleshy, loose scales. In spring, bears stems of 1 to 6, or as many as 12, bell-shaped brown flowers that have a black or purple tinge and are flushed with green. 'Martha Roderick' has red-brown or red-purple blooms with greenish white tips. Plants require perfect drainage and dry conditions when dormant. Zones 6 to 9.

F. camschatcensis

f. kam-chat-SEN-sis. Black Sarana, Black Lily. A 1- to 1½-foot-tall species native from Alaska and Canada to China and Japan. Grows from a 1-inch-wide bulb consisting of many densely packed scales that often produce many bulblets around the base. In early summer produces one to eight nodding, cup-to bell-shaped 1¼-inch-long flowers that are black-purple in color. Best in partial shade with rich, moist soil. Zones 3 to 8.

F. davisii   P. 100
f. dah-VIS-ee-eye. Fritillary. Species native to Greece that grows from 1-inch-wide bulbs and reaches 6 inches. Bears stems of from one to three 1-inch-long bell-shaped green flowers in spring that commonly have yellow petal edges and checkered brown markings. Plants require perfect drainage and dry conditions when dormant. Zones 6 to 9.

F. glauca
f. GLAW-kuh. Siskiyou Lily. A 5- to 7-inch-tall species found in California and Oregon that grows from very tiny bulbs with two to three scales. In spring, bears solitary, nodding, bell-shaped 1-inch-wide yellow flowers mottled with brown. 'Goldilocks' bears stems of three to five yellow flowers flushed with green and sometimes flecked with red-brown. Plants require perfect drainage and dry conditions when dormant. Zones 6 to 9.

F. hermonis ssp. *amana*
f. her-MON-iss ssp. ah-MAN-uh. A 6- to 12-inch-tall species from Turkey and Lebanon. Grows from ¾-inch-bulbs that often are surrounded by bulblets at the base and sometimes produce stolons. In spring, bears 1½-inch-long green flowers lightly checkered with purple or brown. The inner tepals have purple-brown edges, and flowers are solitary or borne in pairs. Plants require perfect drainage and dry conditions when dormant. Zones 6 to 8.

F. imperialis   P. 101
f. im-per-ee-AL-iss. Crown Imperial. Vigorous, easy-to-grow, old-fashioned flower, originally native to Asia, that ranges from 2 to 4 feet in height. In early spring, bears umbels of three to as many as eight, downward-pointing 2½-inch-long flowers topped by a sheaf of leaflike bracts. Bulbs reach about 4 inches in diameter and have a skunklike odor. Orange-, yellow-, and red-flowered forms are available. Cultivars include 'Lutea Maxima', with yellow flowers; 'Aurora', with burnt orange flowers; 'Rubra Maxima', in bright orange; and 'Prolifera' with double orange-red blooms. Zones 5 to 8.

F. meleagris
P. 101

f. me-lee-AG-riss. Checkered Lily, Guinea-hen Flower, Snake's Head Fritillary. An 8- to 12-inch-tall European native growing from 1-inch-wide bulbs consisting of two large scales. Bears nodding, broadly bell-shaped 1¾-inch-long flowers in spring, singly or sometimes in pairs. Flowers can be pinkish purple, red-purple, nearly black, or white and are checked with purple-pink. 'Alba' bears white flowers. Zones 4 to 8.

F. michailovskyi
P. 102

f. mik-ah-LOF-skee-eye. Fritillary. A 4- to 8-inch-tall species, best in rock gardens or raised beds, that grows from 1-inch-wide bulbs. Bears pendent, broadly bell-shaped purple-brown flowers edged in yellow in late spring or early summer. Blooms are borne singly or in clusters of up to four. Plants require rich but very well drained soil and dry conditions when dormant. Zones 5 to 8.

F. pallidiflora
P. 102

f. pal-lid-ih-FLOR-uh. Fritillary. A vigorous ½- to 2-foot-tall species from Siberia and northwestern China. Grows from 1- to 2-inch-wide bulbs and in late spring and early summer bears clusters of six to as many as nine bell-shaped, nodding creamy yellow flowers blushed with green and sometimes marked with red-brown. Best in partial shade. Zones 3 to 8.

F. persica
P. 103

f. PER-sih-kuh. Fritillary. A vigorous, stately species from southern Turkey that produces racemes of 20 to 30 or more mauve-purple flowers on 1- to 3-foot plants in spring. Individual blooms are ¾ inch long. Bulbs are about 2 inches tall and consist of one large scale and several tightly packed smaller scales. Best in a hot, sun-baked site. Zones 5 to 8.

F. pontica
P. 103

f. PON-tih-kuh. Fritillary. A 6- to 8-inch-tall species from the Balkans, including Turkey and Greece, that grows from a 1- to 1¼-inch-wide bulb. In spring, produces solitary or sometimes paired flowers that are nodding, bell shaped, and 1¾ inches long. Blooms are green with brown or maroon at the base. Zones 5 or 6 to 8.

F. pudica
P. 104

f. PEW-dih-kuh. Yellow Fritillary. Native wildflower from western North America that reaches 3 to 6 inches and grows from small disc-shaped bulbs with two to four scales, usually with many small bulblets around the base. Plants produce pendent, bell-shaped, 1-inch-long flowers in spring that are solitary or carried in pairs. Blooms are golden yellow to orange-yellow. Plants require perfect drainage and dry conditions when dormant. 'Fragrance' bears fragrant yellow flowers. Zones 4 to 9.

F. purdyi

f. PUR-dee-eye. A 6- to 8-inch-tall species native to the Southwest that grows from small bulbs that have three to four fleshy scales. Plants bear from one to four nodding, bell-shaped, ¾-inch-long whitish to beige flowers veined and mottled with red- or purple-brown. Plants require perfect drainage and dry conditions when dormant. Zones 5 to 8.

F. thunbergii

f. thun-BER-jee-eye. Sometimes listed as *F. verticillata* var. *thunbergii*. A 1- to 2½-foot-tall native of China growing from 1½-inch-wide bulbs. Bears loose clusters of two to six bell- to cup-shaped 1½-inch-long flowers that are creamy white and checkered with pale green. Zones 6 to 8.

F. uva-vulpis   P. 104

f. OO-vah VUL-pis. Fritillary. A 6- to 8-inch-tall species from western Asia, including Turkey, Iraq, and Iran. Plants grow from 1¼-inch-wide bulbs that usually produce a few bulblets at the base. In spring they produce solitary, nodding, bell-shaped, 1-inch-long flowers that are purple-brown with yellow edges on the tips of the tepals. Plants require perfect drainage and dry conditions when dormant. Zones 5 to 8.

F. verticillata

f. ver-tih-sih-LAH-tuh. A 1- to 3-foot tall species from central Asia and western Siberia that grows from ¾- to 1½-inch-wide bulbs with two bulb scales. Leaves at the tops of the stems have tendril-like tips. In spring, bears from one to six nodding, bell-shaped white or yellow flowers flecked with green or purple. Zones 4 to 8.

❦ Galanthus

gah-LAN-thus. Amaryllis family, Amaryllidaceae.

The dainty blooms of *Galanthus* species, better known as snowdrops, are among the earliest flowers to mark the beginning of a new growing season. About 19 species belong to the genus, all hardy perennials native from Europe to Asia that grow from tunicate bulbs and usually produce grassy, strap-shaped leaves. Each bulb normally produces a single pendent bloom on an arching stem. The flowers have six petal-like tepals; the three outer tepals are teardrop-shaped and markedly larger than the inner three, which they nearly conceal. Flowers may be all white or green and white in color, and they appear in late winter to midspring. While the botanical name *Galanthus* is derived from the Greek *gala*, milk, and *anthos*, flower, the common name is thought to have a German derivation. It is from *schneetropfen*, which were pendants or earrings popular in Germany in the 16th and 17th centuries. Snowdrop bulbs are mildly poisonous, and contact with the foliage can cause skin irritations: their poisonous nature seems to extend to rodents, because these bulbs are generally left alone by mice, voles, and their kin. They are sometimes confused with their close relatives, the snowflakes (*Leucojum* spp.), which bear one to as many as eight flowers per stem and have six tepals of equal size.

HOW TO GROW
Select a site in partial shade with rich, moist, well-drained soil. They are best in soil that remains evenly moist, but not wet, in summer. Snowdrops thrive under deciduous trees and are ideal for naturalizing in shade and woodland gardens as well as along shrub borders. Plant the bulbs in fall, setting them 3 inches deep. Set them at least 3 inches apart because they produce both offsets and self-sown seedlings in abundance and will form nice-sized clumps in fairly short order. Clumps can be left undisturbed for years and will become quite large—ones that become too crowded will push bulbs up to the soil surface. (These are easy to pot up for forcing or can be moved to a new spot.) Propagate by digging the bulbs in summer just as the foliage dies back. Gardener's lore suggests that snowdrops are happiest when moved "in the green" (with foliage). Or sow seeds.

G. caucasicus
g. caw-KASS-ih-kus. A 4- to 6-inch-tall species with 5- to 6-inch-long leaves that are about 1 inch wide. From late fall to early spring it bears white 1¼-inch-long flowers with inner tepals dipped in green. Zones 5 to 9.

G. elwesii   P. 105
g. el-WEH-see-eye. Giant Snowdrop. A 5- to 9-inch-tall species bearing fragrant white ¾- to 1¼-inch-long flowers with green markings on the inner tepals. Zones 3 to 9.

G. ikariae

g. ih-KAR-ee-ee. Sometimes listed as *G. latifolius* or *G. ikariae* var. *latifolius*. A 4- to 6-inch-tall plant with broad leaves up to 6 inches long and 1¼ inches wide. Bears white ½- to 1¼-inch-long flowers with green markings on the inner tepals from late winter to early spring. Zones 3 to 9.

G. nivalis

P. 105

g. nih-VAH-liss. Common Snowdrop. A 4-inch-tall species bearing fragrant white ½- to ¾-inch-long flowers in late winter to very early spring. Each inner tepal has an inverted green V at the tip. Many cultivars have been selected, but most are very hard to find. 'Flore Pleno' is a vigorous selection with double flowers. 'Viridapicis', also vigorous, has white flowers with green marks on both outer and inner tepals. 'S. Arnott' (sometimes sold as 'Sam Arnott'), a vigorous hybrid selection, bears very fragrant 1-to 1½-inch-long flowers with large green V-shaped marks on the inner tepals. Zones 3 to 9.

G. plicatus

g. ply-KAY-tus. An 8-inch-tall species with white ¾- to 1¼-inch-long flowers that have a green mark on the tip of each inner tepal. *G. plicatus* ssp. *byzantinus* has green marks on both the tip and the base of the inner tepals. Zones 3 to 9.

❦ Galtonia

gal-TOE-nee-uh. Lily family, Liliaceae.

Commonly known as summer hyacinths. *Galtonia* species are bulbs native to South Africa. As their common name suggests, they bloom in summer — late summer to be exact — producing graceful, erect racemes of pendent or nodding, bell-like flowers that are white or tinged with green. The individual blooms are trumpet shaped or tubular and have six lobes. The plants have tunicate bulbs and produce a clump of basal, narrow lance-shaped leaves that are partially erect. Four species belong to the genus.

HOW TO GROW

Select a site in full sun with rich, well-drained, deeply prepared soil. Unlike many South African natives, summer hyacinths are hardy and thrive in soil that remains moist, but not wet, through the growing season. Plant the bulbs in spring after the last frost date with the bases of the bulbs at least 6 inches below the soil surface: be sure to prepare the soil several inches below that. Plants are happiest when left undisturbed once they are planted, so space them fairly widely—at about 1 foot apart or three to four bulbs per square foot. Where hardy, they can be left undisturbed for years. In areas where they are marginally hardy, protect them over winter with a heavy mulch of evergreen boughs, pine needles, salt hay, or coarse leaves in late fall after the ground has frozen. In the North, either grow these bulbs in large containers, which can be sunk to the rim in the garden in summer, or dig the bulbs in fall after the foliage turns yellow, dry them off for a few hours, brush off excess soil, and store them indoors over winter. In or out of containers, overwinter the bulbs in a cool (35° to 45°F), dry spot. Propagate by digging the clumps in spring or fall and separating the offsets or by seeds.

G. candicans

P. 106

g. KAN-dih-kans. Summer Hyacinth. Formerly *Hyacinthus candicans*. Graceful 3- to 4-foot-tall species that produces erect, showy racemes of 15 to 30 fragrant white 2-inch-long flowers in late summer. *G. princeps* is a similar species reaching 3 feet in height and bearing 1-inch-long green-tinged white flowers, also in late summer. *G. princeps* is hardy from Zones 7 or 8 to 10, while *G. candicans* is hardy from Zone 6 to 10 and to Zone 5 with heavy winter mulch.

G. viridiflora

g. ver-id-ih-FLOR-uh. A 3-foot-tall species with arching racemes of 15 to 30 pale green ¾- to 2-inch-long flowers in late summer. Zones 7 or 8 to 10.

᭞ Gladiolus

glad-ee-O-lus. Iris family, Iridaceae.

A familiar sight in formal flower arrangements, glads—or gladioli as they are also called—are easy-to-grow, summer-blooming plants that nearly always arise from corms (the genus also contains a few rhizomatous species). Hybrids are far more familiar to gardeners than the species: about 180 species belong here, primarily native to South Africa, but there also are *Gladiolus* native to other parts of Africa as well as Europe and western Asia. All produce spikes (sometimes branched) of funnel-shaped flowers with six petal-like tepals. The flowers usually are arranged on one side of the spike, but some species bear spikes with flowers arranged in two parallel rows. Individual flowers usually have three lower tepals that form a lip (these often are smaller than the other tepals), a large upper tepal, and two wing tepals at the side. The linear- or sword-shaped leaves are basal and arranged in fans. The botanical name, which means little sword, refers to the leaves: it is from the Latin *gladius,* sword.

HOW TO GROW

Select a site in full sun with light, evenly moist soil rich in organic matter. Plant corms of tender glads in spring, setting small corms (½ inch diameter) 3 inches deep, medium ones (½ to 1 inch) 4 to 5 inches deep, and large corms (over 1 inch) 6 to 8 inches deep. Spacing depends on their size as well—set them from 3 to 6 inches apart. Hardy glads, including *G. communis,* can be planted in spring or fall. Work a balanced organic fertilizer into the soil at planting time. When planting common glads in spring, for best results dig a shallow trench and fill it with soil as the plants grow. Plant new corms of common gladiolus at two- to three-week intervals from spring to midsummer to prolong the bloom season. Deep planting helps reduce the need to stake plants, but stake them if necessary. Interplanting with perennials or annuals also helps support the stems. In areas where the plants are not hardy, let the foliage ripen for 6 weeks after flowering. Then dig the corms after the leaves turn yellow, cut off the foliage, and set them in a warm, dry place for a few hours to dry. Separate the new corms and small cormels from the old withered one, which will not bloom again. Dust the corms with sulfur or another fungicide and store them in a cool (40° to 50°F), dry place over winter.

G. callianthus   P. 106

g. cal-ee-AN-thus. Formerly *Acidanthera bicolor* var. *murieliae* and *A. murieliae.* A 2- to 3½-foot-tall species that produces loose, showy spikes of up to 10, fragrant, funnel-shaped flowers in late summer and fall. Individual blooms are white with a dark purple-red blotch at the center. Zones 7 to 10.

G. carneus

g. CAR-nee-us. Formerly *G. blandus, G. blandus* var. *carneus.* A South African species ranging from 8 inches to about 3 feet in height. Bears loose spikes of 3 to 12 funnel-shaped 2-inch-wide flowers in late spring and early summer. Individual blooms are cream, white, or pink and usually are marked with red or sometimes yellow on the lower tepals that form the lip. Zones 7 to 10.

G. communis ssp. byzantinus
P. 107

g. com-YEW-niss ssp. bih-zan-TYE-nus. Hardy Gladiolus. Formerly *G. byzantinus*. A 2- to 3-foot-tall species bearing graceful spikes of 10 to 20 funnel-shaped 2-inch-wide flowers in late spring and early summer. Blooms are magenta-pink striped with white or pale pink on the lower tepals that form the lip. Spreads freely by cormlets. Zones 5 to 10.

G. hybrids
P. 107

Common Gladiolus, Garden Glad. Sometimes listed as *G.* × *hortulanus*. Gladiolus hybrids produce dense spikes of showy flowers that open from the bottom of the spike to the top. The spikes range from 1 to 3 feet in length and have as many as 28 buds. Literally hundreds of gladiolus cultivars are available in an amazing range of colors, including shades of yellow, orange, red, pink, maroon, lavender, violet, green, cream, and white. Many selections bear bicolor blooms. Plants are 3 to 4 feet tall in bloom. Zones 8 to 10, but to Zone 7 with a thick winter mulch.

G. italicus

g. ih-TAL-ih-kus. Field Gladiolus. Formerly *G. segetum*. A 1½- to 3-foot-tall species native to southern Europe bearing loose spikes of 5 to 15 flowers in early summer. Individual blooms are 1½ inches wide and magenta-pink to purple-pink in color with paler pink markings on the lower tepals that form the lip. Prefers hot, dry conditions in summer once plants go dormant. Zones 6 or 7 to 10.

G. tristis
P. 108

g. TRIS-tiss. A 1½- to 5-foot-tall species bearing loose, graceful spikes of up to 20 funnel-shaped, very fragrant, lilylike flowers in spring. Individual flowers are 2½ inches long and creamy white to pale yellow in color. They often are flushed or dotted with mauve-pink, red, purple, or brown. Zones 8 to 10.

☙ Globba

GLOB-buh. Ginger family, Zingiberaceae.

Native to Southeast Asia, *Globba* species are heat-loving, tropical plants grown for their racemes of exotic-looking flowers that are erect or arching and then pendulous. Each individual flower has a long slender tube, three lobes or "petals," one of which forms a spur, and a large lip. There is a showy bract at the base of each flower. Plants grow from slender, branching rhizomes and produce oblong or lance-shaped leaves arranged in two ranks up the reedlike stems. About 70 species belong to the genus.

HOW TO GROW

Give these plants partial shade and deeply prepared, moist soil rich in organic matter. They thrive in areas with warm summers and high humidity and are ideal for gardens in the tropics and subtropics as well as for adding an exotic touch to more northern gardens during the summer months. Where hardy, grow them outdoors year-round. In the North, plant the rhizomes out in spring after the soil has warmed up and overwinter them indoors by digging the rhizomes after a light frost and cutting back the tops. Store the rhizomes in barely damp vermiculite, peat, or sand in a cool (55°F), dry place. Inspect rhizomes occasionally in winter: discard rotted pieces or cut away rotted portions and dust cuts with sulfur; sprinkle the vermiculite with water occasionally during winter to keep the roots from shriveling. Replant in spring. Or, grow these plants in containers year-round: keep them nearly dry and set them in a cool (60°F) spot in winter. Propagate by dividing the rhizomes in spring. While they seldom produce seeds, bulbils are often produced along the flower stems among the bracts.

G. winitii
P. 108

g. wih-NIT-ee-eye. A 2- to 3-foot-tall species native to Thailand that spreads by fleshy rhizomes to 2 feet or more. Leaves are 8 inches long and lance-shaped with heart-shaped bases. Bears pendent 6-inch-long racemes of yellow flowers with mauve-pink or purple-pink bracts. Zones 8 to 11; to Zone 7 with a very heavy winter mulch.

❦ Gloriosa

glor-ee-O-suh. Lily family, Liliaceae.

As the common names climbing lily and glory lily suggest, *Gloriosa* species are climbers that bear spectacular flowers. The botanical name also celebrates the exotic blooms of these tender perennials: it is from the Latin, *gloriosus,* splendid. The genus *Gloriosa* contains one very variable species that grows from slender, brittle, fleshy tubers. The plants produce ovate- to lance-shaped leaves that have tendrils at the tips. The flowers come in red or yellow or combinations of the two colors and have six petal-like tepals. The tepals are reflexed, meaning they point backward, and the flowers have been described as resembling butterflies. The tepals usually have wavy or crisped margins and the flowers also feature six long prominent spidery stamens along with a long pistil.

HOW TO GROW
Select a site in full sun with rich, well-drained soil. Where hardy, these plants can be grown outdoors year-round; in areas where they are marginally hardy look for a protected, south-facing site and mulch heavily over winter with evergreen boughs, pine needles, or salt hay. When selecting a site, try to follow the old adage commonly applied to clematis, and plant with the "head in the sun and feet in the shade." This refers to the fact that plants prefer cool soil conditions while the tops bloom best in full sun to partial shade. Look for a spot where the roots will be shaded by low-growing shrubs or perennials that aren't too aggressive, or on the north, or shaded, side of shrubs or a low wall. Mulch also helps keep the root run cool. Like clematis, these plants require a trellis or other support so the vines can climb into the sunlight. In the North, grow climbing lilies in containers or plant the tubers outdoors in spring on or slightly after the last frost date. In Zone 6 and north, start tubers indoors several weeks before the last frost date to give them a head start. Plant the tubers horizontally or at a slight angle with the tips 2 or 3 inches beneath the soil surface; just barely cover the tops of the tubers when planting in containers. Always handle the tubers carefully, as they are extremely brittle. To overwinter, dig tubers in fall after the first light frost and store them in dry peat moss or sand at a temperature of about 60°F. Or overwinter container-grown plants by drying out the soil and store them pot and all in a cool, dry place. Propagate by separating the tubers in spring.

G. superba   P. 109
g. soo-PER-buh. Climbing Lily, Glory Lily. Plants once classified as *G. carsonii*, *G. lutea*, *G. minor*, *G. rothschildiana*, and *G. simplex* all belong here. A climbing, tuberous perennial that can reach 6 feet in areas with long growing seasons. Bears 2- to 4-inch-wide flowers with red or purple tepals that often have yellow margins. 'Citrina' bears orangy yellow flowers. 'Rothschildiana' features 3- to 4-inch-wide flowers with scarlet tepals that have yellow bases and edges. Zones 8 to 10, to Zone 7 in a protected site with winter mulch.

❦ Habranthus

hah-BRAN-thus. Amaryllis family, Amaryllidaceae.

Habranthus contains ten species of bulbs native to South America that are grown for their funnel-shaped flowers. The blooms, which are carried on leafless stalks, usually are solitary, or sometimes borne in pairs. They stick out at an angle from the stalk; the blooms of closely related *Zephyranthes* point upward. The flowers have six petal-like tepals and are followed by conspicuous black seeds. Habranthus grow from tunicate bulbs and bear grassy, linear, basal leaves that are either evergreen or deciduous, in which case they appear with or just after the flowers. The botanical name *Habranthus* is from the Greek *habros,* graceful, and *anthos,* flower.

HOW TO GROW

Select a site in full sun with deeply prepared, rich, well-drained soil. Neutral to alkaline soil pH is best. Where hardy, these bulbs can be grown outdoors year-round. They prefer a warm site, and where marginally hardy, a protected spot at the base of a south-facing wall is best. They require fairly dry soil in winter when they are dormant, so where wet winter conditions might be a problem, plant them in raised beds or rock gardens and amend the soil with grit when planting to improve drainage. In the North, grow them in containers, which make it easy to move these plants outdoors for summer and indoors in fall for overwintering. In containers or in the ground, plant the bulbs in spring, setting them with the necks above the soil surface. Keep the soil nearly dry until plants sprout, then keep the soil evenly moist once plants are growing actively. Gradually withhold water as the leaves begin to die back. To overwinter bulbs indoors, bring the containers indoors after the foliage has died back and keep them in a cool (45° to 50°F), dry place. The soil should remain nearly, but not completely, dry. Plants can remain in the same containers for several years. Propagate by offsets in late winter or early spring or by seeds. Where hardy, plants often self-sow.

H. robustus   P. 109

h. ro-BUS-tus. Formerly *Zephyranthes robusta.* An 8- to 12-inch-tall species from Brazil and Argentina with grassy leaves that appear about the time flower stalks emerge. Bears solitary 2½-inch-wide pale pink flowers in summer. Zones 7 to 11.

H. tubispathus

h. too-bih-SPAY-thus. Formerly *H. andersonii, H. texanus, Zephyranthes robusta.* A 4- to 6-inch-tall species found from Texas south to Argentina and Chile. Bears leaves that emerge after the flower stalks and solitary 1-inch-wide trumpets in summer in shades of yellow, orange, and orange-red. Zones 9 to 11.

❦ *Haemanthus*

hee-MAN-thus. Amaryllis family, Amaryllidaceae.

Considering the common name blood lily, it's not surprising *Haemanthus* species produce exotic-looking blooms. About 21 species belong to this genus, all tender perennials that have tunicate bulbs and are native to Africa, especially South Africa. They bear umbels of tiny, tightly packed flowers that resemble a shaving brush or a rounded paint brush. The umbels are surrounded by showy petal-like bracts (technically these are spathe valves) that make the clusters of flowers look as if they were a single bloom. The botanical name *Haemanthus* refers to the red color of the bracts of some species: it is from the Greek *haima*, blood, and *anthos*, flower. The individual flowers in the umbels have six petal-like tepals. They also have six showy, protruding stamens that add to the brushlike appearance. Plants have deciduous or evergreen leaves that are arranged in two ranks, or rows, and range from strap shaped to rounded and vary from 1 to about 1½ feet long. Flowers are followed by showy, round berries.

HOW TO GROW

Select a spot in partial shade with rich, well-drained soil. Neutral to alkaline soil pH is best. Like many South African natives, blood lilies require evenly moist soil when they are growing actively and dry conditions when dormant. Dormancy period varies from species to species. Plant the bulbs in fall with the necks just above the soil surface. Grow these bulbs in containers in all but Zone 10 or 11 gardens that can offer dry conditions when the plants are dormant. Water regularly when plants are growing actively. As the leaves of deciduous species turn yellow, gradually withhold water. Keep evergreen species just barely moist when they are dormant; deciduous species can be stored dry. Overwinter them in a spot that does not drop below about 50°F. Plants resent having their roots and bulbs disturbed, and they thrive for years without needing to be divided.

Also, container-grown blood lilies bloom best when they are pot-bound, so repot only if necessary just when new growth resumes. Propagate by separating offsets in early spring or by seeds.

H. albiflos P. 110

h. AL-bih-floss. Shaving-brush Plant, White Paintbrush. Evergreen 6- to 12-inch-tall species with strap-shaped leaves that rests in summer. In fall, new leaves appear along with brushlike 2- to 3-inch-wide umbels of up to 50 white flowers surrounded by white bracts with green veins. The flowers are followed by white to red berries. Zones 10 to 11.

H. coccineus P. 110

h. cock-SIN-ee-us. Blood Lily, Cape Tulip. Deciduous 10- to 14-inch-tall species with elliptic to strap-shaped leaves. Dormant until mid- to late summer. From late summer to fall, shortly before the leaves appear, plants produce 2- to 4-inch-wide umbels of up to 100 densely packed red flowers with yellow stamens that are surrounded by eight very showy, waxy red bracts. The flowers are followed by clusters of white to pink berries. Zones 10 to 11.

H. katherinae see Scadoxus multiflorus

Hedychium

heh-DEE-kee-um. Ginger family, Zingiberaceae.

Hedychium species, commonly known as gingers, are tender perennials that grow from fleshy, branching rhizomes. About 40 species belong to the genus, nearly all native to the tropics of Asia, especially India. One species is native to Madagascar. Plants bear reedlike stems with large lance-shaped leaves arranged in two rows, or ranks, up the stems. The flowers often are fragrant and are carried in showy, dense, spikelike racemes. Individual blooms are two lipped and tubular to somewhat trumpet shaped and come in white as well as shades of yellow and orange-red.

HOW TO GROW

Give these tropical plants a spot in full sun to partial shade and deeply prepared, moist soil that is rich in organic matter. They thrive in areas with warm summers and high humidity and are ideal for gardens in the tropics and subtropics or for adding an exotic touch to more northern gardens in summer. Where hardy, grow them outdoors year-round. Plant the tubers just below the soil surface. Where marginally hardy, look for a warm, sheltered spot, such as at the base of a south-facing wall, and mulch plants heavily over winter. In the North, plant the rhizomes out in spring after the soil has warmed up. In Zone 7 and north, start the rhizomes indoors several weeks before the last frost date to give them a head start. Or, grow these plants in containers year-round. To overwinter, either bring containers indoors or dig the rhizomes after a light frost and cut back the tops. Overwinter the plants right in the pots—keep the soil nearly dry in winter—or store the rhizomes in barely damp vermiculite, peat, or sand in a cool (50° to 55°F), dry place. Inspect rhizomes occasionally in winter: discard rotted pieces or cut away rotted portions and dust cuts with sulfur. Occasionally sprinkle the vermiculite used to pack them with water to keep the roots from shriveling. Replant in spring. Propagate by dividing the rhizomes in spring.

H. coccineum
P. 111

h. cock-SIN-ee-um. Red Ginger Lily, Scarlet Ginger Lily, Orange Bottlebrush Ginger. A 6-foot-tall species with fragrant 10-inch-long flower clusters from late summer to fall in shades of red, orange-red, orange, pink, and white. Zones 8 to 10.

H. coronarium

h. kor-o-NAIR-ee-um. Garland Flower, White Ginger Lily. A 3- to 6-foot-tall species with extremely fragrant 8-inch-long racemes of white flowers with a touch of yellow at the base of the petals from mid- to late summer. *H. coronarium* var. *chrysoleum* and its cultivar 'Yellow Spot' bears flowers with yellow blotches at the base. Best in partial shade. Zones 7 to 11.

H. gardnerianum
P. 111

h. gard-ner-ee-AH-num. Kahili Ginger. A 4- to 6-foot-tall species. From late summer to fall, bears 10- to 12-inch-long racemes of fragrant yellow flowers that have showy red stamens. Zones 8 to 11.

H. greenii

h. GREE-nee-eye. A 4- to 6-foot-tall species with maroon stems and green leaves tinged with maroon on their undersides. In summer, bears 5-inch-long racemes of bright red flowers that are not fragrant. Zones 7 or 8 to 11.

H. hybrids P. 112

A variety of ginger hybrids have been introduced to the market. 'Kinkaku' is a vigorous selection with very fragrant peach-colored flowers. 'Anne Bishop' bears showy, fragrant orange flowers in summer. 'Lemon Beauty' bears fragrant yellow flowers. 'Elizabeth' bears raspberry pink flowers. Hybrids are hardy from Zones 7 or 8 to 11.

❧ *Hemerocallis*

hem-er-o-CAL-iss. Lily family, Liliaceae.

Hemerocallis species, better known as daylilies, are versatile, long-lived perennials grown for their colorful, trumpet-shaped flowers carried on erect stalks, called scapes. The flowers, each of which lasts for only a day, have six petal-like tepals. The botanical name *Hemerocallis* commemorates the fleeting nature of the blooms; it's from the Greek *hemera*, day, and *kallos*, beauty. Blooms are borne from 1 to as many as 7 feet above low clumps of long, arching, sword-shaped or grassy leaves that are arranged in fans. While only about 15 species belong to the genus—all native to China, Japan, and Korea—literally thousands of cultivars are available. Better selections produce a wealth of buds and bloom over a period of 3 to 4 weeks in summer. The plants have thick, fibrous roots with fleshy, tuberlike swellings on them—as a result, gardeners will find these sturdy perennials displayed among traditional perennials as well as in sales racks and catalogs devoted to bulbs. Well-formed clumps of standard-size plants spread 2 to 4 feet, with the foliage ranging from about 1 to 2 feet in height. Small daylily cultivars spread from 1 to 2 feet.

HOW TO GROW

Select a site in full sun or light shade and average to rich, well-drained soil that is evenly moist. Plant daylilies with the crowns at the soil surface. Modern hybrids bloom best with 8 hours of full sun. Daylilies tolerate poor soil and drought but do not bloom as abundantly. Too-rich soil leads to foliage production at the expense of flowers. Plants bloom best when the soil remains evenly moist, so water during dry weather. Remove faded blooms regularly to keep plants attractive and prevent the limp, old flowers from interfering with new ones that are opening. (Tetraploid daylilies are especially notorious for needing regular deadheading.) Pick off any seedpods that begin to form—cultivars do not come true from seed. Remove bloom stalks after the last flowers fade. Divide plants in early spring or early fall when they become crowded, begin to bloom less, outgrow their space, or for propagation.

H. hybrids

PP. 112, 113

Hybrid daylilies are far more commonly grown than the species and come in many colors, shapes, and sizes. Colors include peach, apricot, yellow-orange, maroon, orange-red, buffy orange, pinkish lavender, plum, and pale yellow or pink blooms that are nearly white. Blooms may be a solid color or feature contrasting colors. Shapes include classic trumpets, recurved blooms with petals curving back to form an almost flat face, and spider- and star-shaped blooms with narrow, widely spaced petals. Some are fragrant. Diploid daylilies have two sets of chromosomes; tetraploids, four—twice the normal number. Tetraploids, which often have ruffled or frilled petal edges, usually are larger plants than diploids, with bigger, more brightly colored flowers.

So-called Miniature daylilies bear flowers under 3 inches across, often on full-size plants. The term "dwarf" is sometimes used to indicate small plants. 'Peach Fairy' bears 2½-inch flowers on 26-inch plants, while 'Mini Pearl' bears 3-inch flowers on 16-inch plants. Both are miniatures.

Daylilies also are classified by bloom season, and selecting a mix of early, midseason, and late cultivars extends the bloom season. Reblooming daylilies produce a main flush of bloom, followed by additional spikes later in the season. 'Happy Returns', 'Pardon Me', 'Little Grapette', and 'Eenie Weenie' are rebloomers. Everbloomers, such as 'Stella de Oro', flower continuously through the season after a first main flush of bloom.

Hybrids may be deciduous (also called dormant), semievergreen, or evergreen. The leaves of evergreen types remain green all winter in the South; protect them with a layer of mulch in winter in Zone 6 and the northern part of Zone 7. Semievergreens are deciduous in the North, semievergreen in the South. Deciduous types go dormant in fall and return in spring wherever they are grown.

Hardiness and heat tolerance varies, so buy from a local grower or mail-order supplier in a climate similar to your own. Cultivars that have received the Stout Medal from the American Hemerocallis Society include 'Fairy Tale Pink' (ruffled pink), 'Mary Todd' (ruffled yellow), 'Ruffled Apricot' (ruffled apricot), 'Barbara Mitchell' (ruffled orchid pink), and 'Ed Murray' (deep red). Zones 3 to 10.

❦ *Hermodactylus*

her-mo-DAK-tee-lus. Iris family, Iridaceae.

The single species that belongs to this genus is commonly known as snake's head iris. Native to southern Europe, northern Africa, and eastward to Israel and Turkey, it produces grassy, linear leaves and grows from a creeping rhizome with tuberous, somewhat fingerlike, roots. The spring-borne flowers resemble those of irises (botanists distinguish between the two genera because *Hermodactylus* bears ovaries with one cell, while *Iris* species have three-celled ovaries). Like irises, *Hermodactylus tuberosus* bears flowers with six petals that point up or out and are called standards, and three petal-like sepals that point out or down and are called falls.

HOW TO GROW

Select a site in full sun with average to rich soil that is very well drained. Alkaline soil pH is best. Plant the tubers in fall or early spring at a depth of about 4 inches. Like many plants of Mediterranean origin, this species is best in a sun-baked spot that remains relatively dry in summer. Where hardy, snake's head iris can be grown in the ground year-round, but be sure to give plants a site with very well drained soil—a raised bed is ideal. Where plants are marginally hardy, look for a warm, protected, south-facing site and mulch heavily over winter. Amend the soil with grit at planting time to improve drainage. Or grow this species in containers overwintered in a cool greenhouse. Dig and divide the clumps as the foliage dies back if the plants become overcrowded. Propagate by dividing the tubers in early summer just as the leaves die back.

H. tuberosus   P. 114

h. too-ber-O-sus. Snake's Head Iris, Widow Iris. An 8- to 16-inch-tall species with arching, grassy gray-green leaves that are four-sided. Bears solitary, fragrant 2-inch-wide flowers in spring that are greenish yellow with velvety black falls. Zones 6 or 7 to 9.

❦ *Hippeastrum*

hip-ee-AS-trum. Amaryllis family, Amaryllidaceae.

Widely known as amaryllis, *Hippeastrum* species are grown for their showy, trumpet- or funnel-shaped flowers. The lilylike flowers are produced in umbels atop leafless stems. They have six petal-like tepals. Plants grow from tunicate bulbs and bear basal leaves that are linear to lance shaped. While the species are native to Central and South America—about 80 species belong here—most gardeners are familiar with the large-flowered hybrids sold for growing indoors in pots.

HOW TO GROW

Outdoors, give these plants a site in full sun to partial shade with deeply prepared, rich, well-drained soil. Where hardy, plant the bulbs in spring or fall with 2 to 3 inches of soil over the tops of the bulbs: be sure the basal plate of the bulb is beneath the frost line. Protect them with evergreen boughs, pine needles, or salt hay over winter. In most of the country, these showy bulbs are grown in containers: plant them in winter or early spring. Select a pot that is 2 inches larger than the diameter of the bulb (to allow for 1 inch of space between the bulb and the pot all the way around). Set the bulbs so that the top two-thirds are above the soil surface. Keep the soil barely moist and set the pots in a cool (55° to 60°F) room until leaves or a flower bud appears to signal that the bulbs are growing actively. Then move the pots to a warmer spot and water regularly. Once the bulbs flower, remove the flower stalks and feed with a dilute, balanced fertilizer every two weeks until mid- to late summer. Then begin to withhold water gradually to encourage the leaves to go dormant. (If the soil remains moist, the leaves will be evergreen and plants will be less likely to flower again.) Some gardeners let the leaves be cut back by a light fall frost. Once the leaves die back, store the bulbs dry, still in their pots, at about 55°F. Let them rest for at least 8 weeks. Topdress the bulbs in midwinter and begin watering again—very cautiously at first until plants are growing actively. Bulbs are easy to bloom the year they are purchased (the flower buds are already formed in the bulbs when you buy them), but often do not bloom the following year. That's because these plants have permanent, perennial roots and resent root disturbance. Bulbs usually have few, if any, roots when they are offered for sale, and after flowering the first year spend their energy replacing them. To minimize root disturbance in subsequent years, repot bulbs only as necessary—every three to four years—and when topdressing, disturb them as little as possible. When growing these plants in the ground, dig them only if absolutely necessary. Propagate by removing offsets in fall.

_H_. hybrids   P. 114

A wide variety of hybrids are offered for sale. Large-flowered types bear umbels of up to four flowers in early spring that are 4 to 6 inches across, and the largest bulbs can produce two flowers on 1- to 2-foot-tall stalks.

Cultivars include 'Apple Blossom', with white, pink-tinged flowers; 'Pico-tee', with white flowers with a thin red edge; 'Jaguar', with red blooms, green at the center, striped with white; and 'Red Lion', bright red. Minia-ture-flowered cultivars bear 3- to 4-inch-wide blooms on 1-foot-tall stalks. Miniature-flowered cultivars include 'Scarlet Baby' with scarlet flowers; 'Pamela' with orange-red blooms; and 'Fairy Tale' with raspberry pink blooms and white veins. Zones 8 to 10.

H. papilio   P. 115

h. pah-PIL-ee-o. Butterfly Amaryllis. An evergreen species that reaches 2 feet in height. Bears umbels of two or three 3½-inch-wide flowers in late win-ter. Blooms are creamy white heavily striped with maroon and have green throats. Zones 10 to 11.

❦ *Homeria*

ho-MAIR-ee-uh. Iris family, Iridaceae.

These South African natives, commonly known as Cape tulips, are grown for their clusters of fragrant, cupped, tuliplike flowers. While each bloom lasts only a day, they are borne in fairly good-size clusters and open in succession for several weeks from spring to summer. About 31 species be-long to the genus, all of which grow from corms. Some species have be-come widely naturalized in Australia. They bear leaves that are mostly basal and range from linear to strap-shaped. The leaves of some species are poisonous to livestock.

HOW TO GROW

Select a site in full sun with rich, well-drained soil. Like many South African species, Cape tulips need evenly moist soil while they are growing actively and dry conditions when they are dormant. Where hardy, plant the corms outdoors in fall at a depth of 4 inches. Amend the soil with grit or sharp sand to provide very good drainage. Where they are marginally hardy, look for a warm, south-facing site and protect plants over winter with evergreen boughs, pine needles, salt hay, or another coarse mulch. In the North, grow them in containers. To overwinter them, gradually re-duce watering after the flowers fade. Store the corms completely dry—in or out of the pots—in a cool (40° to 45°F) place. Propagate by separating the offsets just as the leaves die back.

H. collina
P. 115

h. ko-LYE-nuh. Cape Tulip. Formerly *H. breyniana*. A 6- to 16-inch-tall species with leaves that are poisonous to livestock. From spring to summer it bears fragrant, cup-shaped 3-inch-wide flowers that are pink, peach-pink, or yellow. Zones 9 to 11.

❦ Hyacinthoides

hi-ah-sin-THOY-deez. Lily family, Liliaceae.

Hyacinthoides contains three or four species grown for their charming racemes of spring-borne flowers that come in shades of blue, lavender, violet, pink, and white. The small bell-shaped flowers have six lobes, petal-like tepals that are united at the base. Some species are fragrant. Plants grow from tunicate bulbs that are renewed annually, meaning new bulbs are formed each year to replace the old one that dies. They bear basal, strap- to lance-shaped or linear leaves. *Hyacinthoides* species are closely related to *Scilla* and native to western Europe and northern Africa. They also were once classified in *Endymion*. Some gardeners develop skin allergies if they come in contact with the foliage or flowers.

HOW TO GROW

Select a site in partial or dappled shade with average to rich, moist, well-drained soil. They also tolerate full sun and thrive under deciduous trees, where they receive a good amount of sunshine in spring when they are growing actively. Plant the bulbs in fall at a depth of 3 inches. Since plants produce abundant offsets and can be left in place for many years without needing to be divided, space them generously—about 6 inches apart. Divide clumps only if they become overcrowded and begin to bloom less. Plants also self-sow and are ideal for naturalizing in wild and woodland gardens where they form large handsome clumps with time. They also can be naturalized in grass. Because *Hyacinthoides* renew their bulbs yearly, the bulbs of established clumps are quite deep in the soil. Propagate by separating the offsets in early summer as the foliage dies down or by seeds.

H. hispanica
P. 116

h. hiss-PAN-ih-kuh. Spanish Bluebell. Formerly *H. campanulata, Scilla campanulata, Scilla hispanica, Endymion hispanicus*. Vigorous 10- to 14-inch-tall species with large clumps of glossy leaves topped by showy racemes of 6 to as many as 15 bell-shaped, unscented lavender-blue ¾-inch-long flowers in spring. 'Excelsior' has lavender-blue flowers striped with pale blue. 'Rosabella' bears violet-pink flowers. White- and pink-flowered cultivars also are available. Zones 4 to 9.

H. italica

h. ih-TAL-ih-kuh. Italian Squill. Formerly *Endymion italicus, Scilla italica.* Dainty 4- to 8-inch-tall species with dense, somewhat rounded racemes of 6 to as many as 30 bell-shaped ½-inch-long flowers that face upward. Blooms are blue or sometimes white and appear in spring. Zones 4 to 9.

H. non-scripta   P. 116

h. non-SKRIP-tuh. English Bluebell, Harebell. Formerly *Endymion non-scriptus, Scilla non-scripta,* and *S. nutans.* Vigorous 8- to 12-inch-tall species that bears racemes of 6 to 12 lavender-blue flowers in spring arranged all on one side of the raceme. The individual flowers are narrowly bell-shaped, ½ to ¾ inch long, and have tepals that are very curled back at the tips. Zones 4 to 9.

❦ Hyacinthus

hi-ah-SIN-thus. Lily family, Liliaceae.

These familiar spring-blooming bulbs are prized for their intensely fragrant flowers. While three species belong to the genus, by far the best-known plants that belong here are cultivars of common hyacinths *(Hyacinthus orientalis),* also called Dutch hyacinths. These well-known garden plants produce erect, cylindrical trusses of flowers in shades of pink, lilac-blue, violet, yellow, and white. The blooms are carried on thick stalks above basal, strap-shaped leaves. The individual flowers are bell-shaped and have six petal-like tepals. The tepals are united for about half to two-thirds the length of the flower and have tips that flare widely or curve backward. Some gardeners develop a skin rash when they come in contact with the foliage of these plants.

HOW TO GROW

Select a site in full sun or partial shade with average to rich, well-drained soil. Plant the bulbs in fall at a depth of 4 to 5 inches deep — to 6 or even 8 inches deep at the northern limit of their hardiness. In the North, cover plantings with evergreen boughs, salt hay, or another loose mulch to protect the shoots when they emerge in spring. Remove the mulch after the danger of hard frost has passed. Plants produce the largest blooms the first spring and smaller, looser spikes thereafter—many gardeners consider the blooms borne in later years to be more natural-looking and graceful. When the leaves emerge in spring, feeding plants with a top-dressing of well-rotted manure or a balanced organic fertilizer helps keep the blooms large. For formal plantings with exhibition-sized blooms, replace the bulbs annually (bulbs that have already bloomed can be moved to less formal areas of the garden). Propagate by separating the offsets in summer just as the leaves die down.

H. amethystinus see Brimeura amethystina

H. orientalis P. 117

h. or-ee-en-TAL-iss. Hyacinth. The species that yielded the many cultivars grown today bears loose 8- to 12-inch-tall racemes of 2 to as many as 40 bell-shaped, extremely fragrant flowers that usually are violet-blue. Many cultivars are available: 'Blue Jacket', dark violet-blue; 'Amethyst', lilac-purple; 'Carnegie', creamy white; 'City of Haarlem', primrose yellow turning to creamy white; 'Delft Blue', pale lilac-blue; 'Jan Bos', pinkish red; 'Lady Derby', pale pink; 'Pink Pearl', deep pink with pale pink edges; 'White Pearl', white. Zones 5 to 9; to Zone 4 with deep planting.

Hymenocallis

hi-men-oh-KAL-iss. Amaryllis family, Amaryllidaceae.

Commonly known as Peruvian daffodils, spider lilies, or basket flowers, *Hymenocallis* species are tender bulbs grown for their umbels of fragrant flowers that resemble daffodils. (For another, closely related, species also called Peruvian daffodil, see *Pamianthe*.) The flowers usually are white and have six wide-spreading petal-like tepals that are joined at the base. The tepals usually are narrow, somewhat curled, and spidery in appearance. They surround a daffodil-like cup that is called a staminal cup because it is formed by six stamens that are fused at the base. (A close look at the flowers reveals the stamens protruding from the edge of the cup.) The basal, strap-shaped leaves can be deciduous or evergreen. About 40 species belong here, all native from the southern United States to South America. Several were once classified in the genus *Ismene*. Species that once belonged to *Ismene* (including popular *H. narcissiflora*) have larger staminal cups—from 1½ to 3 inches long—than other members of the genus. These species are usually referred to as basket flowers, or ismenes, and bloom in summer. Species with smaller staminal cups—under 1½ inches—are commonly called spider lilies; these plants bloom in winter, early spring, or summer.

HOW TO GROW

Select a site in full sun or partial shade with rich, evenly moist, well-drained soil. Evergreen species, including *H. caribaea* and *H. harrisiana*, are best in areas with hot, humid summers and frost-free winters, where they can be grown outdoors year-round. They also can be grown in large containers: to overwinter container-grown evergreen species indoors, keep them in a humid spot where temperatures do not drop below 55°F and water just enough to keep the foliage from wilting. Where they are hardy, deciduous species, including *H. × festalis* and *H. narcissiflora*, also can be grown outdoors year-round. These are the species most often seen in the North, because bulbs planted outdoors in late spring bloom quickly—by early to midsummer—and are easy to dig and overwinter indoors. To grow any of these species outdoors in the ground, plant the bulbs in late spring or early summer after the soil has warmed up. Set the tips of the bulbs 3 to 4 inches below the soil surface—slightly deeper if you are trying to grow them outdoors year-round at the northern limit of their hardiness. In containers, plant bulbs with the necks above the soil surface. For any of the species, keep the soil evenly moist while they are growing actively. Feed container-grown plants every other week with a dilute, balanced fertilizer. Dig deciduous species after a light fall frost or when the foliage turns completely yellow. Try to dig the bulbs with as many undamaged roots as possible. Set the bulbs upside down to dry them off (this ensures that moisture from the foliage will drip away from the bulbs). Store the bulbs in nearly dry peat or vermiculite in a cool (55° to 60°F), dry spot. Propagate by separating the offsets in spring.

H. caribaea

h. kah-ree-BAY-uh. Spider Lily. Formerly *Pancratium caribaeum*. Evergreen 2-foot-tall species native to the West Indies. Bears umbels of 8 to 12 fragrant 6-inch-wide white flowers with ¾- to 1-inch-long staminal cups. Blooms are borne from summer to fall. Zones 10 to 11.

H. × festalis

h. × fes-TAL-iss. Basket Lily, Peruvian Daffodil. Formerly *Ismene × festalis*. An *H. longipetala* × *H. narcissiflora* hybrid. A 1½- to 2½-foot-tall deciduous species bearing umbels of two to five fragrant white 3- to 6-inch-wide flowers in late spring or summer. The individual flowers have very narrow tepals and large showy 2-inch-long staminal cups. 'Zwanenburg' bears large flowers with cups that have scalloped edges. Zones 8 to 10; to Zone 7 with heavy winter mulch.

H. harrisiana
P. 117

h. har-ih-see-AH-nuh. Spider Lily. Formerly *Ismene harrisiana*. Deciduous 1-foot-tall species native to Mexico. Bears umbels of up to six starry white flowers tinged with green that have 3-inch-long tepals and short staminal cups. Zones 9 to 11.

H. narcissiflora
P. 118

h. nar-sis-ih-FLOR-uh. Peruvian Daffodil, Basket Lily. Deciduous 2-foot-tall species bearing umbels with two to five very fragrant white flowers sometimes striped with green. Flowers are borne in summer and are 4 inches wide with 2-inch-long cups. Zones 8 to 11.

H. 'Sulfur Queen'
P. 118

A deciduous 2-foot-tall hybrid grown for its umbels of up to six fragrant yellow flowers with green-striped throats. Blooms are about 6 inches wide and appear from late spring to summer. Zones 9 to 11.

❧ Incarvillea

in-kar-VIL-lee-uh. Bignonia family, Bignoniaceae.

Grown for their showy clusters of trumpet-shaped flowers, *Incarvillea* species are annuals and tap-rooted perennials native to Asia. While trumpet-shaped blooms of the most commonly grown species in this genus have earned it the name hardy gloxinia, these members of the bignonia family actually are more closely related to trumpet vines (*Campsis* spp.) and Chilean glory vine (*Eccremocarpus scaber*) than to gloxinias. All of the 14 species that belong to this genus bear racemes or panicles of tubular two-lipped flowers that have five spreading lobes, or "petals." The flowers are borne above mounds of handsome leaves divided in a featherlike (pinnate or pinnatisect) fashion.

HOW TO GROW
Select a site in full sun that is shaded during the hottest part of the day. Rich, moist, well-drained soil is best. Since incarvilleas do not tolerate soil that is very wet in winter, a well-drained site, such as a raised bed, is

best. Plant the crowns (composed of thick, fleshy roots) in spring, setting the crown about 1 inch below the soil surface. Handle them carefully to avoid breaking the brittle roots. Amend the soil with coarse sand or grit if winter moisture might be a problem. Incarvilleas are best left undisturbed once planted, as they resent root disturbance. In areas where they are marginally hardy, mulch plants in late fall with evergreen boughs, pine needles, salt hay, or another coarse mulch. Plants also thrive in containers, which can be overwintered in a cool (40° to 50°F) spot and kept on the dry side. Or, dig the roots and store them in dry peat in a cool spot over winter. Propagate by seeds, by carefully digging and dividing the clumps, or by rooting shoot cuttings of stems that arise at the base of the plant in spring.

I. delavayi
P. 119

i. deh-LAV-ay-eye. Hardy Gloxinia. Handsome, tap-rooted 1- to 2-foot-tall perennial forming 1-foot-wide rosettes of pinnate leaves with coarsely toothed leaflets. From early to midsummer plants bear showy racemes of up to 10 pink 3-inch-wide flowers with yellow throats. 'Snowtop' is a white-flowered cultivar. Zones 6 to 10.

✿ Ipheion

IF-ee-on. Lily family, Liliaceae.

One species in this genus of ten is cultivated — *Ipheion uniflorum,* commonly known as spring starflower. It bears starry, fragrant blooms in spring and like all the members of this genus, it grows from small tunicate bulbs. Bulbs usually produce a single flower stalk, sometimes two, with one or two upward-facing flowers. The individual flowers have a salverform shape, meaning they have a slender tube with a flared and flattened face. Like other lily-family plants, the flowers have six lobes, or petal-like tepals. *Ipheion* species are native to South America. Plants produce basal, linear leaves that have a garlicky odor when bruised.

HOW TO GROW
Give spring starflowers a site in full sun with average soil that is moist and well drained. Where hardy, plant the bulbs in late summer or early fall with the tops of the bulbs 3 inches below the soil surface. Where marginally hardy, look for a protected site, such as at the base of a south-facing wall, and protect the bulbs with a coarse winter mulch of ever-

green boughs, pine needles, salt hay, or coarse leaves such as oak leaves from late fall through winter. These plants also are good candidates for growing in containers: pot the bulbs in fall with the tips about ½ inch under the soil surface. Hold them in a cool (40° to 45°F) room or cold frame and keep the soil just barely moist. After plants have bloomed, water and feed regularly until the leaves turn yellow, then store them nearly dry until the following year. Repot in fall as necessary. Spring starflowers grown in the ground can be left for years without needing to be divided. Dig the clumps in summer, just as the leaves disappear, if they become overcrowded and begin to bloom less, or for propagation. Or propagate by seeds.

I. uniflorum PP. 119, 120

i. yoo-nih-FLOR-um. Spring Starflower. Formerly *Tristagma uniflorum*. A 6- to 8-inch-tall species bearing starry, fragrant 1½-inch-wide flowers in spring. Blooms are normally pale blue with darker blue midribs. 'Wisley Blue' bears darker purplish blue flowers. 'Rolf Fiedler' is a 4- to 5-inch-tall hybrid with rich blue flowers that have overlapping tepals. Zones 6 to 9.

❦ *Ipomoea*

eye-po-MEE-uh. Morning glory family, Convolvulaceae.

While the best-known members of this genus are grown for their showy flowers, *Ipomoea* also contains a tender perennial grown in vegetable gardens for its succulent tubers as well as in flower and container gardens for its handsome leaves: sweet potato, *Ipomoea batatas*. Like many members of the genus, it is a climber or scrambler — the genus name is from the Greek *ips*, worm, and *homoios*, resembling. Closely related to *Convolvulus* species, *Ipomoea* species bear funnel- or bell-shaped flowers, either singly or in clusters in the leaf axils. *Ipomoea* contains nearly 500 species of annuals and perennials as well as shrubby plants. In addition to climbers, the genus contains both prostrate and erect species.

HOW TO GROW

A site in full sun and average, well-drained, evenly moist soil is ideal. Although *I. batatas* has a vinelike habit, it does not twine around strings as do many other morning glories, but it can be trained up trellises or other supports. Or allow plants to sprawl out of containers or over the ground. To grow cultivars selected for their foliage, start with plants (they are not grown from seeds), and transplant them to the garden a few weeks after the last frost once temperatures remain above 45°F. The tubers they produce during the summer can be dug before frost in fall and overwintered indoors. Dry the tubers off thoroughly then store them in a cool (55°F), dry location. Like sweet potatoes grown in the vegetable garden, overwintered tubers of ornamental cultivars can be used to start new plants from slips. (The tubers also can simply be replanted in spring after the last frost date once the soil has warmed up.) To start slips, in late winter, place a tuber in a jar filled halfway up with water (the top two-thirds of the tuber should be out of the water). Keep the jar in a warm (75°F), sunny windowsill. Tubers treated in this manner will form sprouts that have roots at the base: pull the sprouts, or slips, off and pot them up when they are about 6 inches long.

I. batatas   P. 120

i. bah-TAH-tas. Sweet Potato. A tender perennial grown in food gardens for its fleshy, sweet, edible tubers. Plants can climb or spread 10 feet or more in a single season, and to 20 feet or more in frost-free climates. They bear rounded to heart-shaped leaves that can be entire or lobed and 1-inch-wide pale purple flowers in summer. While even cultivars developed for vegetable gardens have attractive foliage often flushed with purple, several cultivars are grown for their leaves alone: 'Blackie' bears dark purple-black maplelike leaves; 'Margarita' has chartreuse heart-shaped leaves; and 'Pink Frost' has arrow-shaped leaves marked with green, white, and pink, which require protection from direct sun. Zones 9 to 11.

ᛗ *Iris*

EYE-riss. Iris family, Iridaceae.

Named in honor of the mythological Greek goddess Iris who rode to earth on a rainbow, *Iris* is a vast genus containing about 300 species— both perennials and bulbs—along with thousands of cultivars. All bear flowers with six petal-like tepals. Three of the tepals point up or out and are called standards, and three point out or down and are called falls. Generally the flowers are borne in small clusters and the buds open in succession, a characteristic that lengthens the display from each flower stalk. The foliage is sword shaped, strap shaped, or grassy. Bulbous species grow from tunicate bulbs.

HOW TO GROW

Give bulbous irises a site in full sun or one that is sunny in spring but shaded in summer by deciduous trees. All need average to rich, well-drained soil. Plant the bulbs in late summer to early fall at a depth of 3 to 4 inches. Like many other spring-blooming bulbs, they die back after flowering. Most require a warm spot with dry soil during their summer dormancy. In areas where they do not receive a dry summer dormant period, the bulbs tend to produce many small nonflowering-sized bulblets and do not bloom reliably after the first year. For this reason, they are frequently grown as annuals or short-lived perennials in areas with wet summers. (In well-drained sites that are dry in summer, these bulblets do eventually reach flowering size.) To help ensure dry conditions in summer, combine them with perennials that do not require watering and locate them along the top of a wall, in a raised bed, or in a rock garden. Or, lift the bulbs after the foliage ripens and store them in paper bags in a warm, dry, dark place over summer. Or, try potting the bulbs in sand and setting the pots in a hot place protected from rain (a cold frame works well). Sprinkle them with water once a month and replant in fall. After flowering, feed with a fertilizer high in phosphorus, such as bonemeal. Dig the bulbs after the foliage has turned yellow or in fall as necessary for transplanting or to divide the clumps for propagation.

Give bearded irises a spot in full sun with average to rich, well-drained soil. Plant them from midsummer to early fall, setting the tops of the fleshy rhizomes just above the soil surface. Rhizomes planted too deeply or covered with mulch are susceptible to rot. Cut back and destroy old foliage and rake up debris around the plants in fall to help control iris borers. Dig and divide bearded irises every 3 years in midsummer or early fall to keep them healthy and vigorous, as well as for propagation. (Discard spongy, old portions along with any rhizomes infested with fat, fleshy iris borer larvae or any rhizomes that smell or are slimy, both signs of bacterial soft rot.) Cut the leaves back by two-thirds, then replant. Water deeply to settle the plants in the soil, and then every 10 days to 2 weeks if the weather is dry. Established plants are quite drought tolerant.

I. bearded hybrids   P. 121

Sometimes listed as *I. germanica*, these hybrids bloom in late spring or early summer with flowers that have fuzzy beards at the top of each fall. They come in various heights and flower sizes, although tall-bearded irises, with 4- to 8-inch-wide blooms atop 27-inch-tall plants, are by far the best known. Other size classes can be as small as 8 inches in height and bloom at slightly different times. Hundreds of cultivars are available in colors from white and pale yellow, through peach, pink, raspberry, bronze-red, lilac, purple, and violet-blue to chocolate brown and red-black. The falls and standards may be the same color, contrasting solid colors, or have margins or mottling in contrasting colors. Many are fragrant. Winners of the American Iris Society's Dykes Medal are all good cultivars, including 'Beverly Sills' (pink), 'Bride's Halo' (white and lemon yellow), 'Dusky Challenger' (purple and violet), 'Edith Wolford' (yellow and blue-violet), 'Honky Tonk Blues' (blue and white), 'Jessy's Song' (white with red-violet, and lemon yellow beards), 'Silverado' (silvery lavender-blue), 'Victoria Falls' (blue and white), and 'Hello Darkness' (violet-black). Zones 3 through 9.

I. bucharica

i. boo-KAR-ih-kuh. An 8- to 16-inch-tall species that belongs to a group called Juno irises, because it has bulbs with fleshy roots attached; handle them carefully at planting time (and when transplanting) to avoid breaking the brittle roots. Bears creamy white and yellow flowers that are 2 to 2½ inches wide in spring. Best for dry, well-drained spots in full sun and good for rock gardens. Zones 5 to 9.

I. danfordiae   P. 121

i. dan-FOR-dee-ee. Danford Iris. A 3- to 6-inch-tall species classified as a reticulated iris because of the brown netlike covering on the bulbs. Bears fragrant yellow 2-inch-wide flowers with brown spots in late winter or early spring. Plant the bulbs with the tops a full 4 inches below the soil surface to discourage them from breaking into many bulblets that are too small to flower. They require warm, dry soil during summer when they are dormant. Zones 5 to 8.

I. Dutch hybrids   P. 122

Dutch irises are 15- to 30-inch-tall plants that belong to a group called the xiphium irises, which also contains Spanish and English irises. *I. xiphium* played a major role in the development of Dutch irises. They produce 3- to 3½-inch-wide flowers in shades of white, yellow, and violet from late spring to early summer. Gardeners who want reliable bloom each year often grow these irises as annuals. They make excellent cut flowers, although cutting generally removes enough foliage that the plants won't return the following year. Zones 6 to 9.

I. histrioides
P. 123

i. hiss-tree-OY-deez. A 4- to 6-inch-tall species classified as a reticulated iris because of the brown netlike covering on the bulbs. Bears violet-blue 2½- to 3-inch-wide flowers in early spring. Best in rich, well-drained soil. Good for naturalizing, but the bulbs may break up into many small bulbs that take several years to achieve flowering size. 'Frank Elder' bears pale violet-blue flowers with darker stripes and a yellow crest on the falls. 'George' bears especially fragrant purple blooms. 'Katharine Hodgkin' has yellow flowers blushed with pale blue and veined and dotted with dark blue. Zones 4 to 9.

I. latifolia

i. lah-tih-FO-lee-uh. English Irises. Formerly *I. xiphioides.* These 20-inch-tall hybrids bear 4- to 5-inch-wide flowers in midsummer in shades of violet-blue, purple, white, and lilac-rose. Grow them in full sun or partial shade with rich, well-drained soil that is constantly moist. They are difficult to accommodate in much of North America, but are relatively easy in the Pacific Northwest and Northeast. Where conditions suit them, they are longer-lived than Dutch and Spanish irises. 'Isabella' bears lilac-rose blooms. 'Mont Blanc' bears white flowers blushed with lilac. 'Mansfield' has purple flowers with a violet-blue blotch and white stripes. Zones 5 to 8.

I. reticulata
PP. 123, 124

i. reh-tik-yoo-LAH-tuh. A 4- to 6-inch-tall species with bulbs that have a netted tunic and grasslike, four-angled leaves. Bears fragrant 2-inch-wide flowers in late winter to early spring in shades of blue and purple. Good for naturalizing, but may not return reliably in areas with hot, wet summers. Several cultivars are available, including 'Cantab', pale blue with a pale yellow blotch on each fall; 'Harmony', deep blue blooms and yellow blotches; 'J.S. Dijt', purple with red-purple falls that are borne late; 'Natascha', pale blue, nearly white, with an orange blotch on each fall; and 'Purple Gem', violet-purple with plum purple falls and purple blotches edged in white. Zones 3 to 8.

I. xiphium
P. 124

i. ZIFF-ee-um. Spanish Iris. The Spanish irises grown in gardens are hybrids, similar to Dutch irises, that bear white, yellow, or violet flowers on 15- to 30-inch plants. They bloom from late spring to early summer; Spanish irises bloom about 3 weeks after Dutch cultivars. Gardeners who want reliable bloom each year often grow these irises as annuals. All make excellent cut flowers, although cutting generally removes enough foliage that the plants won't return the following year. Zones 6 to 9.

❦ *Ismene* see *Hymenocallis*

❦ *Ixia*

IKS-ee-uh. Iris family, Iridaceae.

Ixia species, commonly called ixias, corn lilies, or wand flowers, are South African plants that grow from small corms. They are grown for their showy clusters of star-shaped flowers borne on thin, wiry stems. The plants flower from spring to summer and come in a range of bright colors. Blooms often feature an eye, or center, in a contrasting color. The individual blooms have six petal-like tepals. The flowers can be arranged in loose, graceful spikes or in fairly congested, rounded clusters. The grasslike leaves are mostly basal, although small leaves are borne on the stems, and they are arranged in two ranks or rows. From 40 to 50 species belong to this genus.

HOW TO GROW

Give ixias a site with full sun and rich, well-drained soil. Where hardy, they can be grown outdoors year-round. Like many South African species, they prefer dry soil conditions when dormant. Especially in areas with wet winters, a site with very well drained soil (such as a raised bed) is essential. When growing these corms outdoors year-round, plant them in fall at a depth of 3 to 6 inches. Where they are marginally hardy, look for a protected spot, such as at the base of a south-facing wall, and mulch heavily in fall with a coarse mulch such as evergreen boughs, salt hay, or pine needles. Where ixias are not hardy, treat the corms like those of gladiolus: plant outdoors in spring after all danger of frost has passed at a depth of 3 to 6 inches, then dig the corms in summer after the leaves have died back. Store them dry in net or paper bags in a cool (50° to 60°F), dry, well-ventilated spot. Or grow them in containers by potting the corms in spring (or in late summer for bloom the following year). In pots, set corms at a depth of about 1 inch. Water carefully until plants begin to flower: the soil should stay barely moist, never wet or completely dry. Replace the corms annually or, to hold them for another year's bloom, continue watering after plants flower and feed every other week with a dilute, balanced fertilizer. When the leaves begin to turn yellow and die back gradually, dry off the plants and store the containers in a relatively cool, dry, airy spot. Or clean the soil off the corms and store them in paper bags. Repot in spring. Propagate by seeds or by separating offsets in late summer just as the leaves die down.

I. hybrids   P. 125
Hybrid Corn Lily, Hybrid Wand Flower. Many hybrids have been selected. Most are 12- to 16-inch-tall plants with 1½- to 3-inch-wide blooms from spring to summer. 'Marquette' bears yellow flowers with purple-red centers and petal tips. 'Panorama' bears hot pink flowers with purple centers. 'Mable' bears magenta-pink flowers. 'Blue Bird' bears white flowers with dark purple centers, and the outer petals have a violet-purple streak and purple tip. 'Rose Emperor' bears rose-pink flowers with magenta centers. Zones 9 to 11; to Zone 8 with winter protection.

I. maculata
i. mak-yoo-LAH-tuh. A 6- to 20-inch-tall species bearing spikes of 2½-inch-wide flowers from spring to early summer. Blooms are yellow or orange and have dark purple to purple-black centers. Zones 9 to 11; to Zone 8 with winter protection.

I. viridiflora   P. 125
i. vih-rid-ih-FLOR-uh. Green-flowered Corn Lily. A 1- to 2-foot-tall species bearing spikes of 12 or more pale green flowers with black centers rimmed in violet-purple from spring to summer. Zones 9 to 11; to Zone 8 with winter protection.

❦ *Kaempferia*
kemp-FAIR-ee-uh. Ginger family, Zingerberaceae.

Kaempferia species are tender perennials native to tropical portions of Asia that grow from thick, fleshy, rhizomes; some species have aromatic tubers. They bear rounded leaves that are either clustered at the base of the plant or borne in two rows, or ranks, up short stems. The flowers, which are borne on either leafy or scaly spikes, appear either with the leaves or before the leaves emerge. Each flower has a bract at the base, and individual blooms have three petals with a lower lip that is deeply split into two lobes. About 40 species belong to the genus. The roots of some species are used medicinally and to flavor foods.

HOW TO GROW

Give these plants partial shade and deeply prepared, moist soil that is rich in organic matter. They thrive in areas with warm summers and high humidity and are ideal for gardens in the tropics and subtropics or for adding an exotic touch to more northern gardens. Where hardy, they grow outdoors year-round. In the North, plant the rhizomes out in spring after the soil has warmed up and overwinter them indoors. To overwinter, dig the rhizomes after a light frost and cut back the tops. Store the rhizomes in barely damp vermiculite, peat, or sand in a cool (55°F), dry place. Inspect rhizomes occasionally in winter. Discard rotted pieces or cut away rotted portions and dust cuts with sulfur; sprinkle the vermiculite with water occasionally during winter to keep the roots from shriveling. Replant in spring. Or, grow these plants in containers year-round: keep them nearly dry and in a cool spot over winter. Propagate by dividing the rhizomes in spring.

K. pulchra   P. 126

k. PUL-kruh. Ginger Lily. A low-growing species that reaches about 6 inches and spreads to 12 inches. Bears handsome, rounded leaves marked with dark green and silver-green. Short spikes of 2-inch-wide lilac or lilac-pink flowers appear among the leaves in summer. Zones 10 to 11.

K. roscoeana

k. ros-ko-ee-AH-nuh. Dwarf Ginger Lily, Peacock Lily. A 6-inch-tall species that spreads to about 8 or 10 inches. Bears two rounded dark green leaves that are handsomely marked with lighter green on top and tinged with red-purple underneath. From summer to fall, plants produce short spikes of 2-inch-wide white flowers among the leaves. Zones 10 to 11.

K. rotunda

k. ro-TUN-duh. Resurrection Lily. A 6-inch-tall species, spreading to 1½ feet. Bears 16-inch-long lance-shaped leaves that are silvery green on top and flushed with purple beneath. Spikes of up to six fragrant white 2-inch-wide flowers with purplish bracts appear before the leaves. Zones 10 to 11.

❦ *Lachenalia*

lak-eh-NAIL-ee-uh. Lily family, Liliaceae.

Commonly called Cape cowslips, *Lachenalia* species are tender, bulbous perennials native to South Africa grown for their showy, erect spikes or racemes of flowers that appear from fall to spring. The flowers, which are carried on leafless, often mottled stems, are nodding, held horizontally, or point upward. Individual blooms are bell shaped or tubular to cylindrical and have six petal-like tepals. The tepals are arranged in two whorls, with three outer ones that usually are shorter, somewhat swollen at the tips, and form a fleshy cup or tube. The three inner tepals are longer, and usually wider, and they often feature tips that are a contrasting color and may be recurved. About 90 species belong to the genus, all of which grow from fleshy, tunicate bulbs and produce basal leaves that often are spotted or mottled.

HOW TO GROW

Select a site in full sun with light, rich, well-drained soil. A spot with light shade during the hottest part of the day is best, because it protects plants from heat. Plants require very well drained soil, so if drainage might be a problem, select a spot in a raised bed or rock garden and/or amend the soil with plenty of coarse sand or grit at planting time. Like many South African natives, Cape cowslips are ideal for areas that have Mediterranean climates (such as southern California), characterized by dry summers and mild winters. There, they grow and bloom during the winter months and are dormant during the hot, dry summers. Elsewhere, grow them in containers. In the ground or in containers, plant in late summer or fall. When planting in the ground, set the bulbs at a depth of 3 inches; in containers, set them with the tips just under the soil surface. Water the containers and then hold them over winter in a cool spot (45°F nights; 55°F days) that is well ventilated. Keep the soil just barely moist until the plants begin growing actively; after that, keep the soil evenly moist but never wet. Feed container-grown plants weekly during the growing season. After they bloom, continue watering until the foliage begins to turn yellow, then gradually withhold water. Store the containers in a cool, dry, shady place until late summer, then move them to your overwintering spot in fall to repeat the process. Repot, as necessary, in late summer. Propagate by separating the offsets.

L. aloides   P. 126

l. al-OY-deez. Cape Cowslip. Formerly *L. tricolor*. A 6- to 12-inch-tall species with broadly lance-shaped, 8-inch-long leaves spotted with dull red-purple. In late winter or spring bears erect racemes of 10 to 20 pendent, tubular 1- to 1½-inch-long flowers that are rich yellow with scarlet at the top and bottom. 'Nelsonii' bears golden yellow flowers and leaves that are

not spotted. 'Pearsonii' bears red-orange buds that open into yellow-orange flowers with red-orange bases and leaves mottled with brown.
Zones 9 to 10.

L. bulbifera P. 127

l. bul-BIF-er-um. Cape Cowslip. Formerly *L. pendula*. A 1-foot-tall species
with ovate- to lance- or strap-shaped leaves that are either all-green or
spotted with brownish purple. Bears loose racemes of pendent 1½-inch-
long red or orange flowers with green and purple tips. Zones 9 to 10.

❦ *Lapeirousia* see Anomatheca

❦ *Ledebouria*

leh-deh-BOR-ee-uh. Lily family, Liliaceae.

Ledebouria species are grown for their attractively marked leaves as well
as their racemes of small bell-shaped flowers that somewhat resemble
lilies-of-the-valley *(Convallaria majalis)*. About 16 species belong to this
genus, all once classified in *Scilla*. They are native to South Africa and
grow from small tunicate bulbs. The leaves are basal and usually spotted
with red-green, purple, or a contrasting shade of green. The tiny bell- or
urn-shaped flowers appear in spring or summer.

HOW TO GROW

Give ledebourias a site with light, rich, well-drained soil and full sun.
They also appreciate a spot with light shade during the hottest part of the
day. Like many South African natives, they need a dry summer rest period and, outdoors, are best suited for areas—such as southern California—that have Mediterranean climates (characterized by dry summers
and mild winters). Elsewhere, grow them in containers. Plants require
very well drained soil, so if drainage might be a problem, select a spot in
a raised bed or rock garden and/or amend the soil with plenty of coarse
sand or grit at planting time. They are drought tolerant enough to grow
well with collections of cacti and succulents and make fine houseplants.
Plant the bulbs anytime, setting them partly out of the soil. Keep the soil
just barely moist until the plants begin growing actively; after that, keep
the soil evenly moist but never wet. When the plants begin to grow more
slowly in late summer, gradually withhold water. The leaves may or may
not die back completely. Feed container-grown plants every other week

during the growing season. Overwinter the containers in a cool (40° to 45°F) spot, and keep the soil just barely moist until the following late winter or early spring. Repot, as necessary, in late summer. Propagate by separating the offsets.

L. cooperi

l. KOO-per-eye. Formerly *Scilla adlamii, S. cooperi.* A 2- to 4-inch-tall species that often produces bulbs that are poorly developed. Features 2- to 10-inch-long semievergreen leaves that are oblong to ovate or linear and striped with purple-brown. In summer, bears racemes of up to 50 ¼-inch-long pale purple flowers striped with green. Zones 9 to 11.

L. socialis   P. 127

l. so-shee-AL-iss. Formerly *Scilla socialis, S. violacea.* A 2- to 4-inch-tall evergreen species that grows from crowded clusters of bulbs produced on the soil surface. Features 4-inch-long silver-green leaves marked with dark green and colored purple-green underneath. Bears racemes of about 25 ¼-inch-long purple-green flowers above the foliage in spring and summer. Zones 9 to 11.

❧ Leucojum

lew-KO-jum. Amaryllis family, Amaryllidaceae.

Commonly known as snowflakes, *Leucojum* species are spring- or fall-blooming bulbs grown for their dainty, nodding, bell-shaped flowers. About 10 species belong to the genus, all of which grow from tunicate bulbs and are native to western Europe, the Middle East, and northern Africa. The plants bear basal, strap-shaped to linear leaves and produce their flowers atop erect, leafless stalks with one to as many as eight flowers carried per stalk. The flowers are white and have six petal-like tepals. *Leucojum* species are closely related to snowdrops (*Galanthus* spp.), which bear their flowers singly, or sometimes in pairs. (In some areas *Leucojum* species also are commonly called snowdrops.) In *Galanthus,* the three outer tepals are markedly larger than the inner three, which they nearly conceal, while in *Leucojum* all six are of equal size.

HOW TO GROW

For *L. aestivum* and *L. vernum*, select a site in full sun or partial shade with rich, moist, well-drained soil. They are best in a spot that is protected from hot afternoon sun and prefer soil that remains evenly moist, but not wet, in summer. Mulch the plants with compost or chopped leaves in summer to keep the soil moist, rich, and cool. Both species are ideal for naturalizing in dappled shade and along shrub borders. *L. autumnale* can be trickier to establish but is well worth the effort. Give it full sun or very light shade and perfectly drained soil that is rich in organic matter. This species is native to dry, sandy soils, so plant it in raised beds or rock gardens that offer good drainage, and amend the soil at planting time with plenty of coarse sand or grit. When planting any of the species, plant the bulbs in late summer or early fall, as early as you can buy them. Set them with the tops 2 inches below the soil surface. Snowflakes may take a year or two to become established and begin to bloom happily, and once planted they are best left undisturbed. Propagate by digging the clumps and separating the offsets in late spring or early summer just as the foliage dies back. Or sow seeds.

L. aestivum P. 128

l. ES-tih-vum. Summer Snowflake. A 1½- to 2-foot-tall species with 1½-foot-long leaves. Bears dainty stems of three to as many as eight bell-shaped ¾-inch-long 1-inch-wide white flowers with a green spot on each tepal. Despite the common name, and the fact that *aestivum* is from the Latin for summer, plants bloom in spring. Flowers are faintly fragrant. 'Gravetye Giant' reaches 3 feet and bears 1- to 1½-inch-long flowers. Zones 4 to 9.

L. autumnale

l. aw-tum-NAL-ee. Autumn Snowflake. A dainty 4- to 6-inch-tall species that bears threadlike or grassy leaves. Sprays of two to four white bell-shaped ½- to ¾-inch-long flowers tinged with pink appear in late summer or early fall. Zones 5 to 9.

L. vernum P. 128

l. VER-num. Spring Snowflake. An 8- to 12-inch-tall species bearing strap-shaped 10-inch-long leaves. Produces erect stems with one or sometimes two white 1-inch-long bell-shaped flowers that have a green spot at the tip of each petal in early spring. Zones 4 to 8.

☙ *Liatris*

lee-AT-riss. Aster family, Asteraceae.

Commonly called gayfeathers or blazing stars, *Liatris* species are native North American perennials that produce erect feather- or wandlike spikes or racemes of flowers that open from the top of the stalk down.

Each fuzzy-textured wand consists of many buttonlike flower heads arranged along the stalk. The individual flower heads are made up of all tubular disk florets (they lack ray florets, or "petals") and come in shades of pinkish purple, purple, and white. The plants produce clumps of linear to lance-shaped leaves at the base, with smaller leaves growing up the flower stalks. They grow from thick, flattened rootstocks that are tuber- or cormlike. About 40 species belong to the genus.

HOW TO GROW

Select a site in full sun with average to rich, well-drained soil. Unlike other gayfeathers, which succumb to crown rot in damp soil, *L. spicata* also grows in evenly moist conditions. *L. aspera* and *L. punctata* are suitable for a dry, well-drained site. Too-rich soil leads to plants that require staking. Liatris are sold in containers like conventional perennials, but the tubers or corms also are available in bulb displays: plant the dormant tubers just under the soil surface. Established plants of all species are quite drought tolerant and can remain undisturbed for years. Divide plants, which generally form 1½- to 2-foot-wide clumps, only if they outgrow their space or die out in the center. Propagate by dividing the clumps or separating corms or tubers in early spring or fall or by seeds. Several cultivars, including 'Kobold', come true from seeds.

L. aspera

l. ASS-per-uh. Rough Blazing Star, Rough Gayfeather. A 3- to 6-foot-tall species with tuberous roots. Bears 1½- to 3-foot-long spikes of ¾- to 1-inch-wide lavender purple flower heads in late summer and early fall. Zones 3 to 9.

L. punctata

l. punk-TAH-tuh. Dotted Blazing Star. Compact 6- to 14-inch-tall species with tuberous roots. Bears dense 6- to 12-inch-long spikes of ⅛-inch-wide rosy purple flower heads in late summer. Zones 2 to 8.

L. pycnostachya

l. pik-no-STAY-kee-uh. Kansas Gayfeather, Prairie Blazing Star. A 3- to 5-foot-tall species bearing 1- to 2½-foot-long spikes of densely packed ½-inch-wide mauve-purple flower heads in midsummer. Zones 3 to 9.

L. scariosa

l. scare-ee-O-suh. Tall Gayfeather. A 2½- to 3-foot-tall species with 1- to 1½-foot-long spikes of pale purple 1-inch-wide flower heads in late summer and early fall. Zones 4 to 9.

L. spicata

P. 129

l. spih-KAH-tuh. Spike Gayfeather. Handsome 2-to 5-foot-tall species with erect 1½- to 2-foot-long spikes of densely packed ½-inch-wide pinkish purple flower heads from mid- to late summer. Compact mauve-violet-flowered 2- to 2½-foot-tall 'Kobold' (also sold as 'Gnom') is the most widely available cultivar. 'Floristan White' has white flowers on 3-foot plants. Zones 3 to 9.

❦ Lilium

LIL-ee-um. Lily family, Liliaceae.

Showy, exotic-looking lilies are among the most dramatic flowers grown in gardens. *Lilium* species often are referred to as true lilies because literally hundreds of plants share their common name, including daylilies (*Hemerocallis* spp.), magic lilies (*Lycoris* spp.), and trout lilies (*Erythronium* spp.). True lilies bear their large flowers on erect unbranched stems and have individual blooms that consist of six petal-like tepals. The blooms may point up, out, or down. Flower shapes vary as well: lilies can bear blooms that are trumpet, star, cup, bowl, funnel, or bell shaped. Lilies with recurved or reflexed blooms have tepals that curve back from the center of the flower toward the stem. Blooms come in fiery hues such as orange, red, hot pink, and yellow as well as pastel pinks, rose-reds, cream, and white. The leaves are narrow and lance shaped or grassy and borne up the stems. Lily bulbs consist of fleshy, overlapping scales that are attached at the base of the bulb but loose at the top. (The scales are not tightly packed and are covered with a papery protective tunic as are bulbs of daffodils and tulips, which grow from tunicate bulbs.) Lilies also may produce bulbs at the ends of rhizomes or stolons.

There are about 100 species of lilies, numerous hybrid groups, and countless cultivars within those groups. The North American Lily Society has divided the hybrids into nine divisions based on the origin of the plants along with the shape and position of the flowers, plus a tenth division for the true species. Today, hybrids are grown more commonly than the species, although species lilies are still popular. Not only are hybrids showy, vigorous, and easy to grow, but most are resistant to common lily diseases, including the viruses that made garden lilies the sickly, problem-prone plants they were 50 years ago.

HOW TO GROW

In general, give lilies a spot in full sun with rich, evenly moist, well-drained soil. Several species thrive in partial shade, however, and a spot that receives shade during the hottest part of the day protects plants from heat and helps prolong bloom. Look for a site sheltered from strong winds, which can blow over the plants or break them off at the base. Lilies need plenty of soil moisture during the growing season, but their bulbs rot if the soil remains too wet. Well-drained soil is essential in winter when the bulbs are dormant. Like clematis, lilies like their heads in the sun and their feet in the shade. Look for a spot where the bulbs will be shaded by nearby shallow-rooted perennials. Lilies that tolerate partial shade include Martagon Hybrids (Division II), American Hybrids (Division VI), *L. canadense, L. henryi, L. pardalinum, L. speciosum,* and *L. superbum.* These still need good light to bloom well, and a site with morning sun and afternoon shade is ideal. Or grow them in bright, dappled, all-day shade.

By selecting plants from several different divisions, it's possible to have lilies in bloom from early summer (mid- to late June) right through fall (October). Bloom peaks in midsummer, from July to August, in most areas. Expect bloom times to overlap — lilies that bloom in early summer won't be finished when the earliest midsummer bloomers begin. Also, cultivars in each division can bloom at different times. For example, early- to midseason-blooming Asiatic lilies can flower in mid-June, late June, or July. So, the wider the range of lilies you select, the longer, as well as more consistent and varied, the bloom season you can achieve from these garden aristocrats. *NOTE:* When purchasing bulbs of native lily species, ask about the origin of the bulbs you buy. Look for a source that offers nursery-propagated plants: do not buy wild-collected bulbs, as collectors devastate native populations.

Inspect lily bulbs carefully before you buy, or before you accept a mail-order shipment. They should have plump, fleshy scales and, ideally, should have fleshy roots attached to the bottom of the bulb. (Some dealers cut off the roots before shipment, but bulbs with roots generally recover from shipping and transplanting more quickly.) Always handle the bulbs carefully, as they are easily bruised or damaged. They also dry out easily. Reject bulbs that have dry, withered scales or roots, as well as any that have signs of rot or mold. Some garden centers offer clumps of potted lilies. Although these are usually more expensive than bulbs, and you may have a more limited choice of cultivars, potted lilies get off to a fast start in the garden. Plant bulbs in early spring or in fall up to about a month before the last fall frost date, as soon as possible after you buy them. Unlike hardy spring bulbs such as daffodils, lily bulbs are not completely dormant when they are shipped. The bulbs come packed in moist peat moss or other material; do not allow them to dry out before planting. If you can't plant right away, store the bulbs in the refrigerator or a dark, cool (40°F) place. Prepare the soil before you plant—and ideally before you buy—by working compost, leaf mold, or other organic matter into the soil to a depth of 2 feet. Planting depth varies: in general, plant lily bulbs with the tops at a depth of two to three times the height of the bulb—that usually translates to a depth of 6 to 9 inches. Plant smaller bulbs slightly closer to the surface. Many lilies produce roots along the stem *above* the bulb, which help anchor the plant, and deep planting encourages this. *L. candidum* and *L.* × *testaceum* are the exceptions to the deep planting rule: plant them with only 1 inch of soil over the noses of the bulbs. Space all lilies 1 to 1½ feet apart and, for best effect, plant them in clumps of at least three to five. Mark the locations of the bulbs to avoid digging into them by accident.

Once planted, many lilies thrive for years with only minimal care. When new growth emerges in spring, feed the plants with well-rotted manure or a balanced organic fertilizer. Taller lilies require staking: insert stakes in spring when the new growth is about 1 foot tall and loosely tie the stems to the stakes with soft yarn or strips of nylon stockings. Mulch the plants to control weeds and keep the soil cool, but keep mulch away from the stems to prevent rotting. When plants are actively growing, water them deeply whenever the weather is dry. As the flowers fade, deadhead them to direct the plant's energy into next year's flowers. Let species lilies set some seeds if you want to save them or let plants self-sow; hybrids generally don't come true from seeds. Dig and destroy stunted plants or plants with leaves that are mottled with yellow, as these symptoms indicate plants that are infected with viral diseases. Cut stalks to the ground in fall.

Divide clumps in early spring or late summer to early fall for propagation, if they outgrow their space, or if they become overcrowded, a condition signaled by lots of stems but relatively few flowers. Be sure to dig very deeply around the edges of the clump to avoid slicing into the bulbs by mistake. Some lilies produce pea-sized purple-black bulbils in the leaf axils; others produce small bulblets near the base of the stems, under the soil just above the bulbs. To use these for propagation, plant them in pots or in a nursery bed at a depth of two to three times their height. Scaling is another method used to propagate lilies. Dig up a bulb immediately after the flowers fade and pull off a few of the thick scales on the outside, near the base of the bulb. Replant the parent bulb. Dust the scales with sulfur and plant them immediately, pointed end up, in a flat filled with moist, soilless mix. Cover the flat with a plastic bag suspended on a wire frame and set it in a shady, protected spot outdoors or a warm, bright place indoors out of direct light. Keep the medium moist but not wet. In 6 weeks to 2 months, the scales should produce small bulblets at their bases, which can be potted up.

Divisions and species are listed separately below.

DIVISIONS

Asiatic Hybrids (Division I)   PP. 130, 133, 139

Early to midsummer bloomers, Asiatic Hybrids bear 4- to 6-inch-wide flowers on 2- to 5-foot-tall plants. They are hybrids of several Asian species, including *L. bulbiferum, L. cernuum, L. concolor, L. davidii, L. lancifolium,* and *L. maculatum.* Flowers can point up, out, or down and are not fragrant. They come in a wide range of colors, including orange, yellow, red, pink, purple, cream, and white, and can be a solid color or two-tone. Many have spots in contrasting colors. Asiatics seldom need staking and are vigorous, long-lived plants that form clumps in the right site — well-drained soil in sun. Cultivars include 'America', deep burgundy-red; 'Avignon', bright red-orange; 'Connecticut King', deep yellow; 'Citronella', lemon yellow with recurved tepals speckled with pale reddish or black spots; 'Côte d'Azur', pale pink with recurved tepals; 'Enchantment', orange with brownish speckles; 'Montreux', deep rose-pink; 'Jetfire', rose-pink with yellow centers; 'Fire King', red-orange with recurved tepals and centers spotted with purple; and 'Mont Blanc', white lightly spotted with brown. 'Tiger Babies' bears small peachy salmon flowers with recurved, heavily spotted tepals. Mid-century and Harlequin Hybrid lilies also are Asiatics. Zones 3 to 8.

Martagon Hybrids (Division II)   P. 136

Early to midsummer bloomers derived primarily from *L. martagon,* commonly known as Turk's-cap lily, which bears nodding purple-pink 2-inch-wide flowers with recurved petals and dark spots on 3- to 6-foot-tall plants. *L. martagon* var. *album* has white flowers. Martagon Hybrids also are called Turk's-cap Hybrids and bear racemes of nodding 3- to 4-inch flowers with recurved tepals on 3- to 6-foot plants. The species and many of the cultivars have an unpleasant scent. Martagon lilies include the Backhouse Hybrids, including 'Mrs. R. O. Backhouse', which bears orange-yellow flowers flushed with pink, as well as the Paisley and Marhan Hybrids. Both *L. martagon* and the Martagon Hybrids grow in full sun to partial shade. They tolerate a wide range of well-drained soils, from acid to slightly alkaline. Zones 3 to 8.

Candidum Hybrids (Division III) P. 131

Early to midsummer bloomers derived from *L. candidum* as well as other species. *L. candidum,* commonly known as Madonna lily, bears fragrant, waxy white 2- to 3-inch-long flowers in clusters of 5 to 20 blooms on 3- to 6-foot-tall plants. Candidum Hybrids bear erect clusters of 4- to 5-inch flowers on 3- to 4-foot plants. Blooms come in deep red, yellow-orange, and pale yellow to tan. Candidum Hybrid cultivars, which are not as commonly offered as Asiatics and Orientals, include 'Apollo', with tan flowers flushed with apricot, and 'Zeus', which bears red flowers. Nankeen lily *(L. × testaceum),* with yellow-orange flowers, also is classified as a Candidum. Unlike most lilies, *L. candidum* and Candidum Hybrids should be planted with no more than 1 inch of soil over the tops of the bulbs. When planted in fall, they produce a low clump of evergreen leaves before winter. Grow in neutral to slightly alkaline soil. Zones 4 to 9.

American Hybrids (Division VI)

Early to midsummer bloomers, American Hybrids were developed by crossing a variety of native North American species, including well-known Canada lily *(L. canadense)* as well as a number of West Coast natives. They bear clusters of 4- to 6-inch flowers with recurved or sometimes funnel-shaped flowers. The 4- to 8-foot plants require acid soil rich in organic matter. Partial shade is best, especially during the hottest part of the day. Cultivars include the Bellingham Hybrids, such as yellow-orange 'Shuksan' and 'Buttercup', a yellow flower spotted with maroon. Zones 5 to 8.

Longiflorum Hybrids (Division V) P. 135

Early to midsummer bloomers derived primarily from *L. longiflorum,* or Easter lily, and *L. formosanum. L. longiflorum* bears fragrant white 7-inch-long trumpets on 1½- to 3½-foot-tall plants. While the species is not usually considered a garden plant—it is normally hardy only in Zones 7 to 9 and is grown primarily in pots—the cultivar 'Mount Everest' bears fragrant white flowers and can be grown in Zones 5 to 8. Give it a spot in partial shade. Longiflorum Hybrids tolerate alkaline soil.

Trumpet and Aurelian Hybrids (Division VI)

PP. 129, 134

Mid- to late-summer bloomers derived from a variety of Asiatic species, including *L. regale, L. henryi*, and *L. sargentiae*. Many of the lilies in this division have classic trumpet-shaped blooms, but cultivars with bowl-, flat-faced, or recurved blooms also are included here. The flowers, borne in clusters, usually are fragrant and generally face outward or are nodding. Colors include red, pink, gold, yellow, orange, and white; some are purple-red, brown, or green on the back or outside of the flower. Plants range from 4 to 8 feet tall and nearly always require staking. Cultivars include 'Black Dragon', which bears fragrant trumpets that are dark purple-red outside and white inside; 'Bright Star', with fragrant creamy white blooms that have recurved tepals; 'Copper King', with fragrant apricot-orange trumpets with recurved tepals; 'African Queen', with fragrant trumpets that are brown-purple on the outside and golden to orangy yellow inside. Golden Splendor Group cultivars also fall here. Zones 4 to 8.

Oriental Hybrids (Division VII)

PP. 136, 138

Mid- to late-summer bloomers with showy, fragrant flowers that can reach 10 inches across. These are derived primarily from Asian species such as *L. auratum, L. japonicum*, and *L. speciosum*. The blooms usually are bowl shaped, flat faced, or recurved, but trumpet-shaped Orientals also have been developed. White, pink, rose-red, and dark maroon-red are common colors; many cultivars feature flowers striped with yellow or spotted with red. Plants range from 2 to 8 feet tall, and the taller-growing cultivars generally require staking. Cultivars include: 'Black Beauty', with fragrant dark raspberry pink blooms that have recurved tepals edged in white; 'Casa Blanca', with fragrant pure white bowl-shaped blooms; 'Star Gazer', with rose-red blooms spotted with darker red; and 'Tom Pouce', with pink tepals that have recurved tips and a yellow midrib. Zones 4 to 8.

Other Hybrids (Division VIII)

This is a catch-all division of hybrids that have parents in more than one division—an Oriental Hybrid crossed with a Trumpet Hybrid, for example. The cultivar 'Leslie Woodruff' is one example. It bears dark red flat-faced flowers that have a light fragrance and slightly recurved tepals tipped in white. 'Scheherazade' bears dark red flat-faced flowers edged in yellow that have recurved tepals tipped in white. Both are late-season bloomers. Zones 5 to 8.

SPECIES

Division IX includes all true species lilies.

L. auratum   P. 130
l. aw-RAH-tum. Goldband Lily. Mid- to late summer– or fall-blooming species with fragrant 12-inch-wide bowl-shaped flowers that usually face outward. Blooms are white with a yellow stripe on each recurved tepal and borne in clusters of about 12. Plants range from 2 to 5 feet tall. Susceptible to viral diseases. Requires well-drained, acid soil; wet soil in winter is fatal. Zones 5 to 8.

L. bulbiferum
l. bul-BIF-er-um. Orange Lily, Fire Lily. A species that blooms in midsummer, producing one- to five-flowered clusters of erect, bowl-shaped 4- to 6-inch-wide orange-red flowers that have tepals spotted with maroon or maroon-black. Produces bulbils in the leaf axils. Zones 3 to 8.

L. canadense   P. 131
l. kan-ah-DEN-see. Canada Lily, Meadow Lily. Mid- to late summer–blooming lily that is a native North American wildflower that spreads via rhizomatous bulbs. Bears yellow-orange 3-inch-wide flowers on 3- to 6-foot-tall plants. Flowers are pendent, have slightly recurved tepals, and are spotted with maroon. Grows in damp to evenly moist, acid soil in full sun or partial shade. Zones 3 to 7.

L. candidum   P. 131
l. kan-DEE-dum. Madonna Lily. *See* Candidum Hybrids

L. cernuum
l. SIRN-yoo-um. Nodding Lily. A midsummer bloomer that produces racemes of 6 to 12 or more fragrant, pendent 1¼- to 2-inch-wide blooms in lilac, lilac-pink, or purple. Tolerates alkaline soil, but best in peaty, acidic conditions. Zones 2 to 6.

L. columbianum   P. 132
l. ko-lum-bee-AH-num. Columbia Tiger Lily, Oregon Lily. A 5-foot-tall species native to the Pacific Northwest. Bears clusters of 6 to 10 or more pendent 2-inch-wide flowers with recurved tepals. Blooms are yellow to orange-red in color and spotted with maroon. Zones 5 to 8.

L. concolor   P. 132

l. KON-kuh-lor. Star Lily, Morning Star Lily. A 3-foot-tall species that blooms in midsummer and bears clusters of up to 10 erect, star-shaped scarlet 1½-inch-wide flowers. Zones 3 to 7.

L. davidii

l. dah-VIH-dee-eye. A 3- to 4-foot-tall midsummer bloomer that bears clusters of 10 to as many as 20 3-inch-wide red flowers with recurved tepals and purple-black spots. Bulbs may spread by stolons. Zones 3 to 7.

L. formosanum   P. 134

l. for-mo-SAH-num. Formosa Lily. Late summer– to fall-blooming species bearing white 3- to 8-inch-long trumpet-shaped flowers on 4- to 7-foot-tall plants. Susceptible to viral diseases. Requires evenly moist, acid soil and spreads via rhizomatous bulbs. Plants are easy and fast from seeds sown indoors in midwinter; seedlings can begin blooming the first year from seed. *L. formosanum* var. *pricei* is a dwarf form that reaches about 2 feet in height. Zones 5 to 9.

L. grayi

l. GRAY-eye. Orange Bell Lily, Gray's Lily. A native wildflower from the eastern United States that bears clusters of up to 12 fragrant, nodding 2½-inch-long red flowers that are paler yellowish red inside and spotted with purple. Requires moist, acid soil. Zones 4 to 7.

L. henryi

l. HEN-ree-eye. Henry Lily. Mid- to late summer–blooming species producing 2½- to 3-inch-wide orange flowers with recurved tepals spotted with maroon. Blooms are borne in clusters of 10 to 20 on 3- to 10-foot plants. Grows in partial shade in neutral to alkaline soil. Self-sows, and seedlings bloom in about 3 years. Zones 4 to 8.

L. lancifolium   P. 135

l. lan-sih-FO-lee-um. Formerly *L. tigrinum*. Tiger Lily. Orange-red 5- to 9-inch-wide flowers with dark purple-black spots in late summer to fall on 3- to 5-foot plants. Grows in evenly moist acid to slightly alkaline soil. Plants can be infected with viral diseases without showing symptoms. To avoid spreading viral diseases to other lilies, buy certified virus-free bulbs. Zones 3 to 9.

L. longiflorum
I. lon-jih-FLOR-um. *See* Longiflorum Hybrids

P. 135

L. martagon
I. MAR-tah-gon. *See* Martagon Hybrids

P. 136

L. pardalinum

P. 137

I. par-dah-LYE-num. Leopard Lily, Panther Lily. A 5- to 8-foot-tall species native to the western United States. Bears clusters of up to 10 nodding 3½-inch-wide flowers in midsummer. Blooms are orange-red to red in color, spotted with maroon, and have recurved tepals. Best in moist soil in full sun. Tolerates alkaline soil. Zones 5 to 8.

L. philadelphicum
I. fil-ah-DEL-fih-kum. Red Lily, Wild Orange Lily, Wood Lily. A 1- to 3-foot-tall species native to eastern North America. In midsummer, bears racemes of one to three upward-facing orange-red 3- to 4-inch-wide bowl-shaped flowers with slightly recurved tepals spotted with maroon. Zones 2 to 6.

L. pumilum

P. 137

I. pew-MIL-um. Coral Lily. Formerly *L. tenuifolium*. Early- to midsummer-blooming species bearing fragrant 2-inch-wide scarlet flowers with recurved tepals on 1- to 2-foot-tall plants. Full sun to partial shade. Requires acid soil. Bulbs are short-lived, lasting 2 to 4 years, but plants self-sow. Deadheading prolongs the life of the bulbs, but leave some flowers to form seedpods. Zones 3 to 7.

L. regale

P. 138

I. reh-GAL-ee. Regal Lily, Royal Lily. Mid- to late summer–blooming species bearing clusters of up to 25 fragrant 6-inch-long trumpet-shaped flowers on 2- to 6-foot-tall plants. Blooms are white inside and purple- to wine-colored on the outside. Vigorous and easy in well-drained soil but will not grow in very alkaline conditions. Plants emerge early in spring and can be killed by late frosts. Cover emerging plants with bushel baskets or burlap if a late frost threatens. Self-sows, and seedlings begin blooming in about 2 years. Zones 3 to 8.

L. speciosum
I. spee-see-O-sum. Japanese Lily. Mid- to late summer–blooming species bearing clusters of about 12 fragrant 7-inch-wide flowers on 3- to 5½-

foot-tall plants. Blooms, which may face out or down, have recurved petals and come in pale pink or white, usually flushed deeper pink in the center and spotted with red. *L. speciosum* var. *rubrum* has deep pink flowers. A vigorous species that grows in full sun or partial shade and requires rich, evenly moist, very well drained acid soil. Wet soil in winter is fatal. Susceptible to viral diseases and has been largely replaced by the Oriental Hybrids. Zones 4 to 8.

L. superbum
l. soo-PER-bum. American Turk's-cap Lily. Mid- to late summer–blooming species native to North America. Bears clusters of up to 40 orange-red 3-inch-wide flowers with recurved tepals that are spotted with maroon on 4- to 8-foot-tall plants. Grows in damp to evenly moist, acid soil in full sun or partial shade. Established plants tolerate drought. Spreads via rhizomatous bulbs. Zones 4 to 9.

☙ Lycoris
lye-KOR-iss. Amaryllis family, Amaryllidaceae.

Native to China and Japan, *Lycoris* species are grown for their showy clusters of flowers borne from spring to fall, depending on the species. From 10 to 12 species belong to the genus, all perennials that grow from tunicate bulbs and produce linear- to strap-shaped leaves. The flowers are produced in umbels atop fleshy, leafless stems, and the blooms appear when the leaves are dormant—the common name magic lily refers to this characteristic, since the bloom stalks seem to arise suddenly from bare ground. The leaves either die back before the flowers emerge or appear after the flowers fade. The individual flowers have six petal-like tepals. Flowers have six prominent stamens that stick out. The tepals, which are joined together only at the base to form a short tube, are recurved and spreading. Blooms either have broad tepals (so the blooms resemble lily-like trumpets) or are spidery looking. Species with spidery blooms have narrow, strongly reflexed tepals with wavy edges along with prominent stamens.

HOW TO GROW
Select a site in full sun or partial shade with deeply prepared, rich, well-drained soil. Where hardy, plant the bulbs in fall with the tops of the bulbs 4 to 6 inches below the soil surface, and space them about 9 inches

apart. Mark the location of the plants so you don't dig into them by acci-dent after the foliage dies back in spring. Where they are marginally hardy, protect the plants in late fall with a dry winter mulch of evergreen boughs, salt hay, pine needles, or coarse leaves, such as oak leaves. Top-dress before the foliage emerges with a balanced organic fertilizer. Out-doors, combine *Lycoris* species with perennials such as hostas or low-growing asters, which will provide a foil for the blooms. Or overplant the bulbs with annuals. Where they are not hardy, grow them in containers with the tops of the bulbs set just at the soil surface. When container-grown plants are growing actively, keep the soil evenly moist and feed every other week with a dilute, balanced fertilizer. Gradually withhold water as the leaves turn yellow and die back. Let the soil dry out com-pletely, then overwinter the bulbs indoors — still in their containers — in a cool (45° to 50°F), dry spot. Container-grown plants need repotting only every few years. Outdoors, undisturbed plants gradually form large clumps. They can be propagated by separating the offsets, but plants are best left undisturbed as long as possible. (Disturbing them can prevent their flowering for one or two seasons). Or propagate by seeds.

L. albiflora
l. al-bih-FLOR-uh. A 1½-foot-tall species that bears umbels of four to six white flowers in late summer and early fall. Individual blooms are 1½ to 2 inches long and spidery in appearance, with reflexed, wavy-margined tepals. Leaves appear after the flowers. This species is similar to *L. radiata* and may well be a variety of that species. Zones 9 to 10.

L. aurea
l. OR-ee-uh. Golden Spider Lily, Golden Hurricane Lily. A 2-foot-tall species that bears umbels of five or six golden yellow flowers in late spring or summer. Individual blooms are 4 inches wide and spidery in appearance, with wavy-margined tepals reflexed at the tips. Leaves appear after the flowers. Zones 8 to 10.

L. radiata   P. 139
l. ray-dee-AH-tuh. Red Spider Lily. A 1- to 2-foot-tall species that bears um-bels of four to six deep red or deep pink flowers in late summer and early fall. Individual blooms are 1½ to 2 inches long and spidery in appearance, with very reflexed tepals that have wavy margins. Leaves appear after the flowers. Zones 8 to 10.

L. sanguinea

l. san-GWIH-nee-uh. A 1½- to 2-foot-tall species bearing umbels of about six funnel-shaped red flowers in late summer and early fall. Individual blooms are 2 to 2½ inches long and have slightly reflexed tips. Zones 9 to 10.

L. squamigera   P. 140

l. skwa-mih-JEER-uh. Hardy Amaryllis, Magic Lily, Resurrection Lily. A 1½- to 2-foot-tall species bearing umbels of six to eight fragrant pale to rich pink flowers in summer. Individual blooms are lilylike, 3 to 4 inches long, and have fairly broad tepals that are reflexed at the tips. Leaves appear in spring, before the flowers. Zones 6 to 10; to Zone 5 with protection.

❦ Mertensia

mer-TEN-see-uh. Borage family, Boraginaceae.

Some 50 species belong to the genus *Mertensia,* all perennials, about half of which are native North American wildflowers. They bear loose clusters of pendent, bell-shaped or tubular flowers that have five lobes and rounded to lance-shaped leaves. Blooms commonly come in shades of blue to purple, as well as white and sometimes pink.

HOW TO GROW

Select a site in sun or shade with rich, evenly moist, well-drained soil. *M. pulmonarioides* goes dormant and disappears after flowering in spring, so pick a spot where you will not dig into its stout, fleshy, carrotlike rootstocks by mistake. When adding native mertensias to your garden, look for garden-grown or nursery-propagated plants: avoid wild-collected ones. You may be able to acquire these plants from a neighbor's garden or at a local native plant sale, such as one held by a local botanical garden or conservation organization. To propagate, dig the clumps in early summer before the leaves disappear completely. Plants self-sow, and seedlings are easy to move in spring.

M. pulmonarioides   P. 140

m. pul-mo-nair-ee-OY-deez. Virginia Bluebells, Virginia Cowslip. Formerly *M. virginica.* A 1- to 2-foot-tall wildflower native to the eastern half of North America that grows from fleshy white carrotlike roots and spreads to 1 foot. Produces mounds of bluish green leaves, and in spring bears nodding clusters of pink buds that open into pale lilac-blue to purple-blue ¾-to 1-inch-long bells. Zones 3 to 9.

❦ *Mirabilis*

meer-AB-il-iss. Four-o'clock family, Nyctaginaceae.

Mirabilis contains some 50 species of annuals and tender, tuberous-rooted perennials native to the Americas. They bear ovate leaves and trumpet-shaped flowers that have long tubers and flared, flattened faces that have five spreading lobes or "petals," as they are usually called. One species, a tender, tuberous-rooted perennial, is a popular, old-fashioned plant. The botanical name for the genus is from the Latin word *mirabilis,* meaning wonderful.

HOW TO GROW

Full sun to partial shade and average, well-drained soil are ideal. Start four-o'clocks from seeds sown outdoors on the last spring frost date or indoors 6 to 8 weeks before the last frost date at 55° to 65°F. Germination takes 1 to 3 weeks. From Zone 7 south, sow seeds outdoors in fall for bloom the following year. Either way, just press the seeds onto the soil surface, as light is required for germination. For best bloom, water regularly and feed monthly. North of Zone 10, grow these plants as bedding plants replaced annually or as tender perennials: either start new plants from seeds each year, or dig the tuberous roots after a light fall frost and store them in barely damp vermiculite, peat, or sand in a cool (40° to 50°F), dry place, as you would dahlias. In Zones 10 and 11, grow them outdoors year-round as perennials. Where they are marginally hardy, mulch heavily in fall.

M. jalapa   P. 141

m. jah-LAH-puh. Four-o'clock, Marvel of Peru. A bushy 2-foot-tall perennial, hardy from Zone 10 south but often forming self-sowing colonies north of that zone. Bears ovate leaves and fragrant 2-inch-long flowers in pink, red, magenta, yellow, and white, sometimes with stripes or other markings of more than one color on each flower. Flowers on the same plant can be different colors. Plants bloom from midsummer to fall, and each flower opens in the afternoon and dies by morning. Zones 10 to 11.

❦ *Muscari*

mus-CAR-ee. Lily family, Liliaceae.

Commonly known as grape hyacinths, *Muscari* species are beloved for their dainty, grapelike clusters of small flowers, which are borne in early to midspring. About 30 species belong to the genus, all of which grow from tunicate bulbs and have grassy, somewhat fleshy, basal leaves that usually range from 1 to 1½ feet in length. Leaves may be inversely lance shaped (oblanceolate), linear, or narrowly spoon shaped; in all cases they are quite narrow. They are native to the Mediterranean as well as southwestern Asia. Although in all cases the individual flowers are tiny—usually ⅛ to ⅜ inches long—the racemes are quite showy because the individual flowers are erect and densely packed. Several species bear sterile flowers at the tops of the racemes that are paler in color than the fertile ones. Flowers usually come in shades of violet, purplish blue, pale blue, and white. They may be bell or urn shaped as well as nearly round or tubular, and the flowers may point up, out, or down. Most species bear blooms that have constricted mouths, and it is this characteristic that distinguishes them from their close relatives, the true hyacinths (*Hyacinthus* spp.), which have flowers with wide-open throats. Grape hyacinths also have much smaller flowers than true hyacinths. The botanical name *Muscari* is from the Latin *moschus,* musk, and refers to the fragrance of some species.

HOW TO GROW

Select a site in full sun or light shade with rich, well-drained soil. These are spring-blooming plants that disappear by midsummer, so spots lightly shaded under deciduous trees usually are fine because they offer full sun before the trees leaf out. Plant the bulbs in late summer or early fall at a depth of 3 to 4 inches. Some species produce offsets in abundance and others do not; some species also self-sow. *M. armeniacum, M. botryoides,* and *M. neglectum* can propagate themselves to the point of being invasive; because of their vigor, they also are excellent for naturalizing. While the foliage of all species dies back in midsummer, *M. armeniacum* produces new leaves again in fall. Many gardeners use this characteristic to advantage by overplanting other, more expensive, spring bulbs with this species: the fall grape hyacinth foliage marks the location of the other bulbs and eliminates the danger of digging into established clumps. Propagate grape hyacinths by dividing the clumps in summer, after the leaves turn yellow but before they disappear completely, or sow seeds.

M. armeniacum
P. 141

m. ar-men-ee-AH-kum. Grape Hyacinth. A vigorous 4- to 8-inch-tall species producing dense, cylindrical 1- to 3-inch-long racemes of fragrant violet-blue urn-shaped to tubular flowers in spring. The individual flowers have white around the mouth. Cultivars include 'Blue Spike', with double blue flowers; 'Argaei Album', with white flowers; 'Cantab', with large extra fragrant blue flowers; 'Fantasy Creation', an 8-inch-tall selection with tight racemes of double violet-blue flowers; and 'Christmas Pearl', an early-blooming cultivar with light violet-blue flowers that open in early spring. Zones 4 to 8.

M. aucheri

m. AW-cher-eye. Formerly *M. lingulatum*. A 4- to 6-inch-tall species bearing dense, cylindrical ½- to 1½-inch-long racemes in spring. Individual flowers are rounded-tubular, rich blue in color, and have white or paler blue at the mouth. The racemes usually have a number of pale blue sterile flowers at the top. 'Tubergenianum' (formerly *M. tubergenianum*) is a vigorous 8-inch-tall selection with a conspicuous cluster of pale blue sterile flowers at the top. Zones 6 to 9.

M. azureum
P. 142

m. ah-ZUR-ee-um. Formerly *Hyacinthus azureus, Hyacinthella azurea, Pseudomuscari azureum*. A dainty 3- to 6-inch-tall species bearing racemes of bell-shaped flowers in spring that have nearly unconstricted mouths. Blooms are sky blue with a darker blue stripe on each lobe. *M. azureum* f. *album* bears white flowers. Zones 4 to 9.

M. botryoides
P. 142

m. bo-tree-OY-deez. Grape Hyacinth. A 6- to 8-inch-tall species bearing dense 1- to 2-inch-long racemes of flowers in spring that have a fruity fragrance. Individual flowers are bright blue and urn shaped with white mouths. *M. botryoides* f. *album* bears fragrant white flowers. Zones 3 to 8.

M. comosum

m. ko-MO-sum. Tassel Grape Hyacinth. Formerly *Leopoldia comosa*. An 8-inch to 2-foot-tall species that in spring bears 2½- to 12-inch-long racemes of nodding, fertile, urn-shaped flowers topped by tassel-like clusters of upward-facing, nearly round sterile flowers. The fertile flowers are olive-brown with creamy or yellow-brown lobes, and the sterile flowers are bright violet-purple. 'Plumosum', commonly sold as feather hyacinth and sometimes listed as 'Monstrosum' as well as *M. plumosum,* bears racemes of all-sterile violet-blue flowers that have threadlike tepals. Zones 4 to 9.

M. latifolium
P. 143

m. lat-ih-FO-lee-um. An 8- to 12-inch-tall species bearing 1- to 2½-inch-long racemes of urn-shaped dark violet-blue fertile flowers topped by a cluster of paler sterile flowers. Zones 4 to 8.

M. macrocarpum

m. mak-ro-KAR-pum. Formerly *M. muscarimi* var. *flavum, M. moschatum* var. *flavum.* A 4- to 6-inch-tall species bearing 1½- to 2½-inch-long racemes of fragrant, tubular ¾-inch-long flowers that point outward. The buds are purple-brown and open into yellow-green flowers. In order to flower well, this species requires hot, dry conditions in summer when it is dormant. Zones 7 to 9.

M. neglectum

m. neh-GLEK-tum. Musk Hyacinth. Formerly *M. racemosum.* A 4- to 8-inch-tall species that often produces leaves in fall. In spring, bears dense ½- to 2-inch-long racemes of dark violet-blue urn-shaped flowers with white mouths. Zones 4 to 8.

M. paradoxum see Bellevalia pycnantha

☙ Narcissus

nar-SIS-us. Amaryllis family, Amaryllidaceae.

Although nearly everyone is familiar with golden yellow trumpets of daffodils in spring, this genus offers flowers in a remarkably wide range of shapes, sizes, and even colors. All daffodils grow from tunicate bulbs and bear strap-shaped leaves that begin poking above the soil surface in winter, generally after a spell of mild weather. The bulbs and all parts of the plants are poisonous, and thus are left alone by deer as well as mice and other rodents. The flowers consist of a central trumpet or cup, properly called a corona: the corona is referred to as a trumpet if it is long and a cup if it is short. The corona is surrounded by six "petals," more properly called perianth segments, that are collectively called the perianth. The most common flower colors are yellow, orange, and white, but there also are pink daffodils, which generally emerge yellow and turn pink as they mature. Many cultivars feature bicolor blooms — a yellow perianth with an orange cup or trumpet, for example. Bloom season varies, too, and cultivars are generally rated as early-, midseason-, or late-blooming. By planting some that fall into each category, it's possible to have daffodils in bloom for 3 months or more in spring. While all *Narcissus* species are commonly called daffodils, dwarf daffodils with small cups are sometimes referred to as jonquils.

There are about 50 species of daffodils along with literally thousands of cultivars, which are much more commonly grown in gardens today than the species. These have been divided into 12 divisions based on flower shape and origin, and catalogs and well-labeled nursery displays refer to these divisions when describing their offerings. While you don't necessarily need to know the names of the divisions, knowing they exist will help you make good choices. If you select cultivars from several different divisions, you'll be ensured of an interesting variety of flower shapes and sizes, for example. Most full-size daffodils are 3½ to 4½ inches across, but there are tiny 1½-inch-wide selections. Flowers can be single or double, and a single bulb can bear 1 or up to 20 flowers per stem. Plant sizes vary, too: full-size daffodils are usually 18 inches tall, but there are tiny miniatures that range from 4 to 6 inches. In addition, cultivars in the different divisions tend to bloom at similar times, so choosing cultivars from several different divisions also helps extend the bloom season.

HOW TO GROW

Plant daffodils in full sun to partial shade. A site shaded by deciduous trees is fine, because it provides full sun in spring while the plants are growing actively, and shade isn't a problem once the leaves ripen and the plants are dormant. Well-drained soil is essential: the bulbs of nearly all daffodils rot in damp soil. Beyond that, daffodils aren't particular: they'll grow in sandy to loamy soil and tolerate acid to alkaline conditions — pH 5.0 to 8.0. Ideally, the soil should be evenly moist from fall to spring and drier during summer.

Plant the bulbs in fall. Early planting is best, because it gives the bulbs time to grow roots before cold weather arrives. Bulbs are graded and priced according to size. Landscape-sized or "round" bulbs are 3 years old and produce one or more flower stems the first year. They are the least expensive and generally a good buy. Double-nose or bedding-sized bulbs are 4 years old and usually produce two flower stems the first year. Exhibition-sized or triple-nose bulbs are 5 years old and produce three or more flower stems. Proper planting depth varies according to the size of the bulbs: plant two to three times as deep as the bulbs are tall, generally with the shoulder of the bulb (the point where it swells out from the nose, or top) 4 to 6 inches below the soil surface. Space large hybrids 6 to 10 inches apart, miniatures slightly closer. Bulbs planted at the wider spacing look sparse at first, but they fill in and need dividing less frequently. If you have heavy, wet soil, dig in lots of organic matter such as compost or leaf mold to improve drainage. In this case, planting on the shallow side is best. Planting in raised beds filled with improved soil is another option for dealing with heavy clay and poorly drained sites.

Daffodils need minimal care once they are planted. The plants survive just fine without watering, but if the weather is unusually dry in spring or fall, weekly watering (½ inch per week) is beneficial. Let the leaves ripen for 6 to 8 weeks after the flowers fade so they can make food to support next year's flowers. Where they are marginally hardy, cover the plants in late fall with a coarse mulch of evergreen boughs, salt hay, coarse leaves (such as oak leaves), or pine needles. Propagate by digging the clumps just as the foliage disappears in midsummer and separating and replanting the offsets.

Divisions and species are listed separately below.

DIVISIONS

Trumpet Cultivars (Division 1)   PP. 147, 149

These bear one flower per stem, with a trumpet (corona) as long as or longer than the "petals," or perianth segments. Trumpet hybrids bloom in early to midspring and range from 12 to 20 inches tall. 'King Alfred', introduced in 1899, is one of the best-known cultivars that fall here. It bears all-yellow flowers with pointed perianth segments that are slightly twisted at the tips. Other all-yellow cultivars include 'Arctic Gold', 'Dutch Master', 'Golden Harvest', 'Marieke', 'Unsurpassable', and lemon yellow 'Lemon Glow'. All-white-flowered cultivars include 'Beersheba', 'Empress of Ireland', 'Rashee', and 'Mount Hood', which bears flowers slightly blushed in yellow when they open. Outstanding bicolor cultivars include 'Honeybird', pastel yellow perianth, creamy white, yellow-rimmed trumpet; 'Las Vegas', creamy white perianth, yellow trumpet; and 'Spellbinder', yellow perianth, greenish yellow cup that matures to white. This division also contains miniatures, including 8-inch-tall 'Little Beauty', white perianth, yellow trumpet; 'Little Gem', 6 inches, with all-yellow blooms;

'Midget', a 3- to 4-inch-tall selection with yellow blooms; and 'Topolino', an 8- to 10-inch-tall cultivar with a white perianth and a yellow trumpet. Zones 4 to 8; to Zone 3 with winter protection.

Large-cupped Cultivars (Division 2)   PP. 148, 150, 154, 155

Sometimes called long-cupped daffodils, these bear one flower per stem with a cup (corona) that is more than one-third the length of the "petals," or perianth segments, but not as long as the perianth segments. These cultivars usually bloom in midspring and range from 10 to 20 inches tall. Many cultivars are available. All-yellow selections include 'Carlton', a fragrant, vigorous selection good for naturalizing even in the South, and 'Gigantic Star', with fragrant rich yellow blooms. All-white selections include 'Easter Moon' and 'White Plume'. Bicolors are especially popular in this division and these include 'Fortissimo', yellow perianth, orange cup; 'Ice Follies', white perianth, yellow cup; 'Peaches and Cream', creamy white perianth, pale peach-pink cup; 'Pink Charm', white perianth, with a white cup that has a dark pink band; 'Redhill', creamy white perianth blushed with yellow, red cup; 'Romance', white perianth, rose-pink cup; 'Salome', white perianth, pink cup rimmed with gold; 'Scarlet O'Hara', yellow perianth, red cup. Zones 4 to 8; to Zone 3 with winter protection.

Small-cupped Cultivars (Division 3)   PP. 146, 156

Also called short-cupped daffodils, these cultivars bear one flower per stem with a cup (corona) that is equal to or less than one-third the length of the "petals," or perianth segments. These cultivars usually bloom from mid- to late spring and range from 14 to 18 inches in height. Cultivars include 'Barrett Browning', white perianth, orange-red cup; 'Barrii Conspicuus', an old cultivar introduced in 1869 with a yellow perianth and yellow, red-banded cup; 'Birma' and 'Sabine Hay', both with a yellow perianth, coral-red cup; 'Queen of the North', white perianth, small pale yellow cup; 'Sinopel', white perianth, lime green cup; and all-white "Dream Castle'. Zones 4 to 8; to Zone 3 with winter protection.

Double Cultivars (Division 4)   PP. 146, 155, 156

As their name suggests, these daffodil cultivars bear double flowers — both the corona and/or the "petals" (perianth segments) may be doubled. Flowers are either solitary or borne more than one bloom per stem. Plants range from 14 to 18 inches in height. Double cultivars that bear solitary blooms include 'Acropolis', fragrant white blooms flecked with red in the center; 'Flower Drift', creamy white flecked with yellow-orange in the center; 'Honolulu', fragrant white flowers with red petaloids in the center; 'Manly', pale yellow with rich orange in the center; 'Petit Four', creamy white flowers with apricot centers; 'Delnashaugh', white flowers with apricot-pink segments in the center; and 'Tahiti', yellow petals interspersed with bright orangy red segments. Doubles that bear more than one flower per stem include 'Sir Winston Churchill', clusters of three to five fragrant, creamy white flowers with orange-flecked segments at the center; 'Bridal Crown', clusters of two to three fragrant white flowers with orange-yellow segments interspersed, hardy in Zones 4 to 9; 'Cheerfulness', clusters of two to three fragrant white flowers flecked with yellow, hardy in Zones 4 to 9; and 'Yellow Cheerfulness', with clusters of two to three yellow blooms, hardy in Zones 3 to 9. Early-flowering 'Rip van Winkle' (also listed as *N. minor* ssp. *pumilus* 'Plenus' and *N. pumilus* 'Plenus') is a 4- to-6-inch-tall miniature with yellow dandelion-like blooms that have many pointed perianth segments and green interspersed with the yellow. Hardiness of double cultivars varies: unless otherwise noted, the ones listed here are hardy in Zones 4 to 8; to Zone 3 with winter protection.

Triandrus Cultivars (Division 5)　　　PP. 149, 153

Triandrus daffodils feature umbels of two to six small nodding flowers that usually have short cups and reflexed "petals," or perianth segments. These cultivars bloom in mid- to late spring. Plants are 12 to 14 inches tall. Cultivars include 'Petrel', with clusters of three to five extremely fragrant white flowers that have bell-shaped cups; 'Hawera', an 8-inch-tall miniature with clusters of three to five yellow flowers; 'Stint', with clusters of three to five lemon yellow flowers; and 'Thalia', with clusters of two to three fragrant white flowers. Zones 4 to 9.

Cyclamineus Cultivars (Division 6)　　　PP. 144, 148, 150

Solitary flowers and reflexed "petals," or perianth segments, characterize cyclamineus cultivars. The flowers usually have a long trumpet and point down at an acute angle from the stem. These bloom in early to midspring and are 10 to 14 inches tall. Cultivars include 'Beryl', an 8-inch-tall selection with a yellow perianth and yellow cup banded in orange; 'Jetfire', yellow perianth, orange-red cup; 'Jack Snipe', white perianth, yellow cup; 'Foundling', white perianth, apricot-pink cup; and 'Peeping Tom', a vigorous all-yellow selection. Zones 4 to 9.

Jonquilla Cultivars (Division 7)　　　PP. 154, 157

Jonquilla daffodils feature umbels of one to five flowers with small cups and spreading "petals," or perianth segments. They bloom in mid- to late spring and often have fragrant flowers. Jonquilla cultivars have nearly cylindrical leaves. Plants are 12 to 16 inches tall. Cultivars include 'Baby Moon', an 8-inch-tall miniature with clusters of several all-yellow flowers per stem; 'Chit Chat', another miniature, from 3 to 4 inches tall, with prolific clusters of yellow flowers; 'Bell Song', with clusters of three to five fragrant flowers with creamy white perianths and rose-pink cups; 'Curlew', clusters of fragrant white flowers that open creamy yellow; 'Quail', clusters of two to four bronzy yellow blooms; 'Sundial', an 8-inch-tall miniature with clusters of fragrant golden yellow flowers that have nearly flat cups; 'Stratosphere', with two to three fragrant golden yellow flowers per stem; and 'Sweetness', with very fragrant golden yellow flowers produced one or two per stem. Zones 4 to 9.

Tazetta Cultivars (Division 8) PP. 144, 147

These small-flowered daffodils produce umbels of 3 or 4 to as many as 20 flowers that have small cups and broad "petals," or perianth segments. The flowers are very fragrant. Tazetta cultivars are good daffodils for southern gardens. They range from 12 to 16 inches in height. Cultivars include 'Avalanche', with clusters of 15 to 20 fragrant flowers with white perianths and yellow cups, Zones 6 to 9; 'Geranium', with clusters of three to five fragrant flowers that have white perianths and orange-red cups, Zones 4 to 9; 'Scarlet Gem', with clusters of three to five flowers with yellow perianths and red-orange cups, Zones 5 to 9; and 'Silver Chimes', with 8 to 10 fragrant white flowers per stem, Zones 6 to 9. 'Canaliculatus' is a 4- to 6-inch-tall miniature with four to seven fragrant flowers per stem that have white perianths and yellow cups; hardy in Zones 6 to 10, it is best in a spot that remains hot and dry in summer. Hardiness varies widely in this group, from Zones 4 or 6 to 9, depending on the cultivar.

Poeticus Cultivars (Division 9) P. 143

Tiny disc-shaped red-rimmed cups and broad white "petals," or perianth segments, characterize Poeticus cultivars. The flowers are fragrant and usually borne one per stem. Poeticus cultivars bloom from mid- to late spring and range from 14 to 18 inches tall. The most commonly grown cultivar is 'Actaea', with sweetly fragrant flowers that have broad white perianth segments surrounding a yellow cup edged in dark red. 'Cantabile' bears small fragrant flowers with a white perianth and a green and yellow cup edged in red. Zones 3 to 7.

Wild Species (Division 10)

This division includes all the species daffodils and their variants, several of which are described below under "Species."

Split-corona Cultivars (Division 11)

PP. 145, 153

Split-corona daffodils usually bear solitary flowers that are characterized by a trumpet or cup (corona) that is split for more than half its length. These cultivars bloom from mid- to late spring. Plants range from 14 to 18 inches tall. Cultivars include 'Blanc de Blancs', with all-white flowers and a split cup (blushed with yellow when it opens) that lies flat against the perianth; 'Cassata', with a white perianth and yellow cup that matures to white; 'Colblanc', with a white perianth with a green cup; 'Orangery', with white petals and a wavy-edged tangerine cup; 'Printal', with a white perianth and a frilly yellow cup; and 'Palmares', with a white perianth and a frilly salmon-pink cup. 'Papillon Blanc' has a white perianth with a white cup marked with green and yellow, and 'Broadway Star' has white petals surrounding a split cup that forms an orange star in the center. Zones 4 to 7.

Miscellaneous Daffodils (Division 12)

P. 157

This division contains a variety of daffodils that do not fit into other divisions. Several miniatures fall here. 'Jumblie', a 5- to 6-inch-tall selection, bears clusters of several small flowers that have very reflexed yellow perianth segments surrounding orange-yellow cups; hardy in Zones 4 to 9. 'Quince', a 5- to 6-inch-tall selection, bears clusters of three to four flowers with very reflexed sulphur yellow perianth segments and dark yellow cups; hardy in Zones 4 to 9. 'Tête-à-Tête', is a 5- to 6-inch-tall cultivar with yellow flowers, usually borne in pairs, hardy in Zones 4 to 9.

SPECIES

N. bulbocodium

P. 145

n. bul-buh-KO-dee-um. Hoop Petticoat Daffodil. A diminutive 4- to 6-inch-tall species with nearly round, grasslike leaves. In midspring, bears yellow 1½-inch-wide flowers with tiny, twisted, pointed perianth segments and a megaphone-shaped trumpet. *N. bulbocodium* ssp. *conspicuus* is a vigorous form with deep yellow flowers. Zones 4 to 8.

N. jonquilla

P. 151

n. jon-KWIL-luh. Wild Jonquil. A 12-inch-tall species bearing rounded leaves and very fragrant flowers in late spring. Golden yellow flowers are 1¼ inches across and have pointed perianth segments and a small flat cup. Zones 5 to 9.

N. × medioluteus

n. × meh-dee-oh-LOO-tee-us. Primrose Peerless Narcissus, Poetaz Narcissus, Twin Sisters Narcissus. Formerly *N. × biflorus*. A *N. poeticus × N. tazetta* hybrid. This 10- to 12-inch-tall hybrid blooms in very late spring and usually bears two 1¼- to 2-inch-wide flowers per stalk. Individual blooms have a white perianth and a small yellow cup. Zones 3 to 8.

N. minor   P. 151

n. MY-nor. Sometimes listed as *N. nanus*. A dainty 4- to 6-inch-tall species bearing 1¼-inch-wide yellow flowers in early spring that point slightly downward. Zones 5 to 8.

N. obvallaris

n. ob-val-LAR-iss. Tenby Daffodil. Also listed as *N. pseudonarcissus* ssp. *obvallaris*. A vigorous 12-inch-tall species bearing golden yellow 1½-inch-wide flowers in early spring that face upward. Zones 3 to 8.

N. × odorus   P. 152

n. × o-DOR-us. Campernelle Jonquil. Sometimes listed as *N. campernelli*. A *N. jonquilla × N. pseudonarcissus* hybrid. A 10- to 12-inch-tall hybrid bearing one or two very fragrant yellow flowers per stem in early spring. Blooms are 1½ inches across and have narrow perianth segments surrounding a large cup. 'Plenus' bears double flowers. Zones 5 to 8.

N. poeticus   (*See also* Poeticus Cultivars, p. 356)

n. po-EH-tih-kus. Poet's Narcissus. An 8- to 20-inch-tall species bearing very fragrant, solitary flowers in late spring. Individual blooms are 1¾ to 3 inches across and have a white perianth with a very small yellow redrimmed cup. 'Plenus' (also listed as *N.* 'Albus Plenus Odoratus') bears fragrant double white flowers. *N. poeticus* var. *recurvus*, commonly called Pheasant's Eye, bears 1½-inch-wide flowers with a white perianth and a yellow red-rimmed cup. Unlike other daffodils, *N. poeticus* and its cultivars tolerate moist to wet soil in winter and spring and fairly damp conditions in summer. Zones 3 to 7.

N. tazetta

n. tah-ZET-tuh. Polyanthus Narcissus. A variable 6- to 20-inch-tall species bearing umbels of about 4 to as many as 15 very fragrant blooms in late winter or very early spring. Individual flowers are 1½ inches across and have a white perianth with a yellow cup. Paperwhite narcissus belong here; these bear clusters of fragrant white flowers and are commonly forced in water. Zones 7 or 8 to 9.

N. triandrus

n. tri-AN-drus. Angel's Tears. A dainty 4- to 10-inch-tall species bearing nodding creamy white flowers in umbels of one to as many as six blooms in midspring. Individual blooms are 2½ inches wide and have reflexed perianth segments surrounding a rounded cup. Zones 4 to 9.

❦ Nectaroscordum

nek-tah-ro-SKOR-dum. Lily family, Liliaceae.

Nectaroscordum species bear clusters of flowers that resemble ornamental onions, and, in fact, the three species in this genus were once classified in *Allium*. The botanical name refers to the fact that all parts of these plants smell strongly of garlic when bruised—it is from the Greek *nektar,* nectar, and *skordon,* garlic. The nodding, bell-shaped flowers, which are borne in loose umbels, appear in summer. Like alliums, plants bear individual flowers that are small and have six petal-like tepals. Plants grow from tunicate bulbs and have grassy, linear leaves that emerge in spring and die back as the flowers fade or shortly after they fade.

HOW TO GROW
Select a site in full sun or partial shade with average to rich, well-drained soil. Combine them with low-growing annuals or perennials to hide the foliage as it fades. Plants are good for naturalizing, but self-sow, sometimes with abandon, and can become invasive. Propagate by seeds or dig the bulbs in summer as the leaves fade and separate the offsets.

N. siculum   P. 158

n. SIK-yoo-lum. Honey Garlic. Formerly *Allium siculum.* A vigorous 3- to 4-foot-tall species with linear leaves that have a sharp keel along one side. In summer, plants bear umbels of 10 to as many as 30 nodding creamy white ½- to 1-inch-long flowers that are flushed with pink or purple-red and greenish at the base. *N. siculum* ssp. *bulgaricum* (formerly *Allium bulgaricum, Nectaroscordum discoridis*) bears creamy white flowers that are green at the base and flushed with purple. Zones 6 to 10.

☙ *Nerine*

neh-REE-nee. Amaryllis family, Amaryllidaceae.

Grown for their showy fall flowers, nerines are tender bulbs native to southern Africa. About 30 species belong to the genus, all growing from tunicate bulbs and producing strap-shaped, deciduous leaves that appear either with the flowers or soon after the flowers open. The flowers are produced in umbels of 2 to more than 20 blooms atop fleshy, leafless stems. They have six petal-like tepals. The narrow tepals are joined together only at the base to form a short tube and either stick out straight or spread widely. As a result, the blooms either resemble loose, lilylike trumpets or are spidery in appearance. Species with spidery blooms have narrow, strongly reflexed tepals with wavy edges along with prominent stamens.

HOW TO GROW

Give nerines full sun and rich, very well drained soil. Where they are hardy, plant the bulbs outdoors in spring at a depth of 5 to 6 inches and space bulbs about 5 inches apart. Like many South African natives, these bulbs require a mild climate with a dry dormant period. In areas with dry summers and nearly frost-free winters, they are easily satisfied: they are dormant in summer, and leaves appear in fall and last partway though winter. Where they are marginally hardy or may be exposed to too much summer rain, look for a warm, south-facing site, such as at the base of a wall with very well drained soil, and in late fall protect the plants with a heavy, coarse mulch such as evergreen boughs, pine needles, or salt hay. Or, grow these bulbs in containers, planting the bulbs in spring or early summer with the top half above the soil surface.

Soak the soil at planting time, then water very sparingly until the leaves appear in late summer—the soil should remain nearly, but not completely, dry. Water regularly when plants are growing actively. Plants prefer cool temperatures, but bring them indoors before temperatures dip much below 50°F at night in fall. Begin to withhold water when the leaves start to turn yellow, then store the bulbs—still in their containers—in nearly dry soil in a cool (35° to 50°F), dry place. Bulbs also can be dug and stored out of the ground in a cool, dry place but generally do not perform as well. That's because whether outdoors or in containers, plants are happiest when left undisturbed and will thrive for years without needing division: dig or pot on the bulbs only if they become overcrowded or for propagation. Container-grown plants bloom best when slightly pot-bound; topdress the containers annually in late summer to replenish the soil but try to disturb the roots as little as possible. Propagate by separating the offsets in fall as the leaves die back or by seeds.

N. bowdenii

P. 158

n. bow-DEH-nee-eye. Nerine. Native South African species reaching 1½ feet in height. Bears umbels of six or seven funnel-shaped 3-inch-long pink flowers in fall. Blooms have a musky scent and wavy-edged tepals. 'Pink Triumph' bears dark pink blooms. Zones 8 to 10, to Zone 7 with heavy winter protection.

N. sarniensis

n. sar-nee-EN-sis. Guernsey Lily. A 1½-foot-tall species native to South Africa and naturalized on the island of Guernsey in the English Channel. In fall it bears umbels of 5 to as many as 20 orange-red to red flowers that are 1¼ to 1½ inches across and have wavy-margined, reflexed tepals and showy, protruding stamens. This species is highly variable and is one parent of many hybrids that range in color from rose and salmon-pink as well as pale pink, to scarlet, orange-red, and white. Zones 8 to 10.

☙ Nothoscordum

no-tho-SKOR-dum. Lily family, Liliaceae.

While *Nothoscordum* species resemble their close relatives garlic and onions, they lack the characteristic smell of members of the genus *Allium*. Both common and botanical names signal this relationship: *Nothoscordum* species are commonly known as false garlics, and the botanical name is from the Greek *nothos,* false, and *skordon,* garlic. False garlics grow from tunicate bulbs and produce grassy, linear, basal leaves. The small flowers are borne in loose umbels on leafless stems from spring to summer. Individual blooms have six petal-like tepals. They may be funnel, bell, or star shaped. About 20 species belong to the genus, native to North, Central, and South America.

HOW TO GROW

Select a site in full sun or partial shade with average, well-drained soil that is not too rich. Plant the bulbs in fall at a depth of about 3 inches. They are best used in wild gardens and rock gardens. Plants self-sow, sometimes with abandon; deadhead to curtail this tendency. Propagate by seeds or by separating the offsets in fall.

N. gracile

n. grah-SIL-ee. Sometimes listed as *N. fragrans, N. inodorum.* A 1- to 2-foot-tall species native to Mexico and South America. From spring to summer, bears umbels of 8 to 15 fragrant, funnel-shaped flowers. Individual blooms are ⅜ to ½ inch long and white with brown or pink stripes. Zones 7 to 9.

❧ Ornithogalum

or-nith-o-GAL-um. Lily family, Liliaceae.

Commonly known as stars-of-Bethlehem, *Ornithogalum* species are hardy and tender bulbs primarily native to South Africa and the Mediterranean. Plants grow from tunicate bulbs and bear basal leaves that range from narrow and linear to rounded. Depending on the species, plants bloom from late winter to spring or summer. They produce starry, usually white, flowers that are carried in either erect, spikelike racemes or rounded racemes that resemble umbels or corymbs. Individual blooms consist of six petal-like tepals. The outer tepals are often striped with green on the outside.

HOW TO GROW

Select a site in full sun or light shade with average to rich, well-drained soil. Where they're hardy, plant the bulbs outdoors in fall, setting them at a depth of 4 inches. The two most commonly grown species — *O. nutans* and *O. umbellatum* — are fairly hardy and suitable for naturalizing in grass, along shrub borders, and other semiwild areas. Because of their abundant offsets, both can become invasive (*O. umbellatum* tends to be more invasive). Where marginally hardy, look for a warm, south-facing site with very well drained soil and mulch heavily in late fall with evergreen boughs, salt hay, pine needles, or another coarse mulch. Where these plants are not hardy, or in areas where too much summer rain may cause them to rot, plant them outdoors in spring after the soil warms up or grow them in containers. Overwinter the plants by either digging the bulbs as they go dormant in late summer or fall or drying off the soil in containers and storing them in a cool (50°F), dry spot. Container-grown plants can be brought indoors before the first frost to finish blooming indoors, then gradually dried off for overwintering. Propagate by separating the offsets in fall or early spring or by seeds.

O. arabicum
P. 159

o. ah-RAB-ih-kum. Star-of-Bethlehem. A 1- to 3-foot-tall species native to the Mediterranean. Bears rounded racemes of 6 to 25 cup-shaped 1½-inch-wide pearly white flowers that have a prominent black ovary in the center. Blooms appear in early summer and have a rich, fruity fragrance. Zones 8 to 10.

O. balansae

o. bah-LAN-see. Sometimes listed as *O. oligophyllum.* A diminutive 3-inch-tall species native to the Balkans, Turkey, and the Republic of Georgia. In early spring bears rounded racemes of two to five cup-shaped 1¼-inch-wide white flowers that are green on the outside. Zones 5 or 6 to 10.

O. dubium
P. 159

o. DOO-bee-um. Star-of-Bethlehem. Formerly *O. florescens, O. triniatum.* An 8- to 12-inch-tall species from southern Africa. From late winter to early spring, bears racemes of up to 25 cup-shaped 1-inch-wide flowers in shades of golden yellow, orange, red, and sometimes white. Zones 8 to 10.

O. nutans
P. 160

o. NEW-tans. Nodding Star-of-Bethlehem. An 8- to 18-inch-tall species from Europe and southwestern Asia that is naturalized in parts of North America. In spring, bears one-sided racemes of about 20 fragrant, funnel-shaped, slightly downturned white flowers that are striped with green on the outside. Zones 5 to 10.

O. saundersiae
P. 160

o. sawn-DER-see-ee. Giant Chincherinchee. A 2- to 3-foot-tall species from southern Africa. From late winter to early spring bears rounded racemes of cup-shaped ¾- to 1-inch-wide white or creamy white flowers. Zones 7 or 8 to 10.

O. thyrsoides

o. thyr-SOY-deez. Chincherinchee. A 1- to 2-foot-tall South African native. Bears dense racemes of many starry, cup-shaped ¾-inch-wide flowers in spring and early summer that are white with creamy or greenish bases. Zones 7 or 8 to 10.

O. umbellatum

P. 161

o. um-bel-LAH-tum. Star-of-Bethlehem. A vigorous 6- to 12-inch-tall species native to the Mediterranean. Bears rounded racemes of starry white ¾-inch-wide flowers in early summer that have a broad stripe of green on the backs of the tepals. May be invasive. Zones 4 to 9.

❦ Oxalis

ox-AL-iss. Oxalis or Wood Sorrel family, Oxalidaceae.

Oxalis is a large diverse genus of annuals and perennials (both hardy and tender) as well as a few shrubby species. Primarily native to Africa and South America, they are commonly called wood sorrels or simply oxalis. Plants have bulbous, rhizomatous, tuberous, or fibrous roots. While most species bear shamrock-like, three-leaflet leaves, there are also wood sorrels with up to 20 or more leaflets. All have leaves with leaflets arranged in a palmate (handlike) fashion. Many species have leaves that fold downward at night. The small flowers have five rounded petals and are solitary or borne in clusters (umbel-like cymes). Not surprising for a large genus — about 500 species belong here — *Oxalis* contains some attractive garden plants as well as some pesky weeds, including creeping wood sorrel (*O. corniculata*), and common or yellow wood sorrel (*O. stricta,* formerly *O. europaea*).

HOW TO GROW

Select a site in full sun to partial shade with sandy to gritty soil that is well drained. Outdoors, most wood sorrels are happiest in Mediterranean climates, characterized by cool summers, mild winters, and alternating seasons of wet and fairly dry weather. (Plants tolerate dry soil in summer, but are best with a little moisture.) Nevertheless, most are easy to grow elsewhere. Where summers are hot, look for a cool, north-facing site or one that receives shade during the hottest part of the day. Where winters are wet, grow them in raised beds or rock gardens with very well drained soil: wet feet in winter spells disaster. At the northern limits of their hardiness, protect plants over winter with a coarse mulch such as evergreen boughs, pine needles, or salt hay. The tuberous and bulbous species listed here need a rest period, and most are deciduous. (*O. regnellii,* for example, will keep its leaves over winter if grown indoors as a houseplant or can be dried off like the other species, as described below.)

To grow wood sorrels in containers, plant the tubers or bulbs in pots or bulb pans (shallow pots) at the beginning of their growing season—spring for the species listed here, except for spring-blooming *O. adenophylla*, which should be started in a cool greenhouse in fall. Soak the soil at potting time, then water very sparingly until leaves emerge and the plants begin growing actively. Keep the soil evenly moist and feed regularly throughout the growing season. Plants grow best in cool conditions, so protect them from the hottest sun of the day. In late summer or fall gradually withhold water as the leaves begin to die back. Store the bulbs or tubers—still in their pots—in completely dry soil in a cool (40° to 50°F), dry spot. Repot in spring. Propagate by separating the offsets or dividing the tubers in early spring.

O. adenophylla   P. 161
o. ah-den-oh-FIL-uh. Wood Sorrel, Oxalis. A 4-inch-tall South American species that grows from a tuberous, scale-covered base with leaves that have 9 to 20 or more inversely heart-shaped leaflets. In late spring, bears solitary 1-inch-wide funnel-shaped flowers that are pale purplish pink with white throats and darker purple-pink veins. Zones 6 to 8.

O. bowiei   P. 162
o. BO-wee-eye. Wood Sorrel, Oxalis. Formerly *O. purpurata* var. *bowiei*. An 8- to 10-inch-tall South African species that grows from tunicate bulbs and has leathery, cloverlike, three-leaflet leaves that are green above and sometimes purple below. Bears clusters (umbel-like cymes) of 3 to 12 funnel-shaped 1½-inch-wide flowers from summer to fall that are purple-pink to rose-red with green throats. Zones 8 to 10.

O. depressa
o. dee-PRESS-uh. Formerly *O. inops*. A bulbous South African species that reaches 4 inches in height and bears gray-green three-leaflet leaves that have triangular leaflets and sometimes have dark spots. In summer bears solitary, funnel-shaped ¾-inch-wide dark rose-pink to purple-pink flowers that have yellow throats. Zones 5 to 9.

O. lasiandra
o. lah-see-AN-druh. A bulbous 5- to 12-inch-tall species from Mexico with green leaves that have 5 to 10 narrow wedge-shaped to straplike leaflets. From summer to fall bears umbels of 9 to 25 or more trumpet-shaped ¾-inch-wide flowers that are red or violet with a yellow throat. Plants produce a thick taproot that is covered with small scaly bulbils near the top. Zones 7 to 10.

O. purpurea
P. 162

o. pur-PUR-ee-uh. Wood Sorrel, Oxalis. A variable 4-inch-tall bulbous South African species with three-leaflet leaves. Leaflets range from diamond shaped to rounded and dark green above, purple beneath. Solitary, funnel-shaped flowers, borne in summer to fall, are 1¼ to 2 inches across. They have a yellow throat and come in rose-purple, rose-pink, pale to deep violet, cream, and white. Zones 9 to 10.

O. regnellii
P. 163

o. reg-NEL-lee-eye. Wood Sorrel, Oxalis. A 4- to 10-inch-tall South American species with scale-covered rhizomes. Bears three-leaflet leaves with triangular-shaped leaflets that are green above and burgundy on the undersides. Flowers, borne in three- to seven-flowered umbels, are ⅜ to ¾ inch across and white or very pale pink in color. *O. regnellii* var. *triangularis* bears rich burgundy leaves and pale pink flowers. Zones 7 to 10.

O. tetraphylla
P. 163

o. teh-trah-FIL-uh. Wood Sorrel, Oxalis, Good Luck Plant. Formerly *O. deppei*. A 6-inch-tall bulbous species from Mexico with leaves that have four leaflets that range from triangular to strap shaped and usually are marked with purple at the base. In summer, bears clusters (umbel-like cymes) of 4 to 12 funnel-shaped ¾- to 1¼-inch-wide red-purple to rich rose-pink flowers that have yellow-green throats. 'Alba' has a white triangle on the leaves and pink flowers. 'Iron Cross' has burgundy cross-shaped blotches at the bases of the leaflets and hot pink flowers. Zones 7 to 10.

O. versicolor

o. VER-sih-kuh-lor. Candycane Sorrel. A bulbous 3-inch-tall species from South Africa with three-leaflet leaves that have linear leaflets. From late summer to winter, bears solitary, funnel-shaped ¾- to 1¼-inch-wide white flowers that are edged in either red or purple-violet on the back. Zones 9 to 10.

❦ Pancratium

pan-KRAY-tee-um. Amaryllis family, Amaryllidaceae.

Commonly called sea lilies, *Pancratium* species are tender bulbs grown for their fragrant flowers, which resemble daffodils as well as their close relatives in the genus *Hymenocallis*. About 16 species belong here, all of which grow from tunicate bulbs and are native from the Mediterranean to tropical Asia and western Africa. They bear basal leaves that are linear to strap shaped. The flowers have six narrow, spreading petal-like tepals that are joined at the base. The tepals surround a cup that resembles the cup of a daffodil but is properly called a staminal cup because it is formed by six stamens that are fused at the base. (A close look at the flowers reveals the stamens protruding from the cup.) One difference between *Hymenocallis* species and *Pancratium* species is the fact that the latter produces numerous unwinged seeds in each ovary compartment, while *Hymenocallis* produces two or sometimes up to eight seeds per compartment.

HOW TO GROW
Select a site in full sun or partial shade with rich, evenly moist, well-drained soil. Where they are hardy, plant the bulbs outdoors in late summer or early fall. In the North, plant the bulbs outdoors in late spring or early summer after the soil has warmed up. Either way, set the tips of the bulbs 6 to 8 inches below the soil surface—slightly deeper if you are trying to grow them outdoors year-round at the northern limit of their hardiness. In containers, plant bulbs with the necks just above the soil surface. Keep the soil evenly moist while plants are growing actively, and feed container-grown specimens every other week with a dilute, balanced fertilizer. To overwinter the plants where they are not hardy, dig the bulbs after a light fall frost or when the foliage turns completely yellow. Try to damage the roots as little as possible when digging. Set the bulbs upside down to dry them off (this ensures that moisture from the foliage will drip away from the bulbs). Store the bulbs in nearly dry peat or vermiculite in a cool (55° to 60°F), dry spot. Propagate by separating the offsets in spring or fall when the plants are dormant or by seeds.

P. maritimum P. 164
p. mah-RIH-tih-mum. Sea Lily. A 12-inch-tall species from the Mediterranean bearing umbels of fragrant white 4-inch-wide flowers in late summer. Zones 8 to 11.

ꕤ *Pleione*
plee-O-nee. Orchid family, Orchidaceae.

Pleione species are small orchids native from western India to China and Japan that are sometimes grown for their showy flowers. Plants grow from bulblike organs called pseudobulbs and may be terrestrial (growing in soil) or epiphytic (growing on another plant, but not taking water or nutrients from that plant). Plants bear one or two deciduous leaves per pseudobulb that are lance shaped to rounded and folded lengthwise like a fan. Flowers, which appear before the leaves, are solitary or borne in pairs, usually in shades of pink. They have a prominent, fringed, tubular lip marked with brown, maroon-red, or yellow on the inside, and five spreading petals. One terrestrial species, *P. formosana*, is sometimes offered in bulb catalogs.

HOW TO GROW

Give *P. formosana* a spot in partial to full shade with very well drained soil rich in organic matter. It is native to mountainous areas and prefers cool summer temperatures, so be sure to select a spot shaded from hot sun — a location on the north side of a house or wall with deep, organic soil is suitable. They also require dry soil in winter, so be sure the soil is very well drained: in areas with rainy winters (as well as in the North), it is best overwintered indoors or grown in containers year-round. Plant the pseudobulbs in spring at a depth of 2 inches after the soil has warmed up. Where hardy, they can be left in the ground and protected over winter with a thick, coarse mulch such as evergreen boughs, salt hay, or pine needles. To grow them in containers, plant the pseudobulbs in spring in a light, fast-draining soilless mix, and set them with the top two-thirds above the soil surface. In the ground or in containers, water sparingly at first, then keep the soil evenly moist once the plants are growing actively. In late summer or early fall, gradually withhold water. To overwinter the pseudobulbs indoors, dig them in fall just as the foliage disappears, and store them in dry peat moss or vermiculite. Store pseudobulbs or container-grown plants in a cool (35° to 40°F), dry place. Repot container-grown plants in spring, discarding the old pseudobulbs. Individual pseudobulbs are short-lived, usually lasting one or at most two years: propagate these plants in spring by separating the small pseudobulbs that arise around the parent one.

P. formosana P. 164

p. for-mo-SAH-nuh. A 3- to 6-inch-tall terrestrial species bearing nearly round pseudobulbs, each of which produces a single pleated 5- to 6-inch-long leaf. Bears solitary 3-inch-wide flowers in spring that have rose-pink petals and a white lip mottled with pale red-brown to purplish pink on the inside. Zones 8 to 10.

❦ *Polianthes*

pah-lee-AN-theez. Agave family, Agavaceae.

All of the 13 species that belong to the genus *Polianthes* are tender perennials native to Texas and Mexico. They have tuberous, bulblike bases and thick roots, both of which grow from short rhizomes. Plants bear succulent, lance-shaped or linear leaves and erect spikelike racemes of flowers. Individual flowers are tubular to narrowly funnel shaped and have six lobes. Blooms come in orange-red or white. Surprisingly, as members of the agave family, they are closely related to century plants (*Agave* spp.) as well as yuccas (*Yucca* spp.). One species of *Polianthes* is treasured for its incredibly fragrant white flowers—common tuberose, *P. tuberosa*.

HOW TO GROW

Select a site in full sun with light, evenly moist soil rich in organic matter. Plant the tubers outdoors in spring with the tops about 2 to 3 inches below the soil surface. Where hardy, they can be grown outdoors year-round, and in areas with fairly long growing seasons (roughly Zones 6 and 7) plants will have plenty of time to bloom when planted directly outdoors. Work a balanced fertilizer into the soil at planting time. In areas with shorter growing seasons, start them indoors in containers 5 or 6 weeks before the last frost date; setting containers on a heat mat speeds them along. Set plants outside—or sink containers to the rim in the garden—once the soil has warmed up and nighttime temperatures remain above about 60°F. Indoors or out, moisten the soil at planting time, then withhold water until foliage appears: soil that is too wet rots the tubers unless the plants are actively growing. Once leaves appear, water regularly. Feed container-grown plants every 2 weeks until flowers fade. Tubers may survive Zone 7 winters with an extra-heavy layer of coarse mulch such as evergreen boughs, salt hay, or pine needles. To overwinter the tubers indoors, gradually withhold water as the leaves begin to turn yellow. (If fall frost threatens before the plants have bloomed, bring container-grown plants indoors to allow them to finish flowering.) Dig them after the first light fall frost, dry them off for several hours in a warm, shaded place, then cut off the foliage. Store the tubers in dry peat or vermiculite in a cool (65°F), dry place over winter. Propagate by separating the offsets in spring.

P. tuberosa P. 165

p. too-ber-O-suh. Tuberose. A 2- to 4-foot-tall species with rosettes of basal leaves. From summer to fall, bears erect spikes of 20 or more waxy white 1¼- to 2½-inch-wide flowers that are intensely fragrant. 'The Pearl' bears fragrant, semidouble or double creamy white flowers. Zones 8 to 10; to Zone 7 with winter protection.

❦ *Puschkinia*

push-KIN-ee-uh. Lily family, Liliaceae.

Puschkinia contains a single species of spring-blooming bulb—*P. scilloides,* commonly known as striped squill. Closely related to both *Chionodoxa* and *Scilla,* it hails from the Middle East and grows from a small tunicate bulb. Plants bear basal, linear to strap-shaped leaves and dense racemes of small flowers, which appear in spring. The flowers are borne on leafless stalks and consist of six petal-like tepals.

HOW TO GROW

Select a site with average, well-drained soil that is in full sun or in partial to full shade under deciduous trees so plants receive full sun in spring when they are actively growing. A site that dries out in summer when plants are dormant is beneficial, but not required. Plant the bulbs in fall with the bases at a depth of about 3 inches. For best effect, arrange them in drifts—a plant or two here and there will be lost in the spring garden. Propagate by digging and dividing the clumps and/or separating the offsets and seedlings in early summer just as the foliage dies back.

P. scilloides P. 165

p. sil-OY-deez. Striped Squill. A 6- to 8-inch-tall species bearing erect racemes of 4 to 10 densely packed flowers in spring. Individual blooms are bell shaped, ½ inch wide, and very pale bluish white in color with a darker stripe on each tepal. *P. scilloides* var. *libanotica* (formerly *P. libanotica*) bears racemes of small (¼ to ⅜ inch wide) white flowers that usually lack darker stripes and have pointed tepals. Zones 3 to 9.

❦ *Ranunculus*

rah-NUN-kew-liss. Buttercup family, Ranunculaceae.

Best known as buttercups, *Ranunculus* species are primarily perennials, although there are some annuals and biennials among the 400 species in the genus. Most bear cup-, bowl-, or saucer-shaped flowers with five petals around a cluster of showy stamens. There also are garden-grown forms with double flowers, as well as species that lack petals altogether. Blooms are solitary or carried in clusters. Yellow is by far the most common flower color, although a few species feature white, pink, orange, or red blooms. Buttercups produce a rosette of leaves that vary greatly in shape: they range from deeply cut or lobed in a pinnate (featherlike) fashion to simple with entire or toothed leaf margins. There are buttercups suitable for a wide range of conditions, including boggy spots, rock gardens, shady moist woodlands, and spots with rich soil in sun or partial shade. Depending on the species, plants have fibrous or tuberous roots, and there are species that spread by rhizomes, runners, or stolons. Some can be aggressive spreaders.

HOW TO GROW

Cultivation requirements of the species listed here vary. Give *R. asiaticus* full sun and light, rich, well-drained soil that is evenly moist when the plants are actively growing and dry during the summer, when they are dormant. In areas with mild climates that offer these conditions, including southern California, *R. asiaticus* can be grown outdoors year-round. Elsewhere, grow this species in containers. Plant the tubers outdoors in fall where the plants are hardy. Elsewhere, they can be planted in spring, but for best flowering, plant in pots in fall, then overwinter them in a greenhouse, cold frame, sun porch, or other cool, freeze-free spot. They often are treated as annuals. Water sparingly at planting time and until foliage appears. Once buds appear, feed each time you water with a dilute liquid fertilizer and keep the soil evenly moist.

  R. bulbosus thrives in full sun or partial shade with rich, moist, well-drained soil. *R. ficaria* requires partial to full shade with rich, moist soil. Plant these two species outdoors in fall, where they're hardy, or plant in spring at a depth of 2 inches. For all three species, where they're marginally hardy, cover the beds with mulch over winter, but remove it in late winter. Propagate tuberous species by dividing plants in spring or fall. *R. bulbosus* and *R. ficaria* self-sow.

R. asiaticus
P. 166

r. ay-see-AH-tih-kus. Persian Buttercup. An 8- to 18-inch-tall tuberous-rooted species with rounded, three-lobed 5½-inch-long leaves. Bears branched stems of one to four cup-shaped 1¼- to 2-inch-wide flowers in late spring and early summer. Blooms come in yellow, red, pink, and white and have purple-black centers. Tecolote Mixed cultivars bear double or single 4-inch-wide flowers in shades of yellow, orange, pink, and white. Turban Group cultivars also bear double flowers in a range of colors. Zones 7 to 11.

R. bulbosus

r. bul-BO-sus. Bulbous Buttercup. A 6- to 16-inch-tall species native to Europe and North Africa that has naturalized in North America. Grows from a swollen base that resembles a corm. Bears three-lobed 5-inch-long leaves that are further toothed and divided. In late spring and early summer plants produce clusters of golden yellow ¾- to 1¼-inch-wide flowers. 'F. M. Burton', sometimes sold as *R. bulbosus* var. *farreri*, bears glossy, creamy yellow flowers. Zones 7 to 9.

R. ficaria
P. 166, 167

r. fih-KAH-ree-uh. Lesser Celandine. A 2- to 6-inch-tall tuberous species native from Europe and North Africa to southwestern Asia that has naturalized in parts of North America. Bears handsome heart-shaped leaves with toothed or scalloped margins and often marked with silver, bronze, or black-purple. In early spring, solitary, cup-shaped golden yellow flowers with shiny petals appear. Blooms are ¾ to 1¼ inches wide. Leaves die down in early summer after plants flower. Produces offsets and self-sown seedlings with abandon, and may become invasive. Double-flowered forms produce fewer seeds. Many cultivars are available, including 'Brazen Hussy', with black-purple leaves and golden flowers; 'Collarette', with silver-marbled leaves and yellow flowers with a ruff of petaloid stamens in the center; 'Double Bronze', bearing double golden yellow blooms and leaves marbled in purple and silver; 'Flore Pleno', with double yellow flowers; 'Randall's White', with creamy white flowers and marbled leaves; and 'Salmon's White', with white flowers and leaves veined in dark purple. Zones 4 to 8.

❧ *Rhodophiala*

ro-do-fee-AL-uh. Amaryllis family, Amaryllidaceae.

Closely related to amaryllis (*Hippeastrum* species) *Rhodophiala* species are tender bulbs native to South America that produce trumpet- or funnel-shaped flowers. About 35 species belong here, all of which grow from small tunicate bulbs that have a neck. They bear basal, linear leaves and umbels of lilylike flowers atop leafless stems. The flowers have six petal-like tepals.

HOW TO GROW

Where they are hardy, give these plants a site in full sun to partial shade with deeply prepared, rich, well-drained soil. Plant the bulbs in spring or fall at a depth of 6 to 8 inches. At the northern limit of hardiness, mulch heavily with evergreen boughs, pine needles, or salt hay over winter. In most of the country, they are best grown in containers: plant them in winter or early spring as you would *Hippeastrum* species. Set the bulbs so the top two-thirds are above the soil surface. Keep the soil barely moist and set the pots in a cool (55° to 60°F) room until the bulbs begin growing actively. Once they flower, remove the flower stalks and feed them with a dilute, balanced fertilizer every two weeks until mid- to late summer. Then begin to withhold water gradually to encourage the leaves to go dormant. Once the leaves die back, store the bulbs (still in their pots) dry at about 55°F. Let them rest for at least 8 weeks. Topdress the bulbs in midwinter and begin watering again — very sparingly until plants are growing actively. Like *Hippeastrum* species, these plants have permanent, perennial roots and resent root disturbance. To minimize root disturbance, repot bulbs only as necessary — every 3 to 4 years — and when topdressing, disturb the roots as little as possible. When growing these plants in the ground, dig them only if absolutely necessary. Propagate by removing offsets in fall.

R. advena

r. ad-VEE-nuh. Formerly *Hippeastrum advenum*. A 1- to 2-foot-tall species bearing umbels of two to six funnel-shaped 2-inch-long flowers in late summer or early fall. The flowers come in red, pink, or yellow and appear just before the linear leaves appear. Zones 9 to 10.

R. bifida

P. 167

r. BIF-ih-duh. Formerly *Hippeastrum bifidum*. A 12-inch-tall species bearing showy umbels of two to six narrowly funnel-shaped 2-inch-long deep red flowers in summer that appear either just as, or just before, the leaves linear emerge. Zones 9 to 10.

✿ *Sandersonia*

san-der-SO-nee-uh. Lily family, Liliaceae.

Sandersonia contains a single species native to South Africa grown for its charming, lanternlike flowers. A climber that grows from tuberous roots, *S. aurantiaca* bears lance-shaped leaves often tipped with tendrils. The nodding, nearly round flowers are bell to urn shaped and borne on slender, fairly long stalks in the leaf axils.

HOW TO GROW

Select a site in full sun with rich, well-drained soil. In areas with hot summers, shade during the hottest part of the day is best. Plants need a trellis or other support to climb. Where they are hardy, grow plants outdoors year-round; in areas where they are marginally hardy, look for a protected, south-facing site and mulch heavily over winter with evergreen boughs, pine needles, or salt hay. Mulch in summer to keep the root run fairly cool, and water regularly when plants are growing actively. In the North, grow plants in containers or plant the tubers outdoors in spring on or slightly after the last frost date. Indoors or out, handle the brittle tubers very carefully. Plant them with the tips 5 or 6 inches beneath the soil surface. Although the tubers can be dug in fall after the first light frost and stored indoors over winter in dry peat moss or sand, plants are happiest when left undisturbed for several years, and digging the brittle tubers can damage them. For this reason, in the North keeping them in containers year-round is easiest. (Set containers on a deck or terrace or sink them to the rim in the garden during the growing season and lift them in fall.) Overwinter container-grown plants by gradually drying out the soil at the end of the season and storing plants—pot and all—in a cool (50° to 55°F), dry place. Repot or topdress container-grown plants in spring. Plants may self-sow. Propagate by seeds, potting up self-sown seedlings, or separating the tubers in spring.

S. aurantiaca   P. 168

s. aw-ran-tee-AH-kuh. A 2- to 3-foot-tall climber with lance-shaped leaves. Bears pendent 1-inch-long orange flowers that are nearly round, bell, or urn shaped in summer. Zones 7 to 10.

☙ *Sanguinaria*

san-gwih-NAIR-ee-uh. Poppy family, Papaveraceae.

A single species of woodland wildflower native to eastern North America belongs to this genus. Commonly called bloodroot, it grows from a fleshy rhizome that exudes red bloodlike sap when cut. The dainty white flowers have 8 to as many as 16 petals and somewhat resemble daisies or anemones. They emerge in spring shortly before the leaves appear. Leaves have rounded palmate (handlike) lobes with wavy or toothed edges and usually disappear by midsummer.

HOW TO GROW
Select a site in partial to full shade with rich, evenly moist, well-drained soil. Plants go dormant and disappear by midsummer, so mark the locations of clumps to avoid digging into them by mistake. When adding this species to your garden, be sure to purchase only nursery-propagated plants: wild collection depletes native populations. You may be able to acquire these plants from a neighbor's garden or at a local native plant sale, such as one held by a local botanical garden or conservation organization. Propagate by seeds or by dividing the clumps immediately after they flower. Double-flowered forms must be propagated by division.

S. canadensis   P. 168

s. can-ah-DEN-sis. Bloodroot, Red Puccoon. A slowly spreading, rhizomatous species that reaches 4 to 6 inches in height and spreads to 1 foot. Bears cup-shaped 2½- to 3-inch-wide flowers in spring that open before the scalloped, kidney-shaped leaves unfurl. 'Flore Pleno', also sold as 'Multiplex', bears long-lasting double white flowers. Zones 3 to 9.

☙ *Sauromatum*

saw-ro-MAH-tum. Arum family, Araceae.

Sauromatum species are commonly called voodoo lilies—a name they share with members of *Amorphophallus*, a genus of exotic-looking relatives. Two species belong here, both native to woodlands in parts of Africa as well as the Himalayas. They grow from rounded tubers, each of which produces a single large inflorescence in spring or early summer. The inflorescence resembles those of other members of the arum family, including calla lilies (*Zantedeschia* spp.) and Jack-in-the-pulpits (*Arisaema* spp.). It consists of many tiny flowers clustered on a central stalk, called a spadix. The spadix is surrounded by a modified leaf, called a spathe. After the exotic-looking blooms fade, tubers produce a single long-stalked leaf that is divided into lobes in a fingerlike fashion. The leaves are handsome and add a tropical flair to plantings. The flowers have an unpleasant scent reminiscent of rotting meat, which is alluring to the flies that pollinate them, but less so to the humans who grow them. Site these plants accordingly.

HOW TO GROW

Give these plants a spot in partial to full shade with rich, evenly moist, well-drained soil. Where they are hardy, set the tubers with the tops 3 to 4 inches below the soil surface. Toward the northern limit of their hardiness, plant the tubers a little deeper — to 6 inches — and look for a protected spot; mulch heavily with evergreen boughs, pine needles, coarse leaves, or salt hay in late fall. In northern zones where they are not hardy, grow these plants in containers for overwintering indoors or plant directly in the soil in spring and dig the tubers in early fall after the foliage fades. Mark the locations of tubers to avoid digging into them by mistake. Keep the soil evenly moist while the plants are in leaf, but gradually withhold water later in the summer as they enter dormancy. To overwinter tubers indoors, dig and dry them off, then store them in dry peat in a cool (55° to 60°F), dry place. Tubers also can be stored dry without any packing. Propagate by seeds or by separating offsets when plants are dormant.

S. venosum   P. 169

s. ven-O-sum. Voodoo Lily, Monarch of the East. Tuberous 1- to 1½-foot-tall species that blooms in spring or early summer. Inflorescence consists of a foul-smelling 1-foot-long purple spadix and a 1- to 2-foot-long spathe that is yellowish or greenish and heavily spotted with maroon-purple. Flowers are followed by a single 14-inch-long pedate (handlike, but with the outer "fingers" divided into extra lobes) leaf with deeply cut segments. Zones 8 to 10; to Zone 7 with winter protection.

❦ Scadoxus

ska-DOX-us. Amaryllis family, Amaryllidaceae.

Grown for their showy, rounded brushlike flower heads, *Scadoxus* species share the common name blood lily with their close relatives in the genus *Haemanthus*. Nine species of perennials, all native to tropical regions of Africa, belong here. They grow from either tunicate bulbs or rhizomes and bear umbels of 10 to as many as 200 tiny, tightly packed, tubular flowers. The individual flowers have six petal-like tepals as well as six showy, protruding stamens that add to the brushlike appearance. The leaves are arranged in a spiral (those of *Haemanthus* spp. are borne in two rows), and flowers appear either before or as the leaves emerge. Flowers are followed by showy round berries.

HOW TO GROW

Select a spot in full sun or partial shade with rich, well-drained soil. Neutral to alkaline soil pH is best. These plants require evenly moist soil when they are growing actively and dry conditions when dormant. Where they can be grown outdoors year-round—in Zone 10 and 11 gardens that offer dry conditions when the plants are dormant—plant the bulbs in fall. Where they are marginally hardy, look for a protected, south-facing site and mulch the plants heavily in late fall with evergreen boughs, salt hay, coarse leaves, or pine needles. Elsewhere, plant them in containers or outdoors in spring after the last frost date once the soil has warmed up and nighttime temperatures stay above 60°F. In the ground or in containers, set the bulbs with the necks just above the soil surface. Water regularly when plants are growing actively. To overwinter the bulbs indoors, gradually withhold water toward the end of the season and either bring containers indoors or dig the bulbs before the first light frost of fall. Keep the soil of container-grown plants dry, or pack bulbs in dry peat and store them in a cool, dry spot where temperatures do not drop below 50°F. Plants are happiest when their roots and bulbs are left undisturbed, so keeping them in containers year-round usually is a better option than digging them annually in fall. Where they're hardy, plants thrive for years without needing to be divided. Container-grown blood lilies bloom best when they are pot-bound, so repot only if necessary just when new growth resumes in spring. Propagate by separating offsets in early spring or by seeds.

S. multiflorus

P. 169

s. mul-tih-FLOR-us. Blood Lily. Formerly *Haemanthus multiflorus*. A 1½- to 2-foot-tall species from tropical and South Africa with broad, basal, lance-shaped leaves. In summer it bears round 4- to 6-inch-wide red flower heads followed by orange berries. *S. multiflorus* ssp. *katherinae* (formerly *Haemanthus katherinae*) bears wavy-edged leaves. Zones 9 to 11; to Zone 8 with winter protection.

S. puniceus

P. 170

s. pew-NIH-see-us. Royal Paint Brush, Giant Stove Brush. Formerly *Haemanthus puniceus*. A 20-inch-tall species from eastern and southern Africa with rounded, basal, wavy-edged leaves. From spring to early summer, bears 4-inch-wide cone-shaped flower heads that are pink or red and surrounded by conspicuous red bracts (actually spathe valves). Yellow berries follow the flowers. Zones 9 to 11.

❦ *Schizostylis*

skih-zo-STY-liss. Iris family, Iridaceae.

A single species commonly called crimson flag or kaffir lily belongs to the genus *Schizostylis*. Native to South Africa, it grows from a rhizome — unlike many of its close relatives from that country, including *Gladiolus* and *Ixia* species, both of which grow from corms. Plants bear dense, unbranched spikes of cup-shaped flowers that resemble gladiolus from late summer to fall and into winter in mild climates. Individual blooms have six petal-like tepals. The sword-shaped leaves are produced in fans and are evergreen.

HOW TO GROW

Give these plants a site in full sun or partial shade with average to rich, moist, well-drained soil. In the wild, they are found along streams and rivers, making them good choices for bog gardens or other spots where the soil remains constantly moist but is not completely waterlogged. Where they are hardy, grow them outdoors year-round. Toward the northern limits of their hardiness, look for a sheltered, south-facing site and protect them in fall with an insulating mulch of evergreen boughs, coarse leaves, pine needles, or salt hay. Elsewhere, grow them in containers year-round and move them outdoors in spring after the last frost date. To overwinter them, bring containers indoors before the first fall frost and keep them in a cool (45° to 50°F) spot over winter. The rhizomes can be dug each fall, packed in barely moist peat or sand, and stored over winter in a cool spot, but plants bloom best when they are left undisturbed. Divide or repot in spring when the roots become overcrowded. Propagate by division.

S. coccinea P. 170

s. cock-SIN-ee-uh. Crimson Flag. A rhizomatous 1½- to 2-foot-tall species that spreads to about 1 foot. Bears showy spikes of 1 to as many as 14 cup-shaped ¾-inch-wide red flowers in late summer or fall. 'Major', also sold as 'Grandiflora', bears 2- to 2½-inch-wide red flowers. 'Sunrise' bears 2- to 2½-inch-wide pink flowers. 'Viscountess Byns' bears pale pink 1¼-inch-wide flowers. *S. coccinea* var. *alba* bears white flowers. Zones 7 to 9; to Zones 5 or 6 with winter protection.

❦ *Scilla*

SIL-uh. Lily family, Liliaceae.

Spring-blooming *Scilla* species, commonly called squills, are treasured for the erect clusters of rich blue flowers they bring to the garden. The flowers appear in spring, late summer, or fall, depending on the species (spring-blooming species are best known). They are bell shaped or starry and carried in few- to many-flowered clusters. The individual flowers consist of six petal-like tepals. The tepals are split all the way to the base of the flower; in *Chionodoxa*, with which *Scilla* species are often confused, the tepals are united at the base to form a tube. *Scilla* flowers also have wide-spreading stamens. While blue is the most common color, selections with purple, white, or pink flowers also are available. Plants grow from small, usually tunicate, bulbs and produce a few to several grassy, basal, linear to somewhat rounded leaves. About 90 species belong to the genus, native to Europe, Africa, and Asia.

HOW TO GROW

Select a site with average, well-drained soil that is in full sun or in partial to full shade under deciduous trees so plants receive full sun in spring when they are actively growing. Plant the bulbs in fall with the bases at a depth of 3 to 4 inches. For best effect, arrange them in drifts—a plant or two here and there will be lost in the spring garden, while drifts of 20 to 50 or more bulbs are stunning. Plants produce offsets freely and also self-sow: they are ideal for naturalizing and when left undisturbed form large showy colonies. Propagate by digging and dividing the clumps and/or separating the offsets and seedlings in early summer as the foliage dies back.

S. bifolia
P. 171

s. bi-FO-lee-uh. Twin-leaf Squill. A 3- to 6-inch-tall species bearing two linear leaves and starry-shaped purple-blue flowers in early spring. The 1- to 1½-inch-wide flowers are carried in loose, one-sided racemes of up to 10 blooms. Zones 4 to 8.

S. campanulata see Hyacinthoides hispanica

S. litardierei

s. lih-tar-DEE-er-ee-eye. Formerly S. pratensis, S. amethystina. A 4- to 8-inch-tall species with up to six basal leaves that appear in late spring or early summer with the pale bluish violet ¼-inch-wide flowers. The starry flowers are carried in racemes of 15 to 30 or more. Zones 4 to 9.

S. mischtschenkoana
P. 171

s. mis-shenk-o-AH-nuh. Squill. Formerly S. tubergeniana. A 4- to 6-inch-tall species with up to five leaves that appear in late winter or early spring with racemes of starry ¾-inch-wide flowers. Blooms are borne in two- to six-flowered racemes and are silvery blue with darker stripes. Zones 4 to 8.

S. peruviana
P. 172

s. per-oo-vee-AH-nuh. Cuban Lily, Peruvian Jacinth. A tender, nearly evergreen 6- to 18-inch-tall species from the Mediterranean and southern Africa with up to 15 basal leaves; new leaves develop in fall. Bears rounded racemes of 50 to 100 star-shaped ½-inch-wide flowers in early summer. Blooms come in white and purplish blue. Zones 8 to 9.

S. scilloides

s. sil-OY-deez. Chinese Scilla. Formerly S. chinensis, S. japonica. A 6- to 8-inch-tall species with up to seven leaves that appear in late summer or early fall with starry ⅛-inch-wide mauve-pink flowers. Blooms are borne in racemes of 40 to as many as 80 flowers. Zones 4 to 8.

S. siberica
P. 172

s. sye-BEER-ih-kuh. Siberian Squill, Spring Squill. A 4- to 8-inch-tall species with two to four leaves that appear in spring with deep blue nodding, bell- to bowl-shaped flowers. Blooms are borne in loose clusters of four or five. 'Alba' bears white flowers. 'Spring Beauty' is a vigorous cultivar with dark blue blooms on 8-inch-tall plants. Zones 4 to 8.

❦ *Sparaxis*

spah-RAX-iss. Iris family, Iridaceae.

Commonly known as wand flowers or harlequin flowers, *Sparaxis* species are grown for their showy, brightly colored, funnel-shaped flowers that are carried in loose spikes in spring or summer. The individual blooms, which are often marked with contrasting colors, have six petal-like tepals that are joined at the base to form a short tube. Each corm bears two or more stems with anywhere from 2 to about 10 flowers. Plants grow from small rounded corms and produce lance- or sickle-shaped leaves, usually arranged in fans. About six species belong here, all native to South Africa.

HOW TO GROW

Plant wand flowers in a site with full sun and average to rich, well-drained soil. Where they are hardy, grow them outdoors year-round and plant the corms in fall at a depth of 3 to 4 inches. Like many South African species, they prefer warm days, cool nights, and dry soil conditions when they are dormant. In areas with wet winters, select a site with very well drained soil, such as a raised bed. Toward the northern limits of their hardiness look for a protected spot, such as at the base of a south-facing wall, and mulch heavily in fall with a coarse mulch such as evergreen boughs, salt hay, or pine needles. Where wand flowers are not hardy, grow them in containers or treat them like gladiolus. Pot the corms in late summer, setting them at a depth of about 1 to 2 inches, and keep the containers in a cool (45° to 50°F), well-ventilated place, such as a cold frame, over winter. Or plant the corms outdoors in late spring: either way, move them to the garden only after the last frost date. Water newly planted corms carefully until they begin to flower: the soil should stay barely moist, but never wet or completely dry. Replace the corms annually (they are inexpensive) or, to hold them for another year's bloom, continue watering after plants flower and feed every other week with a dilute, balanced fertilizer. When the leaves begin to turn yellow and die back, gradually dry off the soil and store the corms—still in their containers—in a fairly warm (60° to 75°F), dry, airy spot. Corms also can be dug and stored dry, like gladiolus. In the ground or in containers, plants bloom best when left undisturbed, so dig and divide the clumps only when they become overcrowded. Propagate by seeds or by separating off-sets in late summer or early spring when plants are dormant.

S. elegans   P. 173

s. EL-eh-ganz. Wand Flower, Harlequin Flower. Formerly *Strepthanthera cuprea*, *S. elegans*. A 4- to 12-inch-tall species bearing up to five flower spikes per corm and up to five flowers per stem in spring to summer. Individual blooms are funnel shaped, 1½-inches wide, and come in shades of red, orange, and sometimes white marked with yellow or violet. Zones 9 to 11; to Zones 7 or 8 with winter protection.

S. tricolor   P. 173

s. TRY-kuh-lor. Wand Flower, Harlequin Flower. A 4- to 16-inch-tall species that bears from one to five flowering stems per corm in late spring to early summer. Individual blooms are funnel shaped, 2 to 3 inches wide, and come in shades of red, orange, and purple with dark red or black central blotches. Zones 9 to 11; to Zones 7 or 8 with winter protection.

❧ *Sprekelia*

sprey-KEH-lee-uh. Amaryllis family, Amaryllidaceae.

A single species belongs to the genus *Sprekelia* — *S. formosissima*, a tender bulb native to Mexico and Guatemala. Despite several common names that suggest membership in the lily family — including Aztec lily and Jacobean lily — these plants are more closely related to amaryllis (*Hippeastrum* spp.). They bear flowers singly atop leafless stems that consist of six relatively thin, spidery looking petal-like tepals. The tepals are arranged in an asymmetrical fashion and have almost an orchidlike appearance: three lower tepals point down and look like a lip, two point out, and one points up. Plants grow from tunicate bulbs and bear basal, strap-shaped leaves that appear with the flowers.

HOW TO GROW

Give these plants a site in full sun with deeply prepared, rich, well-drained soil where they are hardy and can be grown outdoors year-round. Perfect drainage in winter is essential. Plant in fall with the top of the bulb just above the soil surface or buried slightly — to about 2 inches. Where marginally hardy, protect them with evergreen boughs, pine needles, or salt hay over winter. In most of the country, grow them in containers year-round and plant them in winter or early spring. Or, plant them outdoors in spring, dig the bulbs in fall, and store them dry over winter. Aztec lilies are happiest and bloom best when their roots are left undisturbed, however, so overwintering in containers is best. In containers, plant the bulbs with the neck and shoulders above the soil surface. Keep the soil barely moist and set the pots in a cool (55° to 60°F) room until they begin growing actively. Once the bulbs flower, remove the flower stalks and feed them with a dilute, balanced fertilizer every 2 weeks until mid- to late summer. Then begin to withhold water gradually to encourage the leaves to go dormant. Once the leaves die back, store the bulbs — still in their pots — in a cool (45° to 55°F), dry spot and keep the soil nearly dry. Topdress the bulbs in midwinter and begin watering again — very cautiously until plants are growing actively. To minimize root disturbance, repot bulbs only as necessary — every 3 to 4 years — and when topdressing, disturb them as little as possible. When growing these plants in the ground, dig them only if absolutely necessary. Propagate by removing offsets in fall.

S. formosissima   P. 174

s. for-mo-SIS-ih-muh. Aztec Lily, Jacobean Lily, St. James Lily. A 4- to 14-inch-tall species that bears solitary bright red 5-inch-wide flowers in spring. Zones 9 to 11; to Zone 7 or 8 with winter protection.

❦ Stenanthium

steh-NAN-THEE-um. Lily family, Liliaceae.

Five species belong to this genus of lily-family relatives, all perennials native to North America as well as Russia's Sakhalin Island. Plants grow from tunicate bulbs and bear arching, grasslike, primarily basal leaves. They produce racemes or panicles of bell- or star-shaped flowers in summer that are white, greenish white, or purple. Individual blooms have six petal-like tepals. The botanical name refers to the fact that the tepals are narrow: it is from the Greek *stenos*, narrow, and *anthos*, flower.

HOW TO GROW

Select a site in partial shade with deeply prepared, moist, well-drained soil that is rich in organic matter. A sheltered spot protected from wind is best. Plants do not do well in hot, dry sites, and shade during the hottest part of the day is important. Neutral to slightly acid pH is best for *Stenan-*

thium gramineum; species native to western North America prefer neutral to slightly alkaline soil. Plant bulbs in fall at a depth of 4 inches. Mulch with compost or chopped leaves to keep the soil moist and cool. Once planted, plants are best left undisturbed unless the clumps become overcrowded. Propagate by seeds sown as soon as they are ripe.

S. gramineum   P. 174

s. grah-MIN-ee-um. Featherfleece. A 3- to 6-foot-tall species native to the eastern United States from Pennsylvania to Illinois. Bears arching 2-foot-long panicles of fragrant, densely packed flowers in summer. Individual flowers are star shaped; ½ to ¾ inch wide; and white, greenish white, or purple in color. Zones 7 to 9.

❦ *Stenomesson*

steh-no-MES-son. Amaryllis family, Amaryllidaceae.

The genus *Stenomesson* contains about 20 species native to the South American Andes that produce umbels of pendent, tubular flowers in bright colors in spring and summer. All grow from tunicate bulbs and bear basal, linear to lance-shaped leaves that elongate as the flowers form.

HOW TO GROW

In areas with frost-free—or nearly frost-free—winters, grow these plants outdoors year-round in a spot with full sun and rich, well-drained soil. When planting outdoors, plant the bulbs in fall, setting the tips just under the soil surface. At the northern limit of their hardiness, look for a protected spot and protect plants with a course mulch such as evergreen boughs, salt hay, or coarse leaves over winter. *Stenomesson* species prefer cool growing conditions, and they require dry conditions during the winter months when they are dormant. Where they are not hardy, grow them in containers, setting the bulbs with the top two-thirds out of the soil surface. Keep the soil barely moist until leaves appear, then evenly moist, but never wet, when the plants are growing actively. Gradually withhold water in late summer and fall as the foliage begins to turn yellow, then hold the bulbs—still in their pots—in a cool (45° to 50°F nights), dry spot through the winter. Keep the soil just moist enough to keep the bulbs from shriveling. Repot every few years, as necessary, in spring. Propagate by removing the offsets or by seeds.

S. miniatum

s. mih-nee-AH-tum. Formerly *Urceolina pendula, U. peruviana.* A 1-foot-tall species from Bolivia and Peru that bears umbels of three to six pendent 1½-inch-long flowers from spring to summer. Blooms come in red or orange and have showy stamens that protrude beyond the tubular blooms. Zones 10 to 11.

S. variegatum

P. 175

s. vair-eh-GAH-tum. Formerly *S. incarnatum.* A 1½- to 2-foot-tall species from Ecuador, Bolivia, and Peru that bears umbels of up to six pendent, tubular 5-inch-long flowers that are white, pink, yellow, or red with a green mark on each tepal. Zones 10 to 11.

✿ Sternbergia

stern-BER-gee-uh. Amaryllis family, Amaryllidaceae.

Although *Sternbergia* species are commonly known as autumn daffodils, at first glance their flowers look more like crocuses. In addition, not all species bloom in fall. The flowers usually are funnel to goblet shaped, although some species bear more star-shaped blooms. The flowers consist of six petal-like tepals. Unlike crocuses, which belong in the iris family and have three stamens, the flowers of *Sternbergia* species have six stamens. And while crocuses grow from corms, *Sternbergia* species grow from tunicate bulbs. The basal leaves are linear to strap shaped and appear with or just after the flowers. About eight species belong to the genus, and they are native from southern Europe and Turkey to Central Asia.

HOW TO GROW

Select a site in full sun to partial shade with very well drained, average to rich soil. Well-drained soil is especially important in winter; a spot in a raised bed or rock garden provides the conditions these plants prefer. Plant the bulbs in late summer — for best results as early as you can obtain them — setting them at a depth of 6 inches. Plant *S. candida* 8 inches deep. Be sure to loosen the soil several inches below this depth to encourage the roots to spread out. Once planted, sternbergias are best left undisturbed. They will form large clumps with time, and plants also self-sow. Propagate by seeds or by separating the offsets just as the leaves die down.

S. candida

P. 175

s. kan-DEE-duh. A late winter– to spring-blooming species that is 4 to 8 inches tall. Bears fragrant, funnel- to goblet-shaped 2-inch-wide white flowers that appear shortly after the leaves. Zones 8 to 10.

S. lutea

P. 176

s. LOO-tee-uh. Autumn Daffodil, Winter Daffodil. A fall-blooming 6-inch-tall species bearing golden yellow goblet-shaped 1½-inch-wide flowers in fall. The narrowly lance-shaped leaves appear with the flowers and last through the winter. Zones 6 to 9.

S. sicula

s. SIK-yoo-luh. A fall-blooming 3-inch-tall species. Bears ½- to 1½-inch-wide flowers that are star shaped and dark yellow in color. Zones 6 to 9.

❦ Streptanthera elegans see Sparaxis elegans

❦ Tecophilaea

tek-o-FIL-ee-ee. Lily family, Liliaceae.

Two species, sometimes called Chilean crocuses, belong to this genus in the lily family. In spring, they bear small crocuslike flowers in rich, true blue or violet. Flowers have six petal-like tepals. They grow from corms and have basal, grassy, narrowly lance-shaped leaves. Both of the species in this genus are native to high altitudes in South America, and one of them is sometimes grown in rock gardens.

HOW TO GROW

Select a site in full sun with sandy, well-drained soil rich in organic matter. Perfect drainage is essential: these are plants best suited to rock gardens and require warm, dry conditions when they are dormant in summer. They also are best in areas with cool summers and mild winters, which duplicates their native Andes. Plant the corms in fall at a depth of 2 inches. In areas where they are not hardy or where winters are excessively rainy, keep them in containers set in a cold frame. Chilean crocuses tend to emerge very early in spring and often are cut down by late frosts, so even in areas where they are hardy, connoisseurs often grow them in containers kept in a cold frame and move them out after the weather has set-

tled in spring. Mulch with pea gravel or granite chips to retain soil moisture and ensure perfect drainage. Keep the soil evenly moist while plants
are actively growing, then gradually dry them off in summer as the leaves
die back. Propagate by seeds or offsets.

T. cyanocrocus P. 176

t. sy-an-o-KRO-kus. Chilean Blue Crocus. A 3- to 4-inch-tall species bearing
1½- to 2-inch-long funnel-shaped flowers in spring that are rich gentian
blue with white striping at the throat. Zones 7 to 9.

❦ Tigridia

tih-GRIH-dee-uh. Iris family, Iridaceae.

Easy-to-grow, summer-blooming tigridias have a number of colorful
common names, including tiger flower, peacock flower, and Mexican
shell flower. The showy flowers have six petal-like tepals. The three outer
tepals are large and showy: they flare out at the top, giving the blooms a
somewhat triangular outline, and come together at the base to form a
deep cup or shallow saucer. The three inner tepals are much smaller and
point up or out. The botanical name refers to the fact that the centers of
the blooms are prominently spotted: it is from the Latin *tigris*, tiger. In
this case, however, tiger refers to the Central American tiger, better
known as the jaguar, since tigridias are native to Mexico and Guatemala.
Individual flowers last only a day, but are borne in succession for several
weeks in summer. Plants grow from tunicate bulbs and bear fans of
lance- to sword-shaped leaves.

HOW TO GROW
Select a site in full sun with light, evenly moist soil rich in organic matter.
Tigridias are grown much like gladiolus: plant bulbs in spring after the
soil has warmed up and nighttime temperatures remain above 55°F. Set
bulbs 4 to 5 inches deep; in heavy or clayey soil plant them at a depth of
about 3 inches. Plant small bulbs fairly shallowly—from ½ to 1 inch deep
until they reach full size. For best results, dig the soil deeply and work organic matter and a balanced organic fertilizer into the soil at planting
time. Then set the bulbs in a shallow trench and fill it gradually with soil
as the plants grow. Deep planting helps eliminate the need to stake plants,
but stake them if necessary. Plant new bulbs every two weeks to extend
the bloom season. In areas where the plants are not hardy, let the foliage

ripen for 6 weeks after flowering. Then dig the bulbs after the leaves turn yellow, cut off the foliage, and set them in a warm, dry place for a few hours. Store the bulbs in a cool (40° to 50°F), dry place over winter. Tigridias are quite inexpensive and often are grown as annuals. They also are effective in containers. Propagate by separating the offsets or by seeds.

T. pavonia   P. 177

t. pah-VO-nee-uh. Peacock Flower, Tiger Flower. A 1½- to 2-foot-tall species bearing somewhat irislike 4- to 6-inch-wide flowers in summer. Blooms come in a range of showy colors, including red, pink, orange, yellow, and white with contrasting, spotted centers. Many cultivars are available, including 'Alba Grandiflora', white with red-spotted centers; 'Aurea', yellow with red-spotted centers; and 'Canariensis', yellow with red centers. Mixtures of many colors are often available. Zones 8 to 10.

❧ *Trillium*

TRIL-ee-um. Lily family, Liliaceae.

Trilliums are spring-flowering perennials native to woodlands in North America as well as eastern Asia. They grow from tuberlike rhizomes and form clumps of erect stems, each topped by a single set of rounded to. ovate or diamond-shaped leaves. The solitary flowers, which are either erect or nodding, are borne above the whorl of leaves. The botanical name *Trillium* is from the Latin word *tres,* meaning three, a reference to the normal number of leaves borne on each stem as well as the number of sepals and petals on each flower.

HOW TO GROW

Select a site in partial to full shade with moist, well-drained soil rich in organic matter. Soil with an acid to neutral pH is best for most species. Mulch plants annually with chopped leaves to keep the soil moist and replenish organic matter. Trilliums are spring ephemerals, meaning they die back after flowering, generally by early summer, so mark the locations of plants to avoid digging into them accidentally. *Do not* collect trilliums from the wild or purchase plants that have been wild collected. See page 13 for information on avoiding wild-collected plants. Propagate by dividing the rhizomes in spring after the plants flower. The divisions may be slow to reestablish. Trilliums also self-sow where happy, although plants take several years to bloom from seeds.

T. erectum

t. ee-REK-tum. Stinking Benjamin. A 1- to 1½-foot-tall native North American wildflower that spreads to about 1 foot. Bears 2- to 3½-inch-wide flowers with ill-smelling maroon to maroon-brown petals in spring. Blooms are on long stalks and point up or out. Zones 4 to 9.

T. grandiflorum   P. 178

t. gran-dih-FLOR-um. Great White Trillium, Wood Lily, Wake-robin. A 1- to 1½-foot-tall native North American wildflower that eventually forms 2-foot-wide clumps. Bears showy, short-stalked 3-inch-wide white flowers that fade to pink. Zones 4 to 8.

❦ Triteleia

tri-TEL-ee-uh. Lily family, Liliaceae.

Triteleia contains about 15 species of cormous perennials native to the western United States. Like their close relatives in the genus *Brodiaea,* they are grown for their showy umbels of funnel-shaped flowers borne atop thin, leafless stalks. The flowers in the umbel are borne on individual stalks and have six petal-like tepals. The tepals are joined at the base to form a short tube. The long leaves are basal and grassy or linear and generally die back as the flowers appear. Like crocuses and gladiolus, triteleias grow from corms, which last only one year but are replaced annually as new ones develop during the growing season.

HOW TO GROW

Select a site in full sun or partial shade that has rich, well-drained soil. Light, sandy loam is ideal. Plant corms in early fall, setting them 3 to 5 inches deep, depending on the size. Triteleias are most effective planted in drifts or clumps with fairly close spacing — 2 to 3 inches apart. Work sand or grit into the soil to improve drainage. Plants require even moisture when they are actively growing, but once the plants go dormant in summer, they require warm, dry conditions. In the West, where triteleias grow naturally in dry grasslands and woodlands, these plants are ideal for naturalizing. In areas where they are marginally hardy, look for a protected, south-facing site and cover the plants over winter with a loose mulch of evergreen branches, pine needles, or salt hay. In the North and in areas with rainy summers, grow them in containers or try them in rock gardens, raised beds, or other sites that offer the excellent drainage and dry summer conditions they require. Container-grown plants are easy to move to a warm, dry site protected from rain to ensure a dry dormancy. Overwinter container-grown plants indoors in a cool (40° to 45°F), dry spot, then repeat the cycle in spring. Since the foliage often is dying back when the plants are flowering, underplant with shallow-rooted annuals to fill in around them. Propagate by separating offsets just as the plants go dormant or by seeds.

T. hyacinthina

t. hi-ah-sin-THY-nuh. Wild Hyacinth. Formerly *Brodiaea hyacinthina, B. lactea.* A 2-foot-tall species bearing 4-inch-wide umbels of 20 or more ½-inch-long flowers in late spring or early summer. Flowers are either white or pale lilac-blue. Zones 7 to 10.

T. ixioides   P. 178

t. iks-ee-OH-deez. Pretty Face, Golden Star. Formerly *Brodiaea ixioides, B. lutea.* A 2-foot-tall species bearing 5-inch-wide umbels of 20 to 25 ½- to 1-inch-wide flowers in early summer. Flowers are yellow with a purple stripe down the center of each tepal. Zones 7 to 10.

T. laxa   P. 179

t. LAKS-uh. Grass Nut, Triplet Lily, Ithuriel's Spear. Formerly *Brodiaea laxa.* A 2-foot-tall species bearing loose 6-inch-wide umbels of 20 to 25 flowers in early summer. Individual blooms are ¾ to 2 inches wide and pale lavender to dark purple-blue in color. 'Queen Fabiola' (also listed as 'Koningin Fabiola' bears 2-inch-long purple-blue flowers. Zones 6 to 10; to Zone 5 with winter protection.

❦ Tritonia

tri-TO-nee-uh. Iris family, Iridaceae.

These South African natives are grown for their showy clusters of flowers that come in a range of bright colors and are carried from spring to summer on thin, wiry stems. Individual blooms are funnel to cup shaped with tubular bases that split into six lobes, or petal-like tepals. The plants, which grow from corms, produce fans of linear to lance-shaped, mostly basal leaves. About 28 species belong to this genus.

HOW TO GROW

Select a site with full sun and rich, well-drained soil. Where hardy, they can be grown outdoors year-round. Like many South African species, they need dry soil conditions when dormant. Especially in areas with wet winters, a site with very well drained soil (such as a raised bed) is essential. When growing these corms outdoors, plant them in fall at a depth of 2 to 4 inches. Where they are marginally hardy, look for a protected spot such as at the base of a south-facing wall, and mulch heavily in fall with a coarse mulch such as evergreen boughs, salt hay, or pine needles. In the North, treat the corms like those of gladiolus: plant them outdoors in spring after all danger of frost has passed, dig them in summer after the leaves have died back, and store them dry in net or paper bags in a warm (60° to 75°F), dry, well-ventilated spot. Or grow them in containers by potting the corms in spring at a depth of about 1 to 2 inches. Water carefully until plants begin to flower: the soil should stay barely moist, but never wet or completely dry. Replace the corms annually or, to hold them for another year's bloom, continue watering after plants flower, and feed every other week with a dilute, balanced fertilizer. When the leaves begin to turn yellow and die back, gradually dry off the plants and store the containers in a cool (50° to 60°F), dry, well-ventilated spot. Or clean the soil off the corms and store them in paper bags. Propagate by seeds or by separating offsets in late summer just as the leaves die down.

T. crocata   P. 179

t. kro-KAH-tuh. Formerly *T. fenestrata, T. hyalina.* An 8- to 12-inch-tall species bearing arching spikes of about 10 flowers in spring. Individual blooms are cup shaped, ½-inch-long, and orange to pinkish red in color. Zones 8 to 10; to Zone 7 with winter protection.

T. disticha

t. DIS-tih-kuh. Formerly *Crocosmia rosea.* A 2- to 3-foot-tall species bearing arching spikes of many ¾-inch-long flowers in mid- to late summer. Individual flowers are funnel shaped and come in shades of orange-red, red, and pink. *T. disticha* ssp. *rubrolucens* (formerly *T. rosea, T. rubrolucens*) bears funnel-shaped 1- to 1½-inch-long pink flowers. Zones 9 to 10; to Zone 8 with winter protection.

❦ Tropaeolum

tro-pee-O-lum. Nasturtium family, Tropaeolaceae.

The genus *Tropaeolum* contains from 80 to 90 species of annuals and perennials native from Mexico to Chile. The plants can be bushy, trailing, or climbing, and many have tuberous roots, which can be lifted for overwintering. Commonly called nasturtiums, they are grown for their showy, spurred flowers, usually in shades of red, scarlet, orange, yellow, or cream. The individual flowers have five sepals, one of which forms the spur at the back of the bloom, and usually five petals with smooth, lobed or fringed edges. The leaves are rounded or lobed and peltate, meaning the stem is attached near the center of the leaf, rather than on the edge. In a confusing twist of nomenclature, nasturtium is the botanical name for watercress, *Nasturtium officinale.*

HOW TO GROW

While all *Tropaeolum* species grow in full sun, soil preferences vary. Give the species listed here well-drained, evenly moist soil of average fertility. *Tropaeolum* species are best in areas with relatively cool summers and do not grow well in the hot, humid Southeast. Grow tuberous species as annuals or tender perennials: to overwinter them, dig the tubers in fall and store them in a frost-free spot, as you would dahlias, in a well-ventilated, cool (36° to 45°F), relatively dry spot in boxes of barely moist vermiculite or sand, in paper bags or wrapped in newspaper, or in plastic bags punched with plenty of air holes. Propagate by dividing the tubers in spring or fall or by seeds. Take cuttings in spring or early summer to propagate plants for the garden or in late summer to overwinter the plants.

T. polyphyllum

t. pol-ee-FIL-um. A trailing 2- to 3-foot-tall tender perennial with a fleshy, rhizomelike tuber. Bears 1½-inch-wide deep yellow flowers that have long spurs over a long season in summer. Zones 8 to 10.

T. tricolorum   P. 180

t. tri-KUH-lor-um. Formerly *T. tricolor*. A 3- to 6-foot-tall tender perennial climber that grows from tuberous roots and bears palmate (handlike) leaves with five to seven lobes. From winter to early summer bears 1-inch-long flowers that have orange-red sepals with maroon tips and orange to yellow petals. The spurs are red, yellow, or purple. Zones 8 to 10.

T. tuberosum

t. too-ber-O-sum. A tender perennial climber that reaches 6 to 12 feet and grows from large yellow tubers mottled with purple. From midsummer to fall, plants bear cup-shaped 1- to 1½-inch-long flowers with yellow to orange-yellow petals and orange-red sepals. Flowers are striped with brown on the inside. Zones 8 to 10.

☙ *Tulbaghia*

tul-BAHG-ee-uh. Lily family, Liliaceae.

Tulbaghia species are rhizomatous or bulbous perennials with grassy to strap-shaped leaves that have a garlic- or onionlike odor when bruised. They bear dainty umbels of starry, tubular flowers in lilac-purple or white atop leafless stems. The individual flowers have six spreading petal-like tepals that are united to form a tube for about half the length of the flowers. A close look at the blooms reveals a crown or cuplike corona in the center formed from six small scales. About 24 species belong to the genus, all native to tropical and southern Africa.

HOW TO GROW
Select a site in full sun and average to rich, well-drained soil. Where they are hardy, grow these plants outdoors year-round. In areas where they are marginally hardy, try a site against a south-facing wall for extra winter protection and mulch with evergreen boughs, pine needles, salt hay, or another coarse mulch over winter. In the North, grow them in containers, which can either be set on decks or terraces or sunk to the rim in the garden during the growing season. Water regularly in summer and feed pot-grown plants monthly. Gradually withhold water in fall and keep plants nearly dry over winter. Overwinter them in a bright, cool (40° to 50°F) spot and water sparingly until active growth resumes in spring. Propagate by dividing the clumps or sowing seeds. Repot or divide in late winter or early spring as necessary.

T. simmleri

t. SIM-ler-eye. Formerly *T. fragrans*. A 2-foot-tall species with attractive umbels of 10 to as many as 30 fragrant flowers in early and midsummer. Individual blooms are ¾ inch long and pale to deep purple in color. Zones 7 to 9.

T. violacea   P. 180

t. vee-oh-LAY-see-uh. Society Garlic, Pink Agapanthus. A clump-forming 1½- to 2-foot-tall perennial with linear gray-green leaves. Bears small umbels of fragrant ¾-inch-long lilac flowers from midsummer to fall. 'Variegata' or 'Silver Lace' bears leaves striped in gray-green and cream and larger flowers than the species. Zones 7 to 10.

❦ *Tulipa*

TOO-lip-uh. Lily family, Liliaceae.

These classic spring-blooming bulbs are treasured for their showy flowers, which come in a wide range of colors, from bold deep reds, violet-purple, golden yellow, and orange to pastel mauve, pink, lavender, and white — everything except true blue. Many tulips feature bicolor blooms — red-and-white or red-and-yellow striped, for example — or flowers may have a contrasting eye, or center. The most familiar tulips have cup-shaped blooms, but bowl-shaped and double-flowered cultivars are available as well as selections with goblet- or star-shaped blooms. There also are tulips with fringed petal edges, ruffled petals, and ones that bear several blooms per stem. Like other plants in the lily family, the individual flowers consist of six petal-like tepals. Tulips grow from somewhat teardrop-shaped, tunicate bulbs and have basal leaves that usually are broadly oval and bluish or gray-green, although some species have strap-shaped or long, very narrow leaves. There are about 100 species of tulips and hundreds of named cultivars, all of which have been organized into 15 divisions based on flower shape and origin. Catalogs and well-labeled nursery displays use these divisions to organize their offerings, and planting tulips from several divisions helps ensure you will have a variety of shapes and sizes of flowers to enjoy. In addition, bloom times vary from division to division — although all cultivars in a division don't necessarily bloom at the same time and there is plenty of overlap. Still, with careful selection, it's possible to have tulips in bloom for 8 weeks or more in spring.

HOW TO GROW

Plant tulips where they will receive at least 5 hours of full sun daily and light shade for the rest of the day. Morning sun and afternoon shade is beneficial in the South, because it protects the flowers from heat. Rich, well-drained soil is best, although plants will bloom satisfactorily for a year or two in a wide range of well-drained soils. For best growth, tulips require a cool, moist winter and a warm, dry summer. Most can be grown in Zones 3 to 8, but actually perform best in Zones 4 to 6. In the Southeast, summer heat and rain tend to diminish their performance. (Some cultivars are better performers in the South than others; a reputable garden center will stock good selections for your area.) In Zones 8 or 9 to 10, where the bulbs don't receive cold enough temperatures in winter to bloom, buy precooled bulbs and treat them as annuals. *T. clusiana, T. sax-*

atilis, T. sylvestris, and *T. tarda* are species tulips that can be grown in southern zones and do not require a cold treatment to flower.

When buying tulips, look for fat, fleshy bulbs with no signs of mold or black, rotted blotches. The brown tunic should be on the bulb and intact. Avoid buying cheap bulbs, which may not have been stored or handled properly. This is especially important because the bulbs resent being exposed to temperatures above 70°F, both in the ground and any time they are stored. Storage at high temperatures reduces or destroys the quality of the bulbs and the flowers they produce. Plant tulips in fall as soon as they are available—early fall in northern zones, toward early winter in the South. Dig the soil deeply at planting time, and work in plenty of organic matter such as compost or leaf mold. Also incorporate a balanced organic fertilizer into the soil. Deep soil preparation is important, because the soil several inches below the bulbs needs to be improved and well drained. (Improving the soil around the bulbs doesn't benefit the roots, which emerge from the base of the bulbs.) Set the bulbs with their bases at least 8 inches below the soil surface—10 inches is better. This keeps them cool in summertime and discourages them from breaking up into lots of smaller nonflowering bulbs after the first year. If you are growing the bulbs as annuals, a depth of 5 or 6 inches is fine. Deep planting also makes it easy to fill in on top of the bulbs with annuals or shallow-rooted perennials. For a planting that blooms uniformly at one time and at one height, excavate the entire bed and plant all the bulbs at the same depth. To discourage chipmunks and other rodents from eating the bulbs, fill in around each bulb on all sides with sharp, crushed gravel as you plant. (This also helps improve drainage.) Blood meal worked into the soil also helps discourage rodents. Another option is to excavate the bed and line the bottom and sides with ½-inch hardware cloth. Set the bulbs in place and refill with soil. Cover the top of the bed with mesh as well, removing it in late winter. Or, plant groups of bulbs in mesh baskets.

Tulips do not require any further care to bloom well. Water if the weather is dry in spring. Deadhead to prevent seed formation, and let the leaves ripen naturally if the bulbs are to flower the following year. Remove them only after they have turned yellow—or nearly so. Another option is to dig the bulbs carefully after the flowers fade, retaining as many roots as possible. Plant the bulbs temporarily in a nursery bed to allow the foliage to ripen fully. Space the bulbs fairly closely together, setting the tops at a 45-degree angle to the soil surface and the bulbs at a depth of 2 to 3 inches. Water as necessary to keep the soil evenly moist, but not wet. When the leaves have turned completely yellow, dig the bulbs and store them in a cool, dry spot with good air circulation and temperatures no higher than 70°F. Be sure to select a rodent-proof location. Replant in fall. Topdress plantings with a balanced fertilizer in fall. Many gardeners treat tulips as annuals — replacing them each fall — because they often bloom spectacularly the first year and peter out thereafter. (They are inexpensive and well worth the minimal investment in time and money it takes to replace them.) Perennial plantings of tulips are possible in Zones 3 to 7, however, provided you select and plant carefully. Species tulips are best known for behaving as perennials, but there also are hybrids that can be depended on for repeat performance. Kaufmanniana tulips are good perennializers, as are Fosteriana tulips, Greigii tulips, and Darwin Hybrids. Species that are especially dependable include *T. saxatilis, T. batalinii, T. humilis,* and *T. tarda.* Good site selection, thorough soil preparation, and deep planting (with the base of the bulb 8 to 10 inches below the soil surface) are the secrets to perennial plantings of tulips. It is also important to let foliage ripen and feed bulbs annually.

Divisions and species are listed separately below.

DIVISIONS

Single Early Tulips (Division 1)   PP. 186, 189

These cultivars bear single, cup-shaped blooms in early to midspring. Flowers are about 3 inches across and are borne on 10- to 18-inch-tall plants. Many are fragrant. Good for forcing. Cultivars include 'Apricot Beauty', with fragrant salmon flowers marked with rose-pink flames on the outer petals; 'Beauty Queen', fragrant flowers marked with a blend of pink, salmon, and apricot; 'Christmas Marvel', with reddish pink blooms; 'Flair', with bright yellow blooms marked with vivid red; 'Generaal de Wet', an old cultivar with orange and yellow blooms that have a musky, sweet fragrance; and 'Purple Prince', with petals that are purple and dusky lilac-purple on the outside and deeper purple inside with golden yellow at the base. Zones 3 to 8.

Double Early Tulips (Division 2)   P. 197

Double earlies bear bowl-shaped, fully double flowers that resemble peonies on strong 12- to 16-inch-tall stems in midspring. Blooms, which reach 3 inches across and may be fragrant, come in shades from red to yellow or white and often are marked with a contrasting color. Good for forcing. Cultivars include 'Abba', with fragrant orangy red flowers; 'Monsella', with long-lasting, fragrant yellow flowers marked with red flames; 'Monte Carlo', with fragrant yellow flowers; 'Electra', with cherry red blooms; 'Mr. Van der Hoef', with fragrant yellow flowers; and 'Peach Blossom', an old cultivar with fragrant rose-pink flowers that have a yellow heart. Zones 3 to 8.

Triumph Tulips (Division 3) PP. 181, 194

Mid- to late spring–blooming cultivars that bear 2½-inch-wide flowers usually on 14- to 24-inch-tall stems. Flowers are single, cup-shaped, and come in a wide range of colors. Triumph tulips are among the best tulips for forcing, and many cultivars have been especially developed for forcing and pot culture; they are not very long-lived perennials, however. Cultivars include 'Barcelona', with fuchsia purple blooms on 2-foot plants; 'Calgary', with white flowers on 8- to 10-inch-tall plants; 'Couleur Cardinal', an old cultivar with fragrant scarlet flowers with darker bases; 'Dreaming Maid', with violet petals edged in white; 'Dynamite', red with an ivory white base; 'Golden Melody', bright buttercup yellow; 'Negrita', red-purple; 'New Design', with pink flowers marked with creamy yellow toward the base on the outside, darker pink on the inside, and variegated leaves edged in pinkish white; 'Sandeman', bright red with a lemon yellow edge; and 'Shirley', a Rembrandt-type cultivar with creamy white flowers streaked, flecked, and edged with purple. Zones 3 to 8.

Darwin Hybrid Tulips (Division 4) PP. 182, 192, 195, 197

Mid- to late spring–blooming cultivars that bear single, rounded blooms that are 3 inches across and borne atop strong 20- to 28-inch-tall stems. Darwin Hybrids are among the best tulips for perennializing. They usually come in bright shades of red, yellow, orange, or pink and often have a contrasting eye at the center. Cultivars include 'Apeldoorn', red with a black central blotch edged in yellow; 'Apeldoorn's Elite', brilliant red flowers feathered with yellow at the edges of the tepals; 'Big Chief', large salmon-rose blooms edged in apricot-pink; 'Burning Heart', a vigorous Rembrandt-type cultivar with creamy flowers flamed in red on the outside and yellow with red on the inside; 'Daydream', yellow blooms that age to apricot orange; 'Golden Parade', bright yellow with a black central eye; 'Ivory Floradale', with ivory white blooms; 'Ollioules', large dark rose-pink blooms with tepals edged in silver-white; 'Parade', red with a yellow base and a black yellow-edged central eye inside; 'Pink Impression', with blooms that are a blend of pink and rose-pink; and 'Silverstream', creamy yellow sometimes streaked with red or white. Zones 3 to 8.

Single Late Tulips (Division 5)   PP. 183, 189, 200

These late spring–blooming tulips bear single 3-inch-wide flowers that are cup or goblet shaped on 18- to 30-inch-stems. This group includes cultivars formerly called Darwin tulips (not to be confused with Darwin Hybrid tulips) and cottage tulips and comes in a wide range of colors. Some cultivars bear more than one bloom per stem. Cultivars include 'Big Smile', with long-lasting golden yellow blooms; 'Blushing Lady', with goblet- or lily-shaped blooms that are orangy yellow flamed in rose-red; 'Candy Club', a multiflowering type with three to five creamy white flowers that have a narrow pinkish purple edging along the tepals; 'Dillenburg', a late-flowering, fragrant selection with burnt orange to terra cotta–colored flowers; 'Dreamland', red blooms with creamy white flames on the outside and rose-pink with a white central blotch on the inside; 'Georgette', a yellow-flowered selection edged and brushed with red that bears several blooms per stem; 'Maureen', a vigorous tetraploid cultivar with white blooms; 'Menton', a vigorous tetraploid selection with blooms in shades of pink from pale violet-pink to rose; 'Mrs. J.T. Scheepers', an outstanding old tetraploid cultivar with brilliant yellow blooms; 'Queen of the Night', an old cultivar with velvety, deep maroon blooms; 'Renown', reddish pink blooms with paler pink at the tepal edges; and 'Sorbet', white blooms striped with red. 'Maureen', 'Menton', 'Mrs. J.T. Scheepers', and 'Renown' also are sometimes listed as "French" Single Late tulips or Scheepers Hybrids: these cultivars are vigorous, tall, long-stemmed selections that also tolerate warmer temperatures than many tulips; they can be grown into Zones 8 and 9. Zones 3 to 7.

Lily-flowered Tulips (Division 6)   PP. 193, 204

Lily-flowered tulips bear single goblet-shaped flowers that have slightly reflexed tepals with pointed tips. Plants bloom in mid- to late spring and range from 18 to 26 inches tall. Cultivars include 'Ballade', reddish purple with white-edged tepals; 'Ballerina', fragrant tangerine to apricot-colored blooms; 'Marilyn', a creamy white Rembrandt-type tulip streaked and flamed with reddish purple; 'Maytime', red violet with white-edged tepals; 'Red Shine', rich, deep red; 'West Point', brilliant yellow; and 'White Triumphator', pure white. Zones 3 to 8.

Fringed Tulips (Division 7)
PP. 188, 190

Mid- to late spring–blooming cultivars that bear single 3-inch-wide cup-shaped flowers that have fringed tepal edges. Fringed tulips come in a wide range of colors, with the fringe often in a second color or shade, and range from 14 to 26 inches tall. Cultivars include 'American Eagle', red-purple with creamy fringe on the tepal edges; 'Blue Heron', violet-purple blooms with paler fringe; 'Burgundy Lace', a burgundy-red that performs well as a perennial; 'Fringed Elegance', a good perennializer with yellow blooms; and 'Swan Wings', pure white. Zones 3 to 8.

Viridiflora Tulips (Division 8)
PP. 188, 201

These 18- to 20-inch-tall cultivars bloom in late spring and produce single flowers that have tepals that are either entirely or predominately green. Blooms are 3 inches wide and may be cup shaped or rounded to bowl shaped. Cultivars include 'Greenland' (sometimes listed as 'Groenland'), with dusky rose-pink petals marked with green flames; and 'Spring Green', with creamy white petals feathered in green. Zones 3 to 8.

Rembrandt Tulips (Division 9)

Rembrandt tulips, sometimes called "broken" tulips, bear single cup-shaped flowers feathered and striped with various colors. The striping is caused by virus-infected bulbs and as a result true Rembrandt tulips are no longer commercially available. Instead, dealers offer Rembrandt-type cultivars in a range of colors: these are not virus infected and fall into a variety of the other divisions. They include 'Burning Heart', a Darwin Hybrid; 'Marilyn', a Lily-flowered tulip; and 'Shirley', a Triumph tulip. 'Flaming Parrot' and 'Estella Rijnveld', both Parrot tulips, also are Rembrandt-type selections.

Parrot Tulips (Division 10)
PP. 185, 199

Late season–flowering Parrot Tulips produce single cup-shaped blooms that are 4 inches across and have tepals that are irregularly cut, fringed, curled, and twisted in a featherlike fashion. They bear their heavy blooms on 14- to 26-inch-tall stems and are best in a spot protected from wind. Cultivars include 'Black Parrot', an old cultivar with dark burgundy blooms; 'Blue Parrot', blue-violet blushed with lavender; 'Carmine Parrot', red with a blue central blotch inside; 'Estella Rijnveld', a Rembrandt-type selection with red blooms marked by creamy yellow flames that mature to white; 'Flaming Parrot', a Rembrandt-type selection with creamy yellow blooms marked with red flames on the outside and bright yellow with dark red on the inside; 'Texas Gold', golden yellow with scalloped tepals edged in red; and 'White Parrot', white blooms, sometimes flecked with green, with scalloped tepals. Zones 3 to 8.

Double Late Tulips (Division 11)   P. 182, 187

These late-flowering tulips bear showy, double, bowl-shaped blooms that resemble roses or peonies—these cultivars are sometimes referred to as peony flowered. Flowers are up to 5 inches across and are borne on 14- to 24-inch-tall stems. Like Parrot tulips, they bear heavy blooms and are best planted in protected sites away from wind. Cultivars include 'Angélique', with pale pink blooms blushed with darker pink and shading to cream at the tepal edges; 'Crème Upstar' with creamy white and pale yellow flushed with pink at the petal edges; 'Lilac Perfection', large lilac-purple blooms; 'Maywonder', deep rose-pink; 'Upstar', pinkish purple and rose with creamy white at the base and tepal edges; 'Wirosa', dark wine red tepals with creamy edges. Zones 3 to 8.

Kaufmanniana Tulips (Division 12)   PP. 190, 193, 201

Sometimes called waterlily tulips, this division includes *T. kaufmanniana* and cultivars derived mainly from that species. The species bears creamy white flowers with a yellow base and tepals often streaked with rose-pink. Both species and cultivars bear single cup- or bowl-shaped blooms that have a starry or waterlily-like appearance when fully open. The individual blooms range from 2 to 5 inches across, often feature a multicolored base, and are borne singly or in small clusters of two to five blooms. Kaufmanniana tulips are dependable perennials that bloom from very early to midspring and often feature handsome, mottled leaves. Plants usually range from 6 to 12 inches tall. Cultivars include 'Ancilla', rose-red and soft pink on the outside and white with a yellow eye circled in red on the inside; 'Heart's Delight', red, rose-pink, and yellow blooms coupled with handsomely mottled leaves; 'Shakespeare', red with salmon tepal edges on the outside and salmon flushed with red on the inside with a yellow central blotch; 'Showwinner', bright red with a yellow base; 'Stresa', red edged with yellow on the outside and yellow marked with red at the base on the inside. Zones 3 to 8.

Fosteriana Tulips (Division 13) PP. 195, 198, 199

This division includes *T. fosteriana* and cultivars derived from that species. The species bears solitary red bowl-shaped flowers with a purple-black central blotch edged in yellow. Cultivars that fall in this division bear single 5-inch-wide blooms in white, yellow, or red that have contrasting blotches or bases. Plants bloom in midspring and carry flowers on 8- to 26-inch-tall stems. Fosteriana tulips are reliable perennials in the garden. The classic, well-known Emperor cultivars fall here, including 'Golden Emperor', yellow; 'Red Emperor', red with a black heart; 'Orange Emperor', orange with a yellow base; and 'White Emperor' and 'Purissima', both white with a creamy yellow base and heart. Other cultivars include 'Juan', orange flowers with a yellow base and attractively purple-mottled leaves; 'Solva', pinkish red flushed with pink; and 'Sweetheart', creamy yellow brushed with creamy white along the edges of the tepals. Zones 3 to 8.

Greigii Tulips (Division 14) PP. 196, 202

This division includes *T. greigii* and cultivars derived from that species. While the species usually bears red flowers with a black blotch, the cultivars come in a range of shades from yellow to red, usually with a blotch or base and often with tepal edges marked with a contrasting color. Greigii tulips bear single 4-inch-wide bowl-shaped flowers in early to midspring on compact 6- to 12-inch-tall plants. They also feature leaves handsomely mottled or striped with purple and are reliable perennials. Cultivars include 'Czar Peter', pinkish red tepals edged in white with burgundy-striped leaves; 'Cape Cod', yellow to apricot tepals flamed with red and purple-mottled leaves; 'Oratorio', watermelon to coral-pink flowers and purple-mottled leaves; 'Pinocchio', creamy white blooms marked with red flames and a bronzy heart atop heavily mottled leaves; 'Red Riding Hood', red blooms with a small black heart and leaves heavily mottled with purple; 'Sweet Lady', pink blooms blushed with apricot-pink and yellow-tinged bronze bases atop leaves striped with dark maroon; and 'Turkish Delight', red blooms that are creamy white inside with a central black blotch marked with red and yellow. Zones 3 to 8.

Miscellaneous Tulips (Division 15)

As the name of this division suggests, it contains a wide range of plants: all species tulips fall here, as do hybrids that are not included in other divisions. See below for information on species tulips and their cultivars.

SPECIES

T. acuminata P. 181

t. ah-kew-mih-NAH-tuh. A 16- to 18-inch-tall species with linear- to lance-shaped gray-green leaves. Bears solitary 4-inch-long flowers in mid-spring. Blooms are red or yellow streaked with red and have very narrow tepals with long pointed tips. Zones 3 to 8.

T. albertii

t. al-BER-tee-eye. A 6- to 8-inch-tall species that produces glaucous blue leaves and orange-red blooms in early spring with tepals that have a yellow-edged, black to purple blotch at the base. Zones 6 to 8.

T. altaica

t. al-TAY-ih-kuh. A 10- to 12-inch-tall species that blooms in midspring and bears cup-shaped rich yellow flowers with pointed tepals that are tinged with red on the outside. Zones 3 to 8.

T. aucheriana P. 183

t. aw-sher-ee-AH-nuh. A 6- to 8-inch-tall species blooming in midspring. Bears starry 3-inch-wide pink flowers that open flat and have a yellow to yellow-brown central blotch. Blooms are usually solitary but are sometimes borne in clusters of two or three. Zones 4 to 8.

T. bakeri

t. BAY-ker-eye. An 8- to 10-inch-tall species that spreads by runners and is very similar to *T. saxatilis*. Plants bear fragrant, star-shaped flowers in mid- to late spring that are 2½ to 3 inches across and come in dark pink to purple-pink. Plants sold under this name are currently thought to be *T. saxatilis*. See *T. saxatilis*. Zones 5 to 9.

T. batalinii P. 184

t. bah-tah-LIN-ee-eye. A 4- to 8-inch-tall species with sickle-shaped gray-green leaves. Blooms in mid- to late spring and produces bowl-shaped 3-inch-wide pale yellow flowers marked with bronze or dark yellow inside. Cultivars include 'Apricot Jewel', apricot-orange blooms that are yellow on the inside; 'Bright Gem', with sulphur yellow blooms flushed with orange; 'Bronze Charm', yellow blooms flushed with bronze; and 'Red Gem', red blooms blushed with apricot pink. Zones 3 to 8.

T. biflora   P. 185

t. by-FLOR-uh. Formerly *T. polychroma*. Diminutive 3- to 5-inch-tall species bearing gray-green leaves and starry, fragrant 1½-inch-wide white flowers that are yellow at the base. Blooms are solitary or borne in clusters of two or three in early spring. Zones 5 to 9.

T. clusiana   P. 186, 187

t. klew-see-AH-nuh. Lady Tulip. Formerly *T. aitchisonii*. A 10- to 12-inch-tall species that has gray-green leaves and blooms in early to midspring. Bowl-shaped 4-inch-wide flowers, borne singly or two to a stem, are starry shaped once they are fully open. Blooms are white with a dark pink stripe on the outer tepals and marked with red at the base on the inside. *T. clusiana* var. *chrysantha* bears clusters of up to three yellow flowers with outer tepals tinged red or brown-purple on the outside. *T. clusiana* var. *chrysantha* 'Tubergen's Gem' bears yellow flowers with red outer tepals. Zones 3 to 8.

T. greigii

T. GREG-ee-eye. *See* Greigii Tulips, p. 401.

T. hageri

t. HA-ger-eye. An 8- to 10-inch tall species that blooms in early to midspring. Bears lance-shaped leaves and star-shaped 2½- to 3½-inch-wide blooms that are dull red with green flames and tepal tips and blue-black centers. Blooms are solitary or produced in clusters of up to four. 'Splendens' bears clusters of three to five flowers that are red flecked with green outside and copper- to bronze-red inside. Zones 3 to 8.

T. humilis   P. 191, 192

t. HUE-mil-iss. A 4- to 6-inch-tall species bearing gray-green linear leaves and starry 3-inch-wide croduslike flowers in early spring. Blooms are rose-pink with a yellow base. Cultivars include 'Lilliput', with scarlet flowers that have violet bases; 'Persian Pearl', with magenta blooms that are yellow at the base and purple-pink inside; and 'Violacea', purple-red with a green-black base. Zones 4 to 8.

T. kaufmanniana

t. kauf-man-ee-AH-nuh. Waterlily Tulip. *See* Kaufmanniana Tulips, p. 400.

T. kolpakowskiana

t. kol-pak-ow-ski-AH-nuh. A 6- to 8-inch-tall species bearing gray-green leaves and bowl-shaped 1½- to 3-inch-wide flowers in early to midspring. Blooms are yellow with a red stripe on the outside and solid yellow inside. Zones 3 to 8.

T. linifolia

t. lih-nih-FO-lee-uh. A 3- to 6-inch-tall species with linear, sickle-shaped leaves and red 3-inch-wide bowl-shaped blooms that have a black blotch at the base. Flowers open nearly flat on sunny days. Leaves are edged in red. Zones 4 to 8.

T. maximowiczii

t. max-ih-mo-WIK-zee-eye. A 3- to 6-inch-tall species with linear, sickle-shaped leaves and red flowers that have a dark blue blotch at the center. Flowers open nearly flat on sunny days. Zones 4 to 8.

T. neustruevae   P. 194

t. new-STRU-vee. A 3- to 4-inch-tall species that bears yellow crocuslike flowers in early spring that have outer tepals marked with greenish brown. Zones 3 to 8.

T. orphanidea   P. 196

t. or-fah-NID-ee-uh. An 8- to 10-inch-tall species that bears lance-shaped leaves sometimes edged in maroon and solitary or clusters of up to four red flowers in early to midspring that are marked with buff blushed with green or purple on the outside of the outer tepals. 'Flava' bears brilliant yellow flowers that shade to red at the tops of the tepals. The insides of the flowers are lemon yellow shading to garnet red. Zones 5 to 8.

T. polychroma

t. pol-ee-KRO-muh. An early spring–blooming 3- to 4-inch-tall tulip listed and sold as a separate species by some sources but currently thought to belong in *T. biflora*. The starry blooms, borne singly or in clusters of up to three, are white with a yellow center and have violet-purple at the tips of the tepals. *See T. biflora*. Zones 5 to 9.

T. praestans   P. 198

t. PRAY-stanz. An 8- to 12-inch-tall species bearing bowl-shaped red-orange blooms in early spring. The 4- to 5-inch-wide flowers are borne singly or in clusters of up to five. A good perennializer where happy. 'Fusilier' bears brilliant red flowers. 'Unicum' bears red flowers and leaves edged in creamy white. Zones 4 to 8.

T. pulchella

t. pul-KEL-luh. A 10- to 12-inch-tall species bearing starry 3-inch-wide flowers in early to midspring. Blooms are red to purple with blue-black central blotches and are solitary or sometimes carried in clusters of up to three. Zones 4 to 8.

T. saxatilis   P. 200

t. sax-AH-tih-lis. An 8- to 10-inch-tall species that spreads by runners. Produces fragrant, star-shaped flowers in mid- to late spring that are 2½ to 3 inches across. The pink to purplish pink blooms are carried singly or in clusters of up to four. Plants sold as *T. bakeri* have darker pink to purple-pink blooms. 'Lilac Wonder' has lilac-pink to rose-purple flowers with yellow centers. Plants need poor soil, mild winters, and hot summers. Requires no cold period to bloom. Zones 5 to 9 or 10.

T. sprengeri

t. SPRING-er-eye. A 12- to 14-inch-tall species bearing linear leaves and solitary, goblet-shaped 2- to 2½-inch-long flowers in late spring. Blooms are red or orange-red and yellow at the base. Zones 4 to 8.

T. sylvestris

t. sil-VES-tris. Formerly *T. australis*. A 14- to 16-inch-tall stoloniferous species bearing linear leaves and starry, fragrant flowers in midspring that are yellow and 2½ to 3 inches across. Blooms are solitary or borne in pairs. Plants do not require a cold period to bloom. Zones 4 to 10.

T. tarda   P. 202

t. TAR-duh. Formerly *T. dasystemon*. A 4- to 6-inch-tall species with lance-shaped leaves and clusters of star-shaped 2½-inch-wide blooms borne in midspring. Blooms carried in clusters of four to six, are golden yellow with white tips. Zones 3 to 8.

T. turkestanica   P. 203

t. tur-kes-TAN-ih-kuh. A 6- to 10-inch-tall species bearing linear gray-green leaves and clusters of up to 12 starry 1- to 2-inch-wide flowers in early to midspring. Blooms are white with yellow or orange at the center, have an unpleasant odor, and close at night and on cloudy days. Zones 4 to 8.

T. uruminensis

t. yoo-room-ih-NEN-sis. A 4- to 6-inch-tall species with linear leaves and starry yellow 2- to 3-inch-wide flowers borne singly or in pairs. Blooms are flushed with cream, lilac, or red-brown on the outside and are borne in early spring. Zones 4 to 8.

T. vvedenskyi   P. 203

t. veh-DEN-skee-eye. A 10- to 12-inch-tall species with lance-shaped gray-green leaves. Bears red blooms in early to midspring that have black or red blotches at the base. Zones 5 to 8.

T. whittallii

t. whih-TAL-lee-eye. An 8- to 10-inch-tall species with lance-shaped leaves sometimes edged in red-purple. Bears star-shaped 1¼- to 2½-inch-wide bronzy orange flowers in early to midspring. Blooms are carried singly or in clusters of up to four and have central black basal blotches sometimes edged in yellow. Zones 5 to 8.

T. wilsoniana

t. wil-son-ee-AH-nuh. A 4- to 6-inch-tall species with wavy-edged gray-green leaves blushed with red. Bears dark blood red flowers that have pointed outer tepals and a central black blotch. Zones 5 to 8.

❦ Urceolina see Stenomesson

❦ Urginea

ur-JIN-ee-uh. Lily family, Liliaceae.

Urginea species are bulbous perennials that produce basal leaves and long racemes of densely packed flowers that resemble the plumelike flowers of foxtail lilies (*Eremurus* spp.), which are closely related. The leafless flower stalks are erect and unbranched. Individual flowers are star or wheel shaped and consist of six petal-like tepals. Some 100 species belong to the genus, and these are primarily native to tropical Africa, although three species are from the Mediterranean. In the wild, the tunicate bulbs of these plants are partially or fully aboveground. The one species commonly grown in gardens— *U. maritima*—has been used medicinally, and a rat poison is extracted from the bulbs.

HOW TO GROW

Select a site in full sun with poor to average soil that is extremely well drained and sandy or rocky. *U. maritima* is a Mediterranean native and requires a hot, dry dormant period during the summer and is also intolerant of wet soil in winter. They are most suitable for gardens in areas with Mediterranean climates, where mild winters and hot, dry summers prevail. Elsewhere, grow them in containers. Plant the bulbs when they are dormant, setting them with at least the top half aboveground. Amend the soil with coarse sand or grit at planting time. Plants produce leaves from late fall to early spring, are dormant in summer, then bloom in fall. Water regularly when plants are growing actively, but keep the soil dry at other times by moving containers to a protected spot or mulching with coarse mulch covered with plastic to ward off rainfall. Propagate by seed or separating the offsets in summer.

U. maritima   P. 204

u. mah-RIH-tih-muh. Sea Onion, Red Squill, Sea Squill. Formerly *Scilla maritima*, *Drimia maritima*. A Mediterranean native with clumps of narrow, linear, basal leaves that emerge from late fall to late winter after the flowers fade. Produces 1- to 3-foot-long racemes of tiny, densely packed ¼-inch-wide white flowers in late summer or fall. Plants reach 5 feet in bloom. Zones 9 to 11.

☙ *Vallota* see *Cyrtanthus*

☙ *Veltheimia*

vel-THY-mee-uh. Lily family, Liliaceae.

Veltheimia species are tender, bulbous perennials that, unlike many bulbs, are grown for their handsome leaves as well as their flowers. Two species belong here, both native to South Africa. They produce rosettes of thick, strap-shaped leaves with wavy margins. Dense, rounded clusters of flowers—somewhat resembling those of red-hot pokers (*Kniphofia* spp.) — are carried on erect stalks above the leaves. Individual flowers are pendent and tubular with six small lobes at the top.

HOW TO GROW

Select a spot in full sun with average, well-drained soil. A spot with shade during the hottest part of the day helps protect the flowers. They can be grown outdoors year-round only in mild climates (Zones 10 and 11, or to Zone 9 with winter protection) that offer dry conditions when the plants are dormant in summer. To grow them outdoors, plant the bulbs in fall with the neck above the soil surface. Where they are marginally hardy, look for a protected, south-facing site and mulch the plants heavily in fall with evergreen boughs, salt hay, coarse leaves, or pine needles. Elsewhere, grow them in containers — they make outstanding container plants, growing indoors from fall to spring and blooming reliably. Pot the bulbs in fall, setting them with the tops about halfway out of the soil in pots that allow at least 1 inch on all sides. These are not tropical plants, and they are best kept over winter in a spot where nighttime temperatures range between 50° and 55°F. Water very carefully until leaves appear, then keep the soil evenly moist but never wet. Feed container-grown plants every few weeks with a balanced fertilizer. Once leaves begin to turn yellow — generally by midsummer — gradually withhold water until the leaves die back completely. Rest plants for at least two months by keeping the soil completely dry. Resume watering in fall. Plants are happiest when their roots and bulbs are left undisturbed, and plants growing in the ground thrive for years without needing to be divided. Repot container-grown plants in late summer or fall only if they become overcrowded. Propagate by separating offsets in late summer or early fall or by seeds. *Veltheimia* species also can be propagated by leaf cuttings: pull off entire mature leaves and root them in sand or vermiculite.

V. bracteata   P. 205

v. brak-tee-AH-tuh. Formerly *V. viridifolia*. A vigorous 1½-foot-tall species with rosettes of glossy, strap-shaped 12- to 14-inch-long leaves with wavy margins. Bears dense rounded racemes of tubular 1½-inch-long pinkish purple flowers in spring. Zones 10 to 11; to Zone 9 with winter protection.

Watsonia

wat-SO-nee-uh. Iris family, Iridaceae.

Watsonias are grown for their showy spikes of flowers that usually resemble those of *Gladiolus*. About 60 species native to South Africa as well as Madagascar belong to the genus, all of which grow from corms and produce basal, sword-shaped leaves. The individual flowers are tubular and curved at the base with six spreading lobes, or petal-like tepals. *Watsonia* flowers, unlike those of *Gladiolus*, are nearly symmetrical: the tube at the base of the flower is slender and has enlarged lobes, or tepals, at the top, while *Gladiolus* flowers are more evenly funnel shaped.

HOW TO GROW

Select a site in full sun with light, evenly moist soil rich in organic matter. Grow these plants as you would glads: plant corms in spring, setting small corms 3 inches deep and large corms 6 to 8 inches deep. Where hardy, they can be planted in fall. For best results, dig a shallow trench and fill it with soil as the plants grow. Deep planting helps minimize the need to stake plants, but stake them if necessary. In areas where the plants are not hardy, let the foliage ripen for at least 6 weeks after flowering. Then dig the corms after the leaves turn yellow, cut off the foliage, and set them in a warm, dry place for a few hours to dry. Separate the new corms and small cormels from the old withered one, which will not bloom again. Dust the corms with sulfur or another fungicide and store them in a cool (40° to 50°F), dry place over winter.

W. borbonica P. 205

w. bor-BON-ih-kuh. Formerly *W. pyramidata*. A 3- to 5-foot-tall species bearing branched spikes of up to 20 pink 1¼-inch-long flowers that have spreading lobes. Zones 9 to 10.

Zantedeschia

zan-teh-DES-kee-uh. Arum family, Araceae.

Zantedeschia species are commonly called calla lilies, although they are not related to true lilies (*Lilium* spp.), which belong to the lily family. Instead, the six species of tender perennials in *Zantedeschia*, sometimes also called arum lilies, are more closely related to Jack-in-the-pulpits (*Arisaema* spp.) and caladiums (*Caladium* spp.). The plants bear fleshy, lance- to arrowhead-shaped leaves and grow from fleshy, tuberous rhizomes. Plants are evergreen or deciduous. Like other arum-family plants, calla lilies bear flowers that are actually an inflorescence consisting of many tiny flowers clustered on a central stalk, called a spadix. The spadix is surrounded by a showy modified leaf, called a spathe. *Zantedeschia* species are native to southern and eastern Africa.

HOW TO GROW

Select a site in full sun or partial shade with rich, moist soil. A spot protected from sun during the hottest part of the day is best. *Z. aethiopica* will grow in boggy soil and in standing water up to a depth of 12 inches; it is commonly used as a marginal plant along the edges of water gardens. Where hardy, calla lilies can be grown outdoors year-round; elsewhere, plan on overwintering them indoors by keeping them in containers or digging them annually in fall. Where they are marginally hardy, look for a protected site and mulch heavily in fall with a dry, coarse mulch such as evergreen boughs, salt hay, or pine needles. However you grow them, plant the fleshy rhizomes in spring: set them just under the soil surface — on their sides if you can't tell top from bottom. Water carefully until the plants are growing actively, then keep the soil evenly moist. Feed container-grown plants every 2 weeks with a balanced fertilizer. In the North, start plants indoors in late winter or early spring and move them to the garden after all danger of frost has passed. To overwinter the rhizomes indoors, dig them in early fall, dry them off, and store them in dry peat or vermiculite in a cool (50° to 55°F), dry, airy place. Or keep plants in containers year-round and gradually reduce watering in late summer until the leaves die back, then store the plants in a cool, dry spot — still in their pots — over winter. Propagate by removing offsets or dividing the rhizomes in spring.

Z. aethiopica   P. 206

z. ee-thee-O-pih-kuh. Calla Lily. A 2- to 3-foot-tall species that bears glossy 16-inch-long arrowhead-shaped leaves that are evergreen in mild climates. From late spring to midsummer, plants produce showy flowers with white 4- to 10-inch-long spathes surrounding a yellow spadix. 'Crowborough' has 4- to 6-inch-long spathes and is supposedly hardier than the species. 'Green Goddess' bears white 6- to 8-inch-long spathes marked with green. 'Pink Mist' bears white spathes blushed with pink. Zones 8 to 11; to Zone 7 or even 6 with winter protection.

Z. albomaculata

z. AL-bo-mak-yoo-LAH-tuh. Spotted Calla. A 12- to 16-inch-tall species bearing dark green arrow-shaped 12- to 18-inch-long leaves spotted with white. Handsome flowers with 5-inch-long white spathes surrounding a yellow spadix appear in summer. Zones 8 to 11; to Zone 7 with winter protection.

Z. elliottiana   P. 206

z. el-lee-ot-ee-AH-nuh. Golden Calla, Yellow Calla. A 2- to 3-foot-tall species bearing dark green heart-shaped 12- to 18-inch-long leaves spotted with white. In summer, bears blooms with 6-inch-long yellow spathes surrounding a yellow spadix. Zones 9 to 11.

Z. hybrids   PP. 207, 208

Several hybrids are available, many with *Z. elliottiana* as an important parent. 'Black-eyed Beauty' bears heavily spotted leaves and creamy white spathes that have a black eye. 'Cameo' and 'Pacific Pink' bear pink blooms. 'Golden Affair' bears solid green leaves and bright yellow spathes. 'Mango' bears red-orange spathes. Zones 9 to 10; to Zone 8 with winter protection.

Z. pentlandii

z. pent-LAN-dee-eye. Formerly *Z. angustiloba*. A 2- to 3-foot-tall species with rounded, lance-shaped 12-inch-long leaves that are only rarely spotted. Bears flowers with bright gold to lemon yellow 5-inch-long spathes in summer that are marked with purple inside at the base and surround a yellow spadix. Zones 8 to 11.

Z. rehmannii   P. 208

z. reh-MAH-nee-eye. Pink Calla. A 12- to 16-inch-tall species with lance-shaped 12-inch-long dark green leaves. Bears flowers in summer that have pink, white, or purple 5-inch-long spathes surrounding a yellow spadix. Zones 9 to 11.

❧ Zephyranthes

zeh-fer-RAN-theez. Amaryllis family, Amaryllidaceae.

The charming plants in this genus have a variety of common names, including rain lilies, rain flowers, zephyr lilies, and fairy lilies. About 70 species belong here, all perennials native from North to South America that grow from tunicate bulbs and produce grassy leaves that are either deciduous or evergreen. The tubular flowers, which point upward, are either funnel shaped and resemble small lilies or are more rounded, in which case they look more like crocuses. Flowers appear from spring to fall and, as the name rain lily suggests, often appear after a period of rainy weather. They come in shades of pink, red, yellow, and white.

HOW TO GROW
Select a site in full sun with rich, moist soil that is very well drained. Where hardy, these bulbs can be grown outdoors year-round. Where they are marginally hardy, look for a warm, sheltered spot such as at the base of a south-facing wall. They require fairly dry soil in winter when they are dormant, so plant them in raised beds or rock gardens and amend the soil with grit when planting to improve drainage. In the North, grow them in containers, which will make it easy to move plants outdoors for summer and indoors in fall. Or, dig them annually in fall and overwinter them indoors. Where hardy, plant the bulbs in fall; elsewhere, plant in spring, setting them at a depth of about 2 inches. Keep the soil evenly moist once plants are growing actively. Gradually withhold water as the leaves begin to die back. To overwinter bulbs indoors, bring the containers indoors after the foliage has died back and keep them in a cool (50° to 55°F), dry place. Dig the bulbs, dry them off, and store them in barely moist peat moss or vermiculite. Container-grown plants need repotting only every four years or so—they bloom best when slightly pot bound. Propagate by offsets in spring or by seeds.

Z. atamasco   P. 209
z. ah-tah-MAS-ko. Atamasco Lily. Wildflower native to the southeastern United States that ranges from 8 to 12 inches tall. Bears white 3-inch-long funnel-shaped flowers in spring or summer. Zones 10 to 11.

Z. candida
z. kan-DEE-duh. Heavy-blooming 4- to 8-inch-tall South American species bearing creamy white crocuslike 1¼-inch-long flowers from summer to early fall. Zones 8 to 10; to Zone 7 with winter protection.

Z. citrina
z. sih-TRY-nuh. A 4- to 6-inch-tall South American species with bright yellow 2-inch-long crocuslike flowers from late summer to fall. Zones 9 to 11.

Z. grandiflora

P. 209

z. gran-dih-FLOR-uh. Rain Lily, Rain Flower, Zephyr Lily, Fairy Lily. Formerly *Z. carinata.* An 8- to 10-inch-tall species from Mexico bearing funnel-shaped pink 3-inch-long flowers from late summer to fall. Zones 9 to 11.

Z. robustus see Habranthus robustus

Z. rosea

P. 210

z. RO-see-uh. Rain Lily, Rain Flower, Zephyr Lily, Fairy Lily. A 6- to 8-inch-tall species from Central America as well as the West Indies and Cuba. Bears funnel-shaped 1¼-inch-long pink flowers with white throats in fall. Zones 10 to 11.

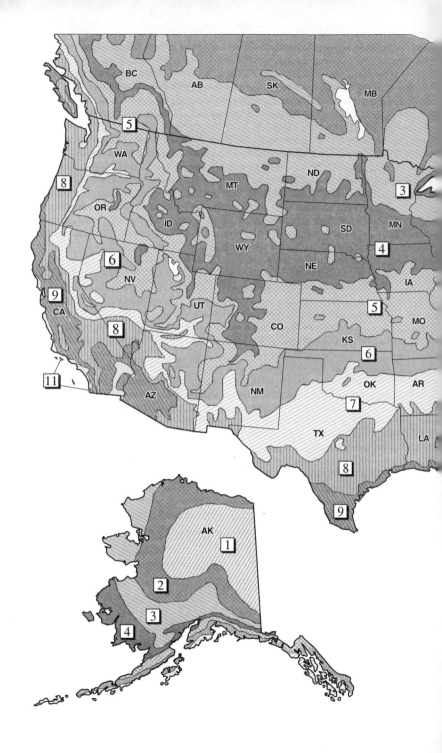

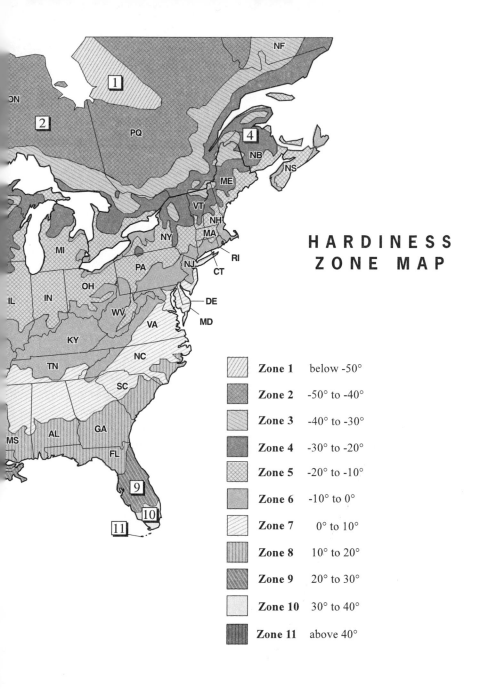

HARDINESS ZONE MAP

	Zone 1	below -50°
	Zone 2	-50° to -40°
	Zone 3	-40° to -30°
	Zone 4	-30° to -20°
	Zone 5	-20° to -10°
	Zone 6	-10° to 0°
	Zone 7	0° to 10°
	Zone 8	10° to 20°
	Zone 9	20° to 30°
	Zone 10	30° to 40°
	Zone 11	above 40°

✌ Photo Credits

BRENT AND BECKY'S BULBS: ii-iii, 11, 12, 30 top, 32 bottom, 33 top, 33 bottom, 34 bottom, 35 bottom, 36 bottom, 40 bottom, 42 bottom, 43 top, 43 bottom, 44 bottom, 45 top, 48 top, 52 bottom, 57 bottom, 58 top, 59 top, 59 bottom, 59 bottom insert, 61 top, 61 bottom insert, 62 top, 62 bottom, 63 top, 63 bottom, 64 bottom, 65 top, 65 bottom, 67 top, 67 bottom, 68 top insert, 70 bottom insert, 71 top, 72 bottom, 73 bottom, 74 bottom insert, 77 top, 77 bottom, 78 bottom, 79 top, 79 bottom, 80 top, 80 bottom, 81 top, 82 top, 82 bottom, 83 bottom, 84 bottom, 85 top, 86 bottom, 87 top, 87 bottom, 89 top, 89 bottom, 92 top, 98 bottom, 100 bottom, 102 bottom, 103 bottom, 104 bottom, 108 bottom, 109 top, 112 top, 114 top, 114 bottom, 116 top, 116 bottom, 117 bottom, 118 bottom, 119 top insert, 122 top, 123 top, 123 bottom, 124 top, 125 top, 125 bottom, 127 top, 128 bottom, 129 bottom, 135 top, 137 bottom, 139 bottom, 144 bottom, 145 top, 146 top, 147 bottom, 148 top, 148 bottom, 151 top, 152 top, 152 bottom, 153 bottom, 154 top, 154 bottom, 155 bottom, 156 top, 156 bottom, 157 top, 158 top, 158 bottom, 159 bottom, 160 top, 163 top, 163 bottom, 164 top, 164 bottom, 167 bottom, 169 top, 169 top insert, 171 top, 175 bottom, 176 top, 176 bottom, 177 bottom, 179 bottom, 180 bottom, 183 bottom, 184 bottom, 185 bottom, 186 bottom, 187 top, 187 bottom, 188 top, 190 top, 191 top, 191 bottom, 192 bottom, 194 top, 194 bottom, 196 top, 196 bottom, 197 top, 200 top, 200 bottom, 204 top, 204 bottom, 207 top, 207 bottom, 208 bottom

DAVID CAVAGNARO: 120 bottom

R. TODD DAVIS PHOTOGRAPHY, INC.: 28-29, 46 bottom, 58 bottom, 61 bottom, 69 top, 71 bottom, 74 top, 85 bottom, 95 bottom, 101 insert bottom, 117 top insert, 121 top, 133 top, 133 bottom, 139 top, 140 bottom, 171 bottom, 181 bottom, 188 bottom, 189 bottom, 190 bottom, 199 top, 201 bottom, 202 top, 208 top

BARBARA W. ELLIS: 41 bottom, 74 bottom, 102 top, 140 top, 149 bottom, 168 bottom insert

DEREK FELL: 10, 27, 30 top insert, 30 bottom, 35 top, 37 top, 40 top, 48 bottom, 55 top, 57 top, 60 bottom, 68 bottom, 69 bottom, 72 top, 76 top, 92 bottom, 93 top, 95 top, 99 bottom, 101 top, 105 top, 106 bottom, 107 bottom, 109 bottom, 111 bottom, 118 top, 121 bottom, 128 top insert, 129 top, 131 top, 142 bottom, 159 top, 161 top, 162 top, 165 top, 166 bottom, 168 top, 175 top, 177 top, 180 bottom insert, 183 top, 189 top, 193 bottom, 195 bottom, 197 bottom, 203 top, 205 bottom insert, 209 top, 209 top insert, 209 bottom, 210

CHARLES MARDEN FITCH: vi-1, 7, 36 top, 42 top insert, 46 top, 46 bottom insert, 53 bottom, 54 top, 75 bottom, 81 bottom, 84 top, 90 bottom, 106 top, 110 bottom, 121 top insert, 126 top, 132 bottom, 138 top, 172 bottom, 178 bottom insert

MARGE GARFIELD: 60 top

NEW ENGLAND WILD FLOWER SOCIETY: 50 top (L. Taylor), 66 bottom (L. Newcomb), 174 bottom (L. Newcomb)

JERRY PAVIA PHOTOGRAPHY, INC.: 15, 24, 31 top, 31 bottom, 32 top, 34 top, 37 bottom, 38 top, 39 top, 39 bottom, 41 top, 42 top, 47 bottom, 49 top, 54 bottom, 55 bottom, 56 top, 64 top, 68 top, 70 top insert, 70 bottom, 73 top, 76 bottom, 86 top, 88 top, 88 bottom, 89 bottom insert, 91 top, 91 bottom, 93 bottom, 96 bottom, 98 top, 99 top, 101 bottom, 104 top, 110 top, 111 top, 112 bottom, 113 top, 113 bottom, 115 bottom, 117 top, 119 top, 119 bottom, 120 bottom insert, 124 bottom, 126 bottom, 131 bottom, 134 bottom, 135 bottom, 136 top, 141 bottom, 143 bottom, 144 top, 147 top, 149 top, 150 top, 150 bottom, 151 bottom, 155 top, 157 bottom, 160 bottom, 161 bottom, 162 bottom, 165 bottom, 166 top, 169 bottom, 170 top, 172 top, 173 top, 173 bottom, 174 top, 181 top, 182 bottom, 185 top, 186 top, 192 top, 193 top, 195 top, 198 top, 198 bottom, 199 bottom, 201 top, 205 top, 205 bottom, 211

MICHAEL S. THOMPSON: 22, 38 bottom, 44 top, 45 bottom, 47 top, 49 top, 50 bottom, 51 top, 51 bottom, 52 top, 53 top, 53 top insert, 56 bottom, 66 top, 70 top, 75 top, 78 top, 83 top, 90 top, 94 top, 94 bottom, 96 top, 97 top, 97 bottom, 100 top, 103 top, 105 bottom, 107 top, 108 top, 115 top, 120 top, 122 bottom, 127 bottom, 128 top, 130 top, 130 bottom, 132 top, 134 top, 136 bottom, 137 top, 138 bottom, 141 top, 142 top, 143 top, 145 bottom, 146 bottom, 153 top, 165 bottom insert, 167 top, 168 bottom, 170 bottom, 178 top, 178 bottom, 179 top, 180 top, 182 top, 184 top, 202 bottom, 203 bottom, 206 top, 206 bottom

❧ Index

Page numbers in italics refer to illustrations.